Design for Liv...
To-night at 8.30 (Hands Across the Sea, Still Life,
Fumed Oak)

"He is simply a phenomenon, and one that is unlikely to occur ever again in theatre history." Terence Rattigan

"His triumph has been to unite two things ever dissociated in the English mind: hard work and wit." Kenneth Tynan

The plays in this volume present the best of Coward's work for the stage in the 1930s.

"Mr. Coward is always at his best when he is fooling," *The Times* said of *Design for Living* in 1939. "Here is the mixture of satire with fooling that is his special talent and his particular confusion."

Of *Cavalcade* in 1931, the *Daily Mail* wrote: "It is a magnificent play in which the note of national pride pervading every scene and every sentence must make each one of us face the future with courage and high hopes."

"It was a big occasion before ever the curtain rose," wrote W. A. Darlington reviewing *Conversation Piece* in 1934. "It became a great one as soon as Yvonne Printemps appeared ... Mr. Coward shares her triumph. Or, rather, since he is author, composer, producer, and chief male actor in this brilliant show, he enjoys a separate triumph all to himself."

Of the three short plays from the *To-night at 8.30* sequence written in 1935 "as acting, singing, and dancing vehicles for Gertrude Lawrence and myself", *Hands Across the Sea* is a gentle satire on the contrasting manners of visiting colonials and London Society; *Still Life* is the original of the film *Brief Encounter*; and *Fumed Oak* is a suburban comedy on the theme of "the worm that turns".

The front cover shows a design from 1935 by Erté, reproduced by courtesy of the Grosvenor Gallery, London. The cartoon of Noël Coward by Max Beerbohm on the back cover is from the Mander and Mitchenson Theatre Collection and is reproduced with permission.

NOËL COWARD

Plays: Three

Design for Living
Cavalcade
Conversation Piece
and
Hands Across the Sea
Still Life
Fumed Oak
from
To-night at 8.30

Introduced by Raymond Mander and Joe Mitchenson

The Master Playwrights
METHUEN – LONDON

A METHUEN PAPERBACK

This collection first published in Great Britain in 1979 in simultaneous
hardback and paperback editions by Eyre Methuen Ltd., 11 New
Fetter Lane, London EC4P 4EE
Reprinted 1983 by Methuen London Ltd

Design for Living was first published in Great Britain in 1933 by
Heinemann and republished in 1934 in Play Parade Vol. 1. It is
reprinted here by arrangement with Davis-Poynter Ltd.

Cavalcade was first published in 1932 by Heinemann and republished in
1934 in Play Parade Vol. 1.

Conversation Piece was first published in 1934 by Heinemann and
republished in 1939 in Play Parade Vol. 2.

To-night at 8.30 was first published in 1936 by Heinemann and
republished in 1954 in Play Parade Vol. 4.

ISBN 0 413 46090 8 (Hardback)
ISBN 0 413 46100 9 (Paperback)

Reproduced, printed and bound in Great Britain by
Cox & Wyman Ltd, Reading

CAUTION
These plays are fully protected by copyright throughout the world.
All applications for performance, etc., should be made *by professionals*
to Dr. Jan Van Loewen Ltd., 81–83 Shaftesbury Avenue, London
W1V 8BX, and *by amateurs* to Samuel French Ltd., 26 Southampton
Street, Strand, London WC2E 7JE. In the case of *Cavalcade* all
inquiries should go to Dr. Jan Van Loewen Ltd.

Contents

Acknowledgements

IN compiling these introductions, we have drawn on Noël Coward's own prefaces to the six volumes of *Play Parade* as well as quoting from *Present Indicative* (Heinemann 1937) and *Future Indefinite* (Heinemann 1952), the two autobiographies, for which we acknowledge our thanks. For the years not covered by these, we have drawn on Sheridan Morley's biography of Coward, *A Talent to Amuse* (Heinemann 1969) and Cole Lesley's *The Life of Noël Coward* (Jonathan Cape) 1976 for which we offer further thanks.

We have had the advantage of compiling our own *Theatrical Companion to Coward* (Rockliff 1957; now under revision), originally produced under the watchful eye of the Master himself, and on this volume we have naturally drawn for information.

We also have to thank Joan Hirst, Coward's London representative, who is always on hand to answer questions, as well as "Quinney", who transposed our disparate thoughts into the printed word, and has always enjoyed casting an eagle eye over our proofs, and lastly Colin Mabberley, Curator of our Collection, who has unflinchingly assisted us in our compilation of these introductions.

Raymond Mander and Joe Mitchenson,
Theatre Collection
August 1982

Introduction

NOËL COWARD was dependent in his formative years, both as an actor and as a writer on the perspicacity of the older generation of the theatre. To Charles Hawtrey, with whom he played boy parts in several productions, Coward acknowledged his debt as the actor who taught him the craft of comedy. Mary Moore, the widow of Charles Wyndham, had faith in the young dramatist, and presented "*I'll Leave it to You.*" And so did Robert Courtneidge who promoted *The Young Idea.*

Noël also had the admiration of a circle of friends of his own generation who felt secure in hitching their wagons to a future star. André Charlot, a wise and successful Anglo-French revue producer, gave Noël his first chance with a number in *Tails Up!* in 1918, and was to be responsible for *London Calling!* in 1923. Charlot's forte was Intimate Revue. We would today call him an "impresario", the term "producer" being now reserved for the "money-bags", or at least the man who can find the "angels" to back his productions, whereas "director" is now used for the man who is responsible for the actual staging of the production. Basil Dean was an example of both producer and director, and to him Coward owed the presentation and staging of many of his plays. Charles B. Cochran, an impresario *in excelsis*, took Charlot's place in Coward's rise to fame as the inspiration of the more artistic and spectacular productions. To him Noël owed *On With the Dance* (1925), *This Year of Grace!* (1928), *Bitter-Sweet* (1929) and *Private Lives*, which opened the new Phoenix Theatre in 1930.

Cavalcade

It was while Coward was appearing in *Private Lives* that, as he said: "I felt the urge to test my production powers on a large scale". He discussed a project with Cochran with the London Coliseum in mind. He tells us:

I toyed for a while with a French Revolution epic, a Pageant of the Second Empire, and various other ideas which might give me enough scope for intimate characterisations against a background of crowd scenes. One day I happened to see in a back number of *The Illustrated London News* a photograph of a troop ship leaving for the Boer War. Very soon after this the whole scheme of the play fell into my mind, and, after relating it to C. B. Cochran and asking him to get me the Coliseum at all costs, I left for New York to play *Private Lives*. A few months later I received a cable from him saying that the Coliseum was unobtainable, but that I could have Drury Lane provided that I would guarantee an approximate opening date. This was slightly agitating, but I cabled back that the play would be ready for production by the end of September.

When I returned to London in May, I carefully examined the facilities of the Drury Lane stage in company with G. E. Calthrop who constructed the whole show with me in addition to designing all the scenery and dresses, and we retired to the country, after a series of conferences to build the play, according to blueprints, time changes, electric installations, and hydraulic lifts. I had not one moment to waste on patriotic fervour.

After a slight delay owing to two extra hydraulic lifts which we had to install, *Cavalcade* was finally launched in October, and with it came the Deluge. A very gratifying Deluge. Letters of congratulation. Crowds in the streets. Superlatives in the Press. I was told, on all sides, that I had done "a big thing" and that a peerage was the least I could expect from a grateful monarch. I was also congratulated on my uncanny shrewdness in slapping on a strong patriotic play two weeks before a general election, which would be bound to result in a sweeping Conservative majority. (Here I must regretfully admit that during rehearsals I was so very much occupied in the theatre, and, as usual, so bleakly un-interested in politics that I had not the remotest idea, until a few days before the production, that there was going to be an election at all! However, there was, and its effect on the box office was considerable.) . . . The only thing that escaped notice in the uproar was the fact that *Cavalcade*, apart from its appeal as a spectacle actually possessed two or three well-written scenes, notably the funeral of Queen Victoria and the outbreak of the war in 1914. These two scenes had dignity and brevity.

Now that the whole thing is done, and has become an "epic", and "the play of the century", and "the picture of the generation", I can meditate blissfully upon the good fortune that prompted me to pick up just that particular number of *The Illustrated London News*, instead of one of a later date, depicting the storming of the Winter Palace at St Petersburg.

The production opened at the Theatre Royal, Drury Lane, on 13 October 1931 and ran for 405 performances, with the following cast:

JANE MARRYOT	Mary Clare
ROBERT MARRYOT	Edward Sinclair
ELLEN BRIDGES	Una O'Connor
ALFRED BRIDGES	Freda Groves
MARGARET HARRIS	Irene Browne
EDITH HARRIS	Alison Leggatt
EDWARD MARRYOT	Arthur Macrae
JOE MARRYOT	John Mills
FANNY BRIDGES	Binnie Barnes
EDITH ⎫	Veronica Vanderlyn
EDWARD ⎬ *as children*	Peter Vokes
JOE ⎪	Leslie Flack
FANNY ⎭	Dorothy Keefe
LAURA MARSDEN (MIRABELLE) ⎫	Stella Wilson
HENRY CHARTERIS (LIEUTENANT EDGAR) ⎬ *Characters in Mirabelle Scene 4*	Eric Purveur
ROSE DARLING (ADA) ⎪	Madie Andrews
MICKY BANKS (TOM JOLLY) ⎭	Billy Fry

Cook		Laura Smithson
Annie		Merle Tottenham
Mrs. Snapper		Edie Martin
Flo Grainger		Dorothy Monkman
George Grainger		Bobby Blythe
Daisy Devon		Moya Nugent
Marion Christie		Betty Hare
Netta Lake		Phyllis Harding
Connie Crawshay		Betty Shale
Tim Bateman		Philip Clarke
Douglas Finn		John Beerbohm
Lord Martlett (Chubby)		Anthony Pélissier
Uncle Harry		Aly Ford
Uncle George	*of "Uncle*	Charles Wingrove
Uncle Dick	*George and*	Walter Rayland
Uncle Jack	*His Merry*	Tod Squires
Uncle Bob	*Men"*	Tom Carlisle
Uncle Jim	*Troupe*	William McGuigan

Freda Weddell	Lena Brand
Olive Frost	Marcelle Turner
Gladys (Parlourmaid)	Dorothy Drover
A Communist	Anthony Blair
A Religious Fanatic	Enid Clinton-Baddeley
A Wireless Announcer	W. A. H. Harrison
Pianist at Night Club	Jack London
Trumpeter at Night Club	Leslie Thompson

It was directed in the grand manner by Coward, with costumes and scenery by G. E. Calthrop.

The first night was fraught with technical hitches and at one moment it was thought that the audience would have to be dismissed. Coward tells the full story in *Present Indicative*, but the conclusion was a triumph. At his curtain speech he said,

"I hope that this play has made you feel that, in spite of the troublous times we are living in, it is still pretty exciting to be English." This brought a violent outburst of cheering, the orchestra frantic with indecision as to whether to play my waltz or "God Save the King", effected an unhappy compromise by playing them both at once. The curtain fell, missing my head by a fraction, and that was that.

On 28 October 1931, King George V and Queen Mary, with the Prince of Wales, the then Duke and Duchess of York, the Duke of Kent, and other members of the Royal Family, saw the play amid scenes of patriotic fervour and loyal enthusiasm. The play was filmed in America, shown in London in 1933, and achieved a Command showing at Windsor Castle. The published version of *Cavalcade* is dedicated "To G. B. Stern. Dear Peter—I am dedicating *Cavalcade* to you in gratitude for a friendship maintained through many of its years. Noël."

Design for Living

With the play a success, Coward went off on his travels in October 1931, this time to South America. On his return, his next production was another revue for Cochran, *Words and Music*, which ran for 164 performances at the Adelphi Theatre from September 1932. Meantime, while on his holiday, the idea of the play for himself and the Lunts had matured, as he tells us:

Design for Living as a project rather than as a play sat patiently at the back of my mind for eleven years. It had to wait until Lynn Fontanne, Alfred Lunt, and I had arrived by different roads, at the exact moments in our careers when we felt that we could all three play together with a more or less equal degree of success.

We had met, discussed, argued, and parted again many times, knowing that it was something we wanted to do very much indeed, and searching wildly through our minds for suitable characters. At one moment we were to be three foreigners. Lynn, Eurasian; Alfred, German; and I, Chinese. At another we were to be three acrobats, rapping out "Allez Oops" and flipping handkerchiefs at one another.

A further plan was that the entire play should be played in a gigantic bed dealing with life and love in the Schnitzler manner. This, however was hilariously discarded, after Alfred had suggested a few stage directions which if followed faithfully, would undoubtedly have landed all three of us in gaol.

Finally, when the whole idea seemed to have sunk out of sight for ever, I got a cable from them in the Argentine, where I happened to be at the moment, saying, "Contract with the Guild up in June—we shall be free—what about it?"

While continuing his holiday the play "suddenly emerged . . . placed firmly in Paris, London and New York". It was tried out in Cleveland, Ohio, on 2 January 1933 before arriving on Broadway on 24 January at the Ethel Barrymore Theatre, with the following cast:

GILDA	Lynn Fontanne
ERNEST FRIEDMAN	Campbell Gullan
OTTO	Alfred Lunt
LEO	Noël Coward
MISS HODGE	Gladys Henson
PHOTOGRAPHER	Ward Bishop
MR. BIRBECK	Philip Tonge
GRACE TORRENCE	Ethel Borden
HELEN CARVER	Phyllis Connard
HENRY CARVER	Alan Campbell
MATTHEW	Macleary Stennett

Coward directed and G. E. Calthrop designed the sets. It ran for 135 performances. The published play is dedicated "To Alexander Woolcott".

Coward said of *Design for Living* in his preface:

It has been liked and disliked, and hated and admired, but never, I think, sufficiently loved by any but its three leading actors. This, perhaps was only to be expected, as its central theme, from the point of view of the average, must appear to be definitely anti-social. People were certainly interested and entertained and occasionally even moved by it, but it seemed to many of them "unpleasant". This sense of "unpleasantness" might have been mitigated for them a little if they had realized that the title was ironic rather than dogmatic. I never intended for a moment that the design for living suggested in the play should apply to anyone outside its three principal characters, Gilda, Otto, and Leo. These glib, over-articulate, and amoral creatures force their lives into fantastic shapes and problems because they cannot help themselves. Impelled chiefly by the impact of their personalities each upon the other, they are like moths in a pool of light, unable to tolerate the lonely outer darkness, and equally unable to share the light without colliding constantly and bruising one another's wings.

The end of the play is equivocal. The three of them, after various partings and reunions and partings again, after torturing and loving and hating one another, are left together as the curtain falls, laughing. Different minds found different meanings in this laughter. Some considered it to be directed against Ernest, Gilda's husband, and the time-honoured friend of all three. If so, it was certainly cruel, and in the worst possible taste. Some saw it as the lascivious anticipation of a sort of carnal frolic. Others with less ribald imaginations, regarded it as a meaningless and slightly inept excuse to bring the curtain down. I as author, however, prefer to think that Gilda and Otto and Leo were laughing at themselves.

Design for Living was filmed in America in 1933, but the play did not reach London until it was produced at the Haymarket Theatre on 25 January 1939 (transferring to the Savoy Theatre) running in all for 233 performances. The run was then broken by the outbreak of the war in September, but resumed in December for another 33 performances. It was directed by Harold French with the following cast:

GILDA	Diana Wynyard
ERNEST FRIEDMAN	Alan Webb
OTTO	Anton Walbrook
LEO	Rex Harrison
MISS HODGE	Dorothy Hamilton
MR. BIRBECK	Cyril Wheeler

GRACE TORRENCE	Everly Gregg
HELEN CARVER	Cathleen Cordell
HENRY CARVER	Ross Landon
MATTHEW	James McIntyre

Conversation Piece

Cochran was eagerly waiting for another Coward musical, and when Noël finished his run with the Lunts in New York, he yet again went cruising in the West Indies. On his return home, he retired to Goldenhurst, his Kentish home, and set to work to meet the challenge. His biographer, Cole Lesley, tells us that Noël

... began to compose the score for *Conversation Piece* with Yvonne (Printemps) in mind. He confided this ambitious project to Cochran as a dead secret, but Cochran at once released it to the Press, and Yvonne cabled from Paris that she would be delighted. He went into retirement at Goldenhurst and slogged away for ten days, but, as with *Bitter-Sweet*, no major waltz theme would materialise. At the end of the tenth day, late at night, he gave up, not so much in despair by then, but in a rage with Cochran for forcing his hand. He made up his mind to cable Cochran and Yvonne the next morning that he had cancelled the whole enterprise, walked to the door of the Big Room and switched off the lights. But the one on the piano remained burning; he marched back in a worse temper than ever to turn it off and sat down and played "I'll Follow My Secret Heart" straight through.

By November 1933, *Conversation Piece* was finished, but the usual casting and production trouble were to follow. Romney Brent, who was to play opposite Printemps was not up to the task and had to be released. Coward had the unenviable task of asking him to go, saying that he had decided to take over the part himself. Romney Brent agreed, saying "Providing you let me still come to rehearsals and watch you find out what a bloody awful part it is".

Conversation Piece was produced at His Majesty's Theatre on 16 February 1934 with the following cast:

SOPHIE OTFORD	Heather Thatcher
MARTHA JAMES	Moya Nugent
MRS. DRAGON	Betty Shale
PAUL, DUC DE CHAUCIGNY-VARENNES	Noël Coward
MELANIE	Yvonne Printemps
ROSE (*her maid*)	Maidie Andrews
THE MARQUIS OF SHEERE	Louis Hayward
THE EARL OF HARRINGFORD	George Sanders
LORD BRACEWORTH *Regency*	Pat Worsley
LORD DOYNING *Rakes*	Antony Brian
MR. HAILSHAM	Sydney Grammer
THE DUCHESS OF BENEDEN	Winifred Davis
THE DUKE OF BENEDEN	Athole Stewart
LADY JULIA CHARTERIS	Irene Browne
HANNAH (*her maid*)	Elizabeth Corcoran
A TIGER	Tommy Hayes
MISS GOSLETT	Everly Gregg
MISS MENTION	Molly Lumley
LORD KENYON	Penryn Bannerman
LORD ST. MARYS	Kim Peacock
FISHERMEN	Reginald Thurgood
	William McGuigan
	Evan Jones, Roy Hall
COUNTESS OF HARRINGFORD	Sheila Pattrick
LADY BRACEWORTH	Betty Elburn
MRS. HAILSHAM	Winifred Campbell
HON. JULIAN KANE	St. John Lauri
MR. AMOS	Alex Robertson
BUTLER	Claude Farrow
MR. JONES	Leonard Michel
COURTESAN	Jean Barnes

Noël of course directed, with settings and costumes by G. E. Calthrop. It ran for 177 performances. Pierre Fresnay took over Coward's part for two periods during the run. The score is dedicated: "A ma chère Yvonne, pour qui a été composée cette musique, et par qui elle est si délicieusement chantée. Affecteusement, Noël", and the book "To G. E. Calthrop, this play is gratefully and affectionately dedicated."

Coward later wrote in *Play Parade*:

Being a fine actress in addition to having one of the loveliest voices it has ever been my privilege to hear, [Yvonne Printemps] endowed the play with a special magic and, in spite of the fact that her English began and ended with "Good moening" "Yes" and "No", she contrived to enchant the public, the critics, the supporting cast, the orchestra, and even the stage hands. It is also an undoubted tribute to her that, by the end of the London and New York runs, most of the company spoke French fluently.

The play itself has, I think, a certain amount of charm in its own right. The lyrics are good and the music excellent. The original production was tremendously enhanced by the exquisite settings and dresses of G. E. Calthrop. Upon re-reading it I find that the story rambles a bit here and there and that there are also two startling anachronisms of which at the time of writing it, I was blissfully unaware. It is never explained for instance why, in the last scene, Melanie has completely dismantled a rented house in Brighton the furniture of which obviously doesn't belong to her! Also the sentimental emphasis on the gleaming lights of the packet-boat sailing to France is unfortunate considering that in 1811, the year in which the action of the play passes, England and France were at war! However apart from these minor defects it is a pleasant entertainment and I hope that one day, if ever we can find an artiste half as good as Yvonne Printempts, it may be revived.

The piece had a disappointing run of only 55 performances in New York, but was recorded in its entirety with Lily Pons and Richard Burton in 1951, with Coward himself speaking a linking narration as well as singing the famous quartets "Regency Rakes", "There's Always Something Fishy About the French" and "There Was Once a Little Village by the Sea" as solos! It has not been issued in this country.

Conversation Piece was to be the last of Noël's works to be produced by Cochran, as Coward had decided to become his own management. The parting with "Cocky" was fairly amicable, with as little rancour as possible. A new company was formed in association with John C. Wilson and the Lunts. "Jack" Wilson, an American stockbroker who gave up Wall Street to become Noël's personal manager, had been a friend since the 'twenties.

The first production of the new management was S. N. Behrman's play *Biography*, which opened at the Globe Theatre in April 1934, with Ina Claire and Laurence Olivier. *Theatre Royal* by Edna Furber and George S. Kaufman followed in October at the Lyric Theatre with Marie Tempest, Madge Titheradge and again Olivier. Coward directed both productions.

At the end of the year, he went to New York to direct *Point Valaine* which he had written during 1934, again for the Lunts. It opened on Broadway in January 1935, but was not a conspicuous success, only running 55 performances. It did not reach this country until 1944, when it was put on by the Old Vic Company in Liverpool during their tenure of the Playhouse. It was seen in London in 1947 in a production at the Embassy Theatre, Swiss Cottage.

To-night at 8.30

When in New York, Coward made his first major film appearance in *The Scoundrel* for Paramount and, after the launching of *Point Valaine*, went off on his usual travels to the East. It was on this holiday that he conceived the idea of a series of one-act plays, to star Gertrude Lawrence and himself. He says in his introduction to the plays:

In the year 1935, upheld by my stubborn faith in the "Star System", I wrote the *To-night at 8.30* plays as acting, singing, and dancing vehicles for Gertrude Lawrence and myself. The success we had had with *Private Lives* both in London and New York encouraged me to believe that the public liked to see us playing together and this belief, happily for us both and the managements concerned, turned out to be fully justified.

The result was eventually an accumulation during the summer of 1935 of ten plays (only nine of which are published). They were presented as *To-night at 8.30*, though on the long tour before they reached London, they had sometimes to be called *To-night at 7.30* to conform with provincial theatre-going.

They opened in Manchester in October 1935, and eventually in London at the Phoenix Theatre in repertoire between January and June 1936. Of the plays, only some were seen on tour; in London new plays were introduced during the run before eventually settling down to three programmes of three plays each. (The tenth play *Star Chamber* was tried out at a matinée but not repeated.) Coward directed and appeared in all the plays, with settings and costumes by G. E. Calthrop, and in all they ran for 157 performances.

In order of production in London the plays are: *Family Album, The Astonished Heart,* and *"Red Peppers"* (First night: Phoenix, 9 January 1936). *Hands Across the Sea, Fumed Oak, Shadow Play* (Second programme, 13 January 1936). The following were introduced later in various combinations; *We Were Dancing, Star Chamber, Ways and Means* and *Still Life,* later becoming a third programme.

In this volume, there are included *Hands Across the Sea, Still Life* and *Fumed Oak.*

Hands Across the Sea (produced 13 January 1936)

WALTERS	Moya Nugent
LADY MAUREEN GILPIN (PIGGIE)	Gertrude Lawrence
COMMANDER PETER GILPIN, R.N.	Noël Coward
LIEUT.-COMMANDER ALASTAIR CORBETT, R.N.	Edward Underdown
MRS. WADHURST	Alison Leggatt
MR. WADHURST	Alan Webb
MR. BURNHAM	Kenneth Carten
THE HON. CLARE WEDDERBURN	Everly Gregg
MAJOR GOSLING	Anthony Pélissier

In his preface, Coward says:

Hands Across the Sea is a satire on the confusions of a London Society woman suddenly faced with the unexpected arrival of two colonials with whom she once stayed while travelling in the Far East. It is a gay, unpretentious little play, and it was acted by Gertie with incomparable brilliance. I cannot think of it without remembering the infinite variety of her inflections; her absurd scatterbrained conversations on the telephone; her frantic desire to be hospitable and charming and her expression of blank dismay when she suddenly realized that her visitors were not who she thought they were at all. It was a superb performance in the highest traditions of high comedy, already now over and done with for ever, but, as far as I am concerned, never to be forgotten.

Still Life (produced 18 May 1936)

LAURA JESSON	Gertrude Lawrence
MYRTLE BAGOT	Joyce Carey
BERYL WATERS	Moya Nugent
YOUNG MAN	Charles Peters
STANLEY	Kenneth Carten
ALBERT GODBY	Alan Webb
ALEC HARVEY	Noël Coward
BILL	Edward Underdown
JOHNNIE	Anthony Pélissier

| MILDRED | Betty Hare |
| DOLLY MESSITER | Everly Gregg |

Still Life was expanded by Coward into a full length film-script *Brief Encounter* made in 1945, with Celia Johnson and Trevor Howard. A radio adaptation of the film was broadcast in 1955. Noël made a version for two voices, which he recorded with Margaret Leighton in 1956. It was staged in Paris as *Brève Rencontre* (paired with *Nous Dansons...*) in 1968, and later paired with *Fumed Oak* as a musical (by other hands) under the title *Mr. and Mrs.,* also in 1968.

Coward says in the preface:

Still Life was the most mature play of the whole series (with the exception of *Hands Across the Sea* which was equally mature but in a different idiom) . . . It is well written, economical and well constructed: the characters, I think, are true, and I can say now, reading it with detachment after so many years, that I am proud to have written it.

Fumed Oak (produced 13 January 1936)

HENRY GOW	Noël Coward
DORIS (*his wife*)	Gertrude Lawrence
ELSIE (*his daughter*)	Moya Nugent
MRS. ROCKETT (*his mother-in-law*)	Alison Leggatt

In his preface, Coward says:

Fumed Oak is a comedy based on the good old "Worm will turn" theme. I loved "Henry Gow" from the moment I started writing him, and I loved playing him more, I think, than anything else in the repertoire. A memorable performance was given in this by Moya Nugent as Elsie, the snivelling schoolgirl.

A further three plays from *To-night at 8.30* are to be found in *Plays: Four.*

RAYMOND MANDER and JOE MITCHENSON

A complete chronology of Noël Coward's work for the stage, with a note on publication, will be found in Volumes 1, 2 and 4 of this series.

DESIGN FOR LIVING

CHARACTERS

GILDA

OTTO

LEO

ERNEST FRIEDMAN

MISS HODGE

MR. BIRBECK

HENRY CARVER

HELEN CARVER

GRACE TORRENCE

MATTHEW

ACT I

Otto's Studio in Paris.

ACT II

Scene I.   Leo's Flat in London. (Eighteen months later.)

Scene II.   The Same. (A few days later.)

Scene III.   The Same. (The next morning.)

ACT III

Scene I.   Ernest's Apartment in New York. (Two years later.)

Scene II.   The Same. (The next morning.)

———

Time : The Present.

ACT I

The Scene is rather a shabby studio in Paris. There is a large window at the back looking out on to roof tops. Down stage, on the Left, there is a door leading on to the stairs, which in turn lead to the street. Up stage, on the Right, there is a door leading into a small kitchen.

When the curtain rises, it is about ten o'clock on a spring morning, and the studio is empty. GILDA comes in from the kitchen carrying a coffee pot and a milk jug. She places them on a table just under the window, which is already laid with cups and plates, etc. GILDA is a good-looking woman of about thirty.

Suddenly there is a knock on the door Left. She gives a quick glance towards it, and then goes swiftly and silently into the bedroom. In a moment she returns, closing the bedroom door carefully behind her. There is another knock on the door. She opens it, admitting ERNEST FRIEDMAN. *He is any age between forty and fifty, rather precise in manner. He carries a large package, obviously a picture. done up in brown paper.*

GILDA : Ernest !

ERNEST : May I come in ?

GILDA : I'd no idea you were back.

ERNEST : I arrived last night.

He comes in and puts down the package.

GILDA · What's that ?

ERNEST : Something exquisite, superb.

3

GILDA :   The Matisse ?

ERNEST :   Yes.

GILDA :   You got it, after all.

ERNEST :   It's unbelievable.

GILDA :   Undo it quickly !

ERNEST :   Otto must see it, too.

GILDA :   He's asleep.

ERNEST :   Wake him up, then.

GILDA :   Not now, Ernest ; he's had the most awful neuralgia all night.

ERNEST :   Neuralgia ?

GILDA :   Yes, all up one side of his face and down the other side.

ERNEST (*undoing the package*) :   Wake him up. One look at this will take away his neuralgia immediately.

GILDA :   No, really. He's only just dropped off. He's been in agony. I've dosed him with aspirin and given him a hot-water bottle here, and another one just there——

ERNEST (*petulantly*) :   I didn't know anyone had so many hot-water bottles.

GILDA :   I still have one more, in case it spreads.

ERNEST :   It really is very irritating. I take the trouble to drag this large picture all the way round here and Otto chooses to have neuralgia.

GILDA :   He didn't choose to have it. He hated having it. His little face is all pinched and strained.

ERNEST :   Otto's face is enormous.

GILDA :   Show me the picture, Ernest, and try not to be disagreeable.

ERNEST (*grumbling*) :   It's an anticlimax.

GILDA :   Thank you, dear.

ERNEST :   It's no use pretending to be hurt. You

know you don't really care for anybody's pictures except Otto's.

GILDA :   Do you want some coffee ?

ERNEST :   Why are there two cups, if Otto has neuralgia ?

GILDA :   Habit.   There are always two cups.

ERNEST (*propping up the picture, facing up stage*): There !

GILDA (*scrutinizing it*) :   Yes, it's good.

ERNEST :   Stand further back.

GILDA (*obliging*) :   Very good indeed.   How much ?

ERNEST :   Eight hundred pounds.

GILDA :   Did you bargain ?

ERNEST :   No, that was their price.

GILDA :   I think you were right.   Dealers or private owners ?

ERNEST :   Dealers.

GILDA :   Here's your coffee.

ERNEST (*taking the cup and still looking at the picture*) : It's strangely unlike all the other work, isn't it ?

GILDA :   What are you going to do with it ?

ERNEST :   Wait a little.

GILDA :   And then resell ?

ERNEST :   I expect so.

GILDA :   It will need a room to itself.

ERNEST :   None of your decorating schemes.   Hands off !

GILDA :   Don't you think I'm a good decorator ?

ERNEST :   Not particularly.

GILDA :   Darling Ernest !

ERNEST (*back at the picture*) :   Otto will go mad when he sees it.

GILDA :   You think Otto's good, don't you ?   You think he's all right ?

ERNEST : Coming along. Coming along very nicely.

GILDA : Better than that. Much better !

ERNEST : Lady Jaguar, defending her young !

GILDA : Otto isn't my young.

ERNEST : Oh, yes, he is. Otto's everybody's young.

GILDA : You think he's weak, don't you ?

ERNEST : Certainly, I do.

GILDA : And that I'm strong ?

ERNEST : Strong as an ox !

GILDA : You've called me a jaguar and an ox within the last two minutes. I wish you wouldn't be quite so zoological.

ERNEST : A temperamental ox, Gilda. Sometimes a hysterical ox ; and, at the moment, an over-vehement ox ! What's the matter with you this morning ?

GILDA : The matter with me ?

ERNEST : There's a wild gleam in your eye.

GILDA : There always is. It's one of my greatest charms ! I'm surprised that you never noticed it before.

ERNEST : The years are creeping on me, Gilda. Perhaps my perceptions are getting dulled.

GILDA (*absently*) : Perhaps they are.

ERNEST : If, in my dotage, I become a bore to you, you won't scruple to let me know, will you ?

GILDA : Don't be an idiot !

ERNEST (*ruminatively*) : Perhaps it was wrong of me to arrive unexpectedly ; I should have written you a little note making an appointment.

GILDA : Be a nice bluebottle and stop buzzing at me, will you ?

ERNEST : You're a striking-looking woman—particularly when a little distrait. It's a pity Otto's paintings of you have always been so tranquil. He's missed something.

GILDA : The next time he paints me, you must be here to lash me with gay witticisms.

ERNEST : Surely, in my rôle of bitter old family friend, I can demand a little confidence ! You could tell me quite safely, you know, if anything's wrong. I might even be able to help, with a senile word or two.

GILDA : Nothing is wrong, I tell you.

ERNEST : Nothing at all ?

GILDA : Shall I make you some toast ?

ERNEST : No, thank you.

GILDA : It's very hot to-day, isn't it ?

ERNEST : Why not open the window ?

GILDA : I never thought of it.

She opens the window almost violently.

There!—I'm sick of this studio ; it's squalid ! I wish I were somewhere quite different. I wish I were somebody quite different. I wish I were a nice-minded British matron, with a husband, a cook, and a baby. I wish I believed in God and the *Daily Mail* and "Mother India" !

ERNEST : I wish you'd tell me what's upsetting you.

GILDA : Glands, I expect. Everything's glandular. I read a book about it the other day. Ernest, if you only realized what was going on inside you, you'd be bitterly offended !

ERNEST : I'm much more interested in what's going on inside you.

7

GILDA : I'll tell you. All the hormones in my blood are working overtime. They're rushing madly in and out of my organs like messenger boys.

ERNEST : Why ?

GILDA : Perhaps it's a sort of presentiment.

ERNEST : Psychic. I see. Well, well, well !

GILDA : Yes, I hear voices. I hear my own voice louder than any of the others, and it's beginning to bore me. Would you describe me as a super-egoist, Ernest ?

ERNEST : Yes, dear.

GILDA : Thinking of myself too much, and not enough of other people ?

ERNEST : No. Thinking of other people too much through yourself.

GILDA : How can anyone do otherwise ?

ERNEST : Detachment of mind.

GILDA : I haven't got that sort of mind.

ERNEST : It's an acquired attitude and difficult to achieve, but, believe me, well worth trying for.

GILDA : Are you presenting yourself as a shining example ?

ERNEST : Not shining, my dear, just dully effulgent.

GILDA : How should I start ? Go away alone with my thoughts ?

ERNEST : With all my detachment I find it very difficult to regard your painful twistings and turnings with composure.

GILDA : Why ?

ERNEST (*blandly*) : Because I'm very fond of you.

GILDA : Why ?

ERNEST : I don't know. A tedious habit, I suppose. After all, I was very attached to your mother.

GILDA : Yes, I know. Personally, I never cared for her very much. A bossy woman.

ERNEST : I don't think you should allude to the dead as " bossy."

GILDA : No reverence. That's my trouble. No reverence.

ERNEST : I feel vaguely paternal towards you.

GILDA : Yes, Ernest.

ERNEST : And your behaviour confuses me.

GILDA : My painful twistings and turnings.

ERNEST : Exactly.

GILDA : What did you mean by that ?

ERNEST : Will you explain one thing to me really satisfactorily ?

GILDA : What ?

ERNEST : Why don't you marry Otto ?

GILDA : It's very funny that underneath all your worldly wisdom you're nothing but a respectable little old woman in a jet bonnet.

ERNEST : You don't like being disapproved of, do you ?

GILDA : Does anybody ?

ERNEST : Anyhow, I don't disapprove of you, yourself—of course, you're as obstinate as a mule——

GILDA : There you go again ! " Strong as an ox ! " " Obstinate as a mule ! " Just a pack of Animal Grab—that's what I am ! Bring out all the other cards. " Gentle as a dove ! " "Playful as a kitten ! " "Black as a crow ! "——

ERNEST : "Brave as a lion ! "——

GILDA : Oh, no, Ernest ! You couldn't think that, disapproving of me as you do.

ERNEST : I was about to explain, when you so

rudely interrupted, that it isn't you, yourself, I disapprove of. It's your mode of life.

GILDA (*laughing slightly*): Oh, I see !

ERNEST: Your life is so dreadfully untidy, Gilda.

GILDA: I'm not a tidy person.

ERNEST: You haven't yet answered my original question.

GILDA: Why I don't marry Otto ?

ERNEST: Yes. Is there a real reason, or just a lot of faintly affected theories ?

GILDA: There's a very real reason.

ERNEST: Well ?

GILDA: I love him. (*She glances towards the bedroom door and says louder*): I love him.

ERNEST: All right ! All right, there's no need to shout.

GILDA: Yes, there is, every need. I should like to scream.

ERNEST: That would surely be very bad for Otto's neuralgia.

GILDA (*calming down*): The only reasons for me to marry would be these : To have children ; to have a home ; to have a background for social activities, and to be provided for. Well, I don't like children ; I don't wish for a home ; I can't bear social activities, and I have a small but adequate income of my own. I love Otto deeply, and I respect him as a person and as an artist. To be tied legally to him would be repellent to me and to him, too. It's not a dashing bohemian gesture to Free Love : we just feel like that, both of us. Now, are you satisfied ?

ERNEST: If you are.

GILDA: You're impossible, Ernest. You sit there looking quizzical, and it maddens me !

ERNEST : I am quizzical.

GILDA : Well, be something else, for God's sake !

ERNEST : I suppose you know Leo is back ?

GILDA (*jumping slightly*) :   What ?

ERNEST : I said, "I suppose you know Leo is back?"

GILDA (*tremendously astonished*) : It's not true !

ERNEST : Didn't he let you know ?

GILDA (*eagerly*) : When did he arrive ? Where's he staying ?

ERNEST : He arrived yesterday on the *Mauretania*. I had a note from him last night.

GILDA : Where's he staying ?

ERNEST : You'll be shocked when I tell you.

GILDA : Quickly !—Quickly !

ERNEST : The George V.

GILDA (*going off into peals of laughter*) : He must be raving ! The George V ! Oh, dear, oh, dear ! Leo, at the George V ! It's a glorious picture. Marble bathrooms and private balconies ! Leo in all that grandeur ! It isn't possible.

ERNEST : I gather he's made a good deal of money.

GILDA : That's not enough excuse. He ought to be ashamed of himself !

ERNEST : I can't understand him, not letting you know he was back.   I fully expected to find him here.

GILDA : He'll appear sooner or later.

ERNEST :   Are you glad he's made money ?

GILDA : Why do you ask that ?

ERNEST :   Curiosity.

GILDA : Of course I'm glad.   I adore Leo !

ERNEST :   And Otto ?   What about Otto ?

GILDA (*irritably*) : What do you mean, " What about Otto ? "

ERNEST : Will he be glad, too ?

GILDA : You're too ridiculous sometimes, Ernest. What are you suspecting ? What are you trying to find out ?

ERNEST : Nothing. I was only wondering.

GILDA : It's all right. I know what you're getting at ; but you're wrong as usual. Everybody's always wrong about Leo and Otto and me. I'm not jealous of Leo's money and success, and Otto won't be either when he knows. That's what you were suspecting, wasn't it ?

ERNEST : Perhaps.

GILDA (*turning away*) : I think you should grasp the situation a little better, having known us all for so long.

ERNEST : Otto and Leo knew each other first.

GILDA : Yes, yes, yes, yes—I know all about that ! I came along and spoilt everything ! Go on, dear——

ERNEST : I didn't say that.

GILDA (*sharply*) : It's what you meant.

ERNEST : I think, perhaps, you may have spoilt yourself a little.

GILDA : Distrust of women frequently sets in at your age, Ernest.

ERNEST : I cannot, for the life of me, imagine why I'm so fond of you. You have such abominable manners.

GILDA : It's probably the scarlet life I live, causing me to degenerate into a shrew.

ERNEST : Very likely.

GILDA (*suddenly, leaning over the back of his chair, with her arms around him*) : I'm sorry—about my bad manners, I mean. Please forgive me. You're a darling, and you love us a lot, don't you ? All three of us ? Me a little less than Otto and Leo because I'm a woman and, therefore, unreliable. Isn't that true ?

ERNEST (*patting her hand*): Quite.

GILDA (*leaving him*) : Your affection is a scared thing, though. Too frightened ; too apprehensive of consequences. Leave us to grapple with the consequences, my dear. We're bound to have a bad time every now and then, but, at least, we know it. We're aware of a whole lot of things. Look at us clearly as human beings, rather peculiar human beings, I grant you, and don't be prejudiced by our lack of social grace. I laughed too loudly just now at the thought of Leo being rich and rare. Too loudly because I was uneasy, not jealous. I don't want him to be any different, that's all.

ERNEST : I see.

GILDA : Do you ? Do you really ? I doubt it. I don't see how anyone outside could. But I would like you to understand one thing absolutely and completely. I love Otto—whatever happens, I love Otto.

ERNEST : I never suggested for a moment that you didn't.

GILDA : Wait. Wait and see. The immediate horizon is grey and forbidding and dangerous. You don't know what I'm talking about and you probably think I've gone mad, and I can't explain—not now. But, darling Ernest, there's a crisis on. A full-blooded, emotional crisis ; and when I need you, which I expect will be very soon, I shall yell ! I shall yell like mad !

ERNEST : I knew you were in a state about something.

GILDA : Nasty shrewd little instincts shooting out and discovering things lurking in the atmosphere. It's

13

funny about atmosphere, isn't it? Strong inside
thoughts make outside impressions. Imprints on the
ether. A horrid sort of spiritual television.

ERNEST: Quite.

GILDA: Well, are you satisfied now? You felt
something was the matter, and you were right. It's
always pleasant to be right, isn't it?

ERNEST: Not by any means.

GILDA: You're right about something else, too.

ERNEST: What?

GILDA: Women being unreliable. There are
moments in life when I look upon my own damned
femininity with complete nausea. There!

ERNEST (*smiling*): Good!

GILDA: I don't like women at all, Ernest; and I
like myself least of any of them.

ERNEST: Never mind.

GILDA: I do mind. I mind bitterly. It humiliates
me to the dust to think that I can go so far, clearly and
intelligently, keeping faith with my own standards—
which are not female standards at all—preserving a
certain decent integrity, not using any tricks; then,
suddenly, something happens, a spark is struck and
down I go into the mud! Squirming with archness,
being aloof and desirable, consciously alluring, snatching and grabbing, evading and surrendering, dressed
and painted for victory. An object of strange contempt!

ERNEST: A lurid picture, perhaps a trifle exag-
gerated.

GILDA: I wish it were. I wish it were.

ERNEST: Drink a little coffee.

GILDA: Perhaps you're right.

She sits down suddenly.

ERNEST (*pouring it out*) :   There !

GILDA :   Thank you, Ernest.   You're a great comfort.   (*She sips a little.*)   It's not very nice, is it?

ERNEST :   Disgusting !

GILDA :   I must have burnt it.

ERNEST :   You did, dear.

GILDA :   How lovely to be you !

ERNEST :   In heaven's name, why ?

GILDA :   You're a permanent spectator.   You deal in pictures.   You look at pictures all day long, good pictures and bad pictures ; gay pictures and gloomy pictures, and you know why they're this or why they're that, because you're critical and knowledgeable and wise.   You're a clever little dear, that's what you are— a clever little dear !   (*She begins to laugh again.*)

ERNEST :   Gilda, stop it !

GILDA :   Take a look at this, my darling.   Measure it with your eyes.   Portrait of a woman in three cardinal colours.   Portrait of a too loving spirit tied down to a predatory feminine carcass.

ERNEST :   This is definitely macabre.

GILDA :   Right, again !

ERNEST :   I think I'd better go.   You ought to lie down or something.

GILDA (*hysterically*) :   Stay a little longer, you'll find out so much.

ERNEST :   I don't want to find out anything. You're scaring me to death.

GILDA :   Courage, Ernest.   Be brave.   Look at the whole thing as a side show.   People pay to see freaks. Walk up !   Walk up and see the Fat Lady and the Monkey Man and the Living Skeleton and the Three Famous Hermaphrodites !——

*There is a noise outside in the passage. The door
bursts open, and* OTTO *fairly bounds into the room.
He is tall and good-looking, wearing a travelling coat
and hat, and carrying a suitcase and a large package of
painting materials.*

GILDA :   Otto !

OTTO (*striking an attitude*) :   I've come home !

GILDA :   You see what happens when I crack the
whip !

OTTO :   Little Ernest !   How very sweet to see
you !   (*He kisses him.*)

GILDA :   When did you leave Bordeaux ?

OTTO :   Night train, dear heart.

GILDA :   Why didn't you telegraph ?

OTTO :   I don't hold with these modern innovations.

ERNEST :   This is very interesting.

OTTO :   What's very interesting ?

ERNEST :   Life, Otto. I was just meditating upon Life.

OTTO (*to* GILDA) :   I've finished the picture.

GILDA :   Really ?   Completely finished it ?

OTTO :   Yes, it's fine.   I brought it away with me.
I made the old fool sit for hours and wouldn't let her
see, and afterwards when she did she made the most
awful scene.   She said it was out of drawing and made
her look podgy ; then I lost my temper and said it was
over-eating and lack of exercise that made her look
podgy, and that it was not only an exquisite painting but
unfalteringly true to life.   Then she practically ordered
me out of the house !   I don't suppose she'll ever pay
me the rest of the money, but to hell with her !   If she
doesn't, I shall have the picture.

ERNEST :   Unwise, but, I am sure, enjoyable.

There is silence.

16

OTTO :   Well ?

GILDA :   Well what ?

OTTO :   What on earth's the matter ?

GILDA :   Why should you think anything's the matter ?

OTTO (*looking from one to the other*) :   Have your faces lit up ?   No.   Have you rushed at me with out-stretched arms ?   No.   Are you, either of you, even remotely pleased to see me ?   Obviously NO !   Something dreadful has happened and you're trying to decide how to break the news to me.   What is it ?   Tell me at once !   What's the matter ?

ERNEST (*with slight malice*) :   Gilda has neuralgia.

OTTO :   Nonsense !   She's as strong as a horse.

GILDA (*laughing wildly*) :   Oh, my God !

OTTO (*to* ERNEST) :   What's she " Oh, my God-ing " about ?

ERNEST :   It's glandular.   Everything's glandular.

OTTO :   Have you both gone mad ?

GILDA :   Don't take off your coat and hat.

OTTO :   What ?

GILDA (*very slowly and distinctly*) :   I said, " Don't take off your coat and hat."

OTTO (*humouring her*) :   Very well, darling, I won't, I promise you.   As a matter of fact, I said to myself only this morning, " Otto," I said, " Otto, you must never, never be parted from your coat and hat !   Never, never, never ! "

GILDA :   There's a surprise for you, darling.   A beautiful surprise !

OTTO :   What ?

GILDA :   You must go to the George V at once.

OTTO :   The George V ?

GILDA : Yes. That's the surprise.

OTTO : Who is it ? Who's at the George V ?

GILDA : Leo.

OTTO : You're not serious ? He couldn't be.

GILDA : He is. He came back on the *Mauretania.*
His play is still running in Chicago, and he's sold the
movie rights and he's made thousands !

OTTO : Have you seen him ?

GILDA : Of course ! Last night.

ERNEST : Well, I'm damned !

GILDA : I told you you didn't understand, Ernest.
(*To* OTTO): If you'd only let me know you were
coming, we could have both met you at the station. It
would have been so lovely ! Leo will be furious.
You must go to him at once and bring him back here
and we'll make some sort of a plan for the day.

OTTO : This is good, good, better than good ! An
excellent, super-homecoming ! I was thinking of him
last night, bumping along in that awful train. I
thought of him for hours, I swear I did. Cross my
hand with silver, lady, I'm so definitely the Gipsy
Queen ! Oh, God, how marvellous ! He'll be able to
go to Annecy with us.

GILDA : He's got to go back to New York, and
then to London.

OTTO : Splendid ! We'll go with him. He's been
away far too long. Come on—— (*He seizes* GILDA's
hand.)

GILDA : No.

ERNEST : What are you going to do ?

GILDA : Stay here and tidy up. You go with
Otto to fetch Leo. You said my life was untidy, didn't
you ? Well, I'm taking it to heart !

OTTO: Come on, Gilda; it doesn't matter about tidying up.

GILDA: Yes, it does. It does! It's the most important thing in the world—an orderly mind; that's the thing to have.

OTTO: He's probably brought us presents, and if he's rich they'll be expensive presents. Very nice! Very nice, indeed. Come along, Ernest, my little honey—we'll take a taxi.

ERNEST: I don't think I'll go.

OTTO: You must. He likes seeing you almost as much as us. Come on! (*He grabs* ERNEST *by the shoulders and shoves him towards the door.*)

GILDA: Of course, go, Ernest, and come back too and we'll all celebrate. I'm yelling! Can't you hear me yelling like mad?

OTTO: What on earth are you talking about?

GILDA: A bad joke, and very difficult to explain.

OTTO: Good morning, darling! I never kissed you good morning.

GILDA: Never mind about that now. Go on, both of you, or he'll have gone out. You don't want to miss him.

OTTO (*firmly kissing her*): Good morning, darling.

GILDA (*suddenly stiffening in his arms*): Dearest——
          OTTO *and* ERNEST *go to the door.*

GILDA (*suddenly*): Otto——!

OTTO (*turning*): Yes?

GILDA (*smiling gaily, but with a slight strain in her voice*): I love you very much, so be careful crossing roads, won't you? Look to the right and the left and all around everything, and don't do anything foolish and impulsive. Please remember, there's a dear——

OTTO : Be quiet, don't pester me with your attentions ! (*To* ERNEST *as they go out*) : She's crazy about me, poor little thing ; just crazy about me.

They go out. GILDA *stands quite still for a moment or two staring after them ; then she sits down at a table.* LEO *comes out of the bedroom. He is thin and nervous and obviously making a tremendous effort to control himself. He walks about aimlessly for a little and finishes up looking out of the window, with his back to* GILDA.

LEO : What now ?

GILDA : I don't know.

LEO : Not much time to think.

GILDA : A few minutes.

LEO : Are there any cigarettes ?

GILDA : Yes, in that box.

LEO : Want one ?

GILDA : No.

LEO (*lighting one*) : It's nice being human beings, isn't it ? I'm sure God's angels must envy us.

GILDA : Whom do you love best ? Otto or me ?

LEO : Silly question.

GILDA : Answer me, anyhow.

LEO : How can I ? Be sensible ! In any case, what does it matter ?

GILDA : It's important to me.

LEO : No, it isn't—not really. That's not what's important. What we did was inevitable. It's been inevitable for years. It doesn't matter who loves who the most ; you can't line up things like that mathematically. We all love each other a lot, far too much, and we've made a bloody mess of it ! That was inevitable, too.

GILDA :   We must get it straight, somehow.

LEO :   Yes, we must get it straight and tie it up with ribbons with a bow on the top.   Pity it isn't Valentine's Day !

GILDA :   Can't we laugh a little ?   Isn't it a joke ? Can't we make it a joke ?

LEO :   Yes, it's a joke.   It's a joke, all right.   We can laugh until our sides ache.   Let's start, shall we ?

GILDA :   What's the truth of it ?   The absolute, deep-down truth ?   Until we really know that, we can't grapple with it.   We can't do a thing.   We can only sit here flicking words about.

LEO :   It should be easy, you know.   The actual facts are so simple.   I love you.   You love me.   You love Otto.   I love Otto.   Otto loves you.   Otto loves me.   There now !   Start to unravel from there.

GILDA :   We've always been honest, though, all of us.   Honest with each other, I mean.   That's something to go on, isn't it ?

LEO :   In this particular instance, it makes the whole thing far more complicated.   If we were ordinary moral, high-thinking citizens we could carry on a backstairs affair for weeks without saying a word about it.   We could lunch and dine together, all three, and not give anything away by so much as a look.

GILDA :   If we were ordinary moral, high-thinking citizens we shouldn't have had an affair at all.

LEO :   Perhaps not.   We should have crushed it down.   And the more we crushed it down the more we should have resented Otto, until we hated him.   Just think of hating Otto——

GILDA :   Just think of him hating us.

LEO :   Do you think he will ?

GILDA (*inexorably*):   Yes.

LEO (*walking about the room*): Oh, no, no—he mustn't ! It's too silly. He must see how un-important it is, really.

GILDA :   There's no question of not telling him, is there ?

LEO :   Of course not.

GILDA :   We could pretend that you just arrived here and missed them on the way.

LEO :   So we could, dear—so we could.

GILDA :   Do you think we're working each other up ? Do you think we're imagining it to be more serious than it really is ?

LEO :   Perhaps.

GILDA :   Do you think, after all, he may not mind quite so dreadfully ?

LEO :   He'll mind just as much as you or I would under similar circumstances. Probably a little bit more. Imagine that for a moment, will you ? Put yourself in his place.

GILDA (*hopelessly*): Oh, don't !

LEO :   Tell me one thing.   How sorry were you last night, when once you realized we were in for it ?

GILDA :   I wasn't sorry at all.   I gave way utterly.

LEO :   So did I.

GILDA :   Very deep inside, I had a qualm or two. Just once or twice.

LEO :   So did I.

GILDA :   But I stamped on them, like killing beetles.

LEO :   A nice way to describe the pangs of a noble conscience !

GILDA :   I enjoyed it all, see ! I enjoyed it thoroughly from the very first moment.   So there !

LEO : All right ! All right ! So did I.

GILDA (*defiantly*) : It was romantic. Suddenly, violently romantic ! The whole evening was " Gala." You looked lovely, darling—very smooth and velvety—and your manner was a dream ! I'd forgotten about your French accent and the way you move your hands, and the way you dance. A sleek little gigolo !

LEO : You must try not to be bitter, dear.

GILDA : There seemed to be something new about you : something I'd never realized before. Perhaps it's having money. Perhaps your success has given you a little extra glamour.

LEO : Look at me now, sweet ! It's quite chilly, this morning light. How do I appear to you now ?

GILDA (*gently*) : The same.

LEO : So do you, but that's because my eyes are slow at changing visions. I still see you too clearly last night to be able to realize how you look this morning. You were very got up—very got up, indeed, in your green dress and your ear-rings. It was " Gala," all right—strong magic !

GILDA : Coloured lights, sly music, overhanging trees, paper streamers—all the trappings.

LEO : Champagne, too, just to celebrate, both of us hating it.

GILDA : We drank to Otto. Perhaps you remember that as well ?

LEO : Perfectly.

GILDA : How could we ? Oh, how could we ?

LEO : It seemed quite natural.

GILDA : Yes, but we knew in our hearts what *you* were up to. It was vile of us.

LEO: I'll drink Otto's health until the day I die! Nothing could change that ever.

GILDA: Sentimentalist!

LEO: Deeper than sentiment: far, far deeper. Beyond the reach of small enchantments.

GILDA: Was that all it was to you? A small enchantment?

LEO: That's all it ever is to anybody, if only they knew.

GILDA: Easy wisdom. Is it a comfort to you?

LEO: Not particularly.

GILDA (*viciously*): Let's have some more! "Passion's only transitory," isn't it? "Love is ever fleeting!" "Time is a great healer." Trot them all out, dear.

LEO: Don't try to quarrel with me.

GILDA: Don't be so wise and assured and knowing, then. It's infuriating.

LEO: I believe I was more to blame than you, really.

GILDA: Why?

LEO: I made the running.

GILDA: *You* made the running! (*She laughs.*)

LEO: A silly pride made me show off to you, parade my attraction for you, like a mannequin. New spring model, with a few extra flounces!

GILDA: That's my story, Leo; you can't steal it from me. I've been wallowing in self-abasement, dragging out my last night's femininity and spitting on it. I've taken the blame on to myself for the whole thing. Ernest was quite shocked; you should have been listening at the door.

LEO: I was.

GILDA: Good! Then you know how I feel.

LEO : Lot of damned hysteria.

GILDA : Possibly, but heartfelt at the moment.

LEO : Can't we put an end to this flagellation party now ?

GILDA : We might just as well go off with it ; it passes the time.

LEO : Until Otto comes back.

GILDA : Yes. Until Otto comes back.

LEO (*walking up and down*) : I expect jealousy had something to do with it, too.

GILDA : Jealousy ?

LEO : Yes. Subconscious and buried deep, but there all the same ; there for ages, ever since our first meeting when you chose Otto so firmly.

GILDA : Another of those pleasant little galas ! The awakening of spring ! Romance in a café ! Yes, sir ! " Yes, sir, three bags full ! "

LEO : A strange evening. Very gay, if I remember rightly.

GILDA : Oh, it was gay, deliriously gay, thick with omens !

LEO : Perhaps we laughed at them too hard.

GILDA : You and Otto had a row afterwards, didn't you ?

LEO : Yes, a beauty.

GILDA : Blows ?

LEO : Ineffectual blows. Otto fell into the bath !

GILDA : Was there any water in it ?

LEO : Not at first.

GILDA (*beginning to laugh*) : Leo, you didn't——?

LEO (*also beginning to laugh*) : Of course I did ; it was the obvious thing to do.

GILDA : Couldn't he get out ?

LEO : Every time he tried, I pushed him back.

GILDA (*now laughing helplessly*) : Oh, the poor darling !——

LEO (*giving way*) : Finally—he—he got wedged——

GILDA : This is hysteria ! Stop it, stop it——

LEO (*sinking down at the table with his head in his hands, roaring with laughter*) : It—it was a very narrow bath, far—far—too narrow——

GILDA (*collapsing at the other side of the table*) : Shut up, for heaven's sake ! Shut up——

> *They are sitting there, groaning with laughter, when* OTTO *comes into the room.*

OTTO : Leo !

> *They both look up, and the laughter dies away from their faces.* LEO *rises and comes slowly over to* OTTO. *He takes both his hands and stands looking at him.*

LEO : Hello, Otto.

OTTO : Why did you stop laughing so suddenly ?

LEO : It's funny how lovely it is to see you.

OTTO : Why funny ?

GILDA : Where's Ernest ?

OTTO : He wouldn't come back with me. He darted off in a taxi very abruptly when we found Leo wasn't at the hotel. He seemed to be in a fluster.

LEO : Ernest's often in a fluster. It's part of his personality, I think.

OTTO : Ernest hasn't got a personality.

GILDA : Yes, he has ; but it's only a very little one, gentle and prim.

OTTO : You've changed, Leo. Your face looks different.

LEO : In what way different ?

OTTO : I don't know, sort of odd.

LEO: I was very seasick on the *Mauretania*. Perhaps that changed it.

GILDA: They call the *Mauretania* " The Greyhound of the Ocean." I wonder why ?

LEO: Because it's too long and too thin and leaps up and down.

GILDA: Personally, I prefer the *Olympic*. It's a good-natured boat and cosy, also it has a Turkish bath.

LEO: I dearly love a Turkish bath.

OTTO: Have you both gone crazy ?

LEO: Yes. Just for a little.

OTTO: What does that mean ?

GILDA: Lots of things, Otto. Everything's quite horrid.

OTTO: I'm awfully puzzled. I wish you'd both stop hinting and tell me what's happened.

LEO: It's serious, Otto. Please try to be wise about it.

OTTO (*with slight irritation*): How the hell can I be wise about it if I don't know what it is ?

LEO (*turning away*): Oh, God ! This is unbearable !

OTTO (*fighting against the truth that's dawning on him*): It wouldn't be what I think it is, would it ? I mean, what's just dropped into my mind. It isn't that, is it ?

GILDA: Yes.

LEO: Yes.

OTTO (*very quietly*): Oh, I see.

GILDA (*miserably*): If only you wouldn't look like that.

OTTO: I can't see that it matters very much how I look.

LEO: We're—we're both equally to blame.

27

OTTO : When did you arrive ? When—when did —don't you think you'd better tell me a little more ?

LEO (*swiftly*) : I arrived yesterday afternoon, and the moment I'd left my bags at the hotel I came straight here, naturally. Gilda and I dined together, and I spent the night here.

OTTO : Oh—oh, did you ?

LEO (*after a long pause*) : Yes, I did.

OTTO : This is the second bad entrance I've made this morning. I don't think I'd better make any more.

GILDA : Otto—darling—please, listen a minute !

OTTO : What is there to listen to ? What is there for you to say ?

GILDA : Nothing. You're quite right. Nothing at all.

OTTO : Have you planned it ? Before, I mean ?

LEO : Of course not.

OTTO : Was it in your minds ?

LEO : Yes. It's been in all our minds, for ages. You know that.

OTTO : You couldn't have controlled yourself ? Not for my sake, alone, but for all that lies between us ?

LEO : We could have, I suppose. But we didn't.

OTTO (*still quiet, but trembling*) : Instead of meanly taking advantage of my being away, couldn't you have waited until I came back, and told me how you felt ?

LEO : Would that have made things any better ?

OTTO : It would have been honest, at least.

LEO (*with sudden violence*) : Bunk ! We're being as honest as we know how ! Chance caught us, as it was bound to catch us eventually. We were doomed to it from the very first moment. You don't suppose we enjoy telling you, do you ?   You don't suppose I like watching the pleasure at seeing me fade out of your eyes ?   If it wasn't that we loved you deeply, both of us, we'd lie to you and deceive you indefinitely, rather than inflict this horror on ourselves.

OTTO (*his voice rising slightly*) :   And what about the horror you're inflicting on me ?

GILDA :   Don't argue, Leo.   What's the use of arguing ?

OTTO :   So, you love me, do you ?   Both of you love me deeply !   I don't want a love that can shut me out and make me feel more utterly alone than I've ever felt in my life before.

GILDA :   Don't say that—it's not true !   You couldn't be shut out—ever !   Not possibly.   Hold on to reason for a moment, for the sake of all of us—hold on to reason !   It's our only chance.   We've known this might happen any day ;   we've actually discussed it, quite calmly and rationally, but then there wasn't any emotion mixed up with it.   Now there is, and we've got to fight it.   It's distorting and overbalancing everything—don't you see ?   Oh, please, please try to see——

OTTO :   I see all right.   Believe me, I see perfectly !

GILDA :   You don't, really—it's hopeless.

OTTO :   Quite hopeless.

GILDA :   It needn't be, if only we can tide over this moment.

OTTO :   Why should we tide over this moment ?   It's a big moment !   Let's make the most of it.

He gives a little laugh.

LEO :   I suppose that way of taking it is as good as any.

GILDA :   No, it isn't—it isn't.

OTTO :   I still find the whole thing a little difficult to realize completely.   You must forgive me for being so stupid.   I see quite clearly ; I hear quite clearly ; I know what's happened quite clearly, but I still don't quite understand.

LEO :   What more do you want to understand ?

OTTO :   Were you both drunk ?

GILDA :   Of course we weren't.

OTTO :   Then that's ruled out.   One thing is still bewildering me very much.   Quite a small trivial thing.   You are both obviously strained and upset and unhappy at having to tell me.   Isn't that so ?

GILDA :   Yes.

OTTO :   Then why were you laughing when I came in?

LEO :   Oh, what on earth does that matter ?

OTTO :   It matters a lot.   It's very interesting.

LEO :   It was completely irrelevant.   Hysteria.   It had nothing to do with anything.

OTTO :   Why were you both laughing when I came in ?

LEO :   It was hysteria, I tell you.

OTTO :   Were you laughing at me ?

LEO (*wildly*) :   Yes, we were !   We were !   We were laughing at you being wedged in the bath.   That's what we were laughing at.

GILDA :   Shut up, Leo !   Stop it.

LEO (*giving way*) :   And I shall laugh at that until the end of my days—I shall roll about on my death-bed thinking about it—and there are other things I shall laugh at, too.   I shall laugh at you now, in this situation, being hurt and grieved and immeasurably calm.   What right have you to be hurt and grieved, any more than Gilda and me ? We're having just as bad a time as you are, probably worse. I didn't stamp about with a martyr's crown on when you rushed off with her, in the first place ; I didn't look wistful and say I was shut out. And I don't intend to stand any of that nonsense from you ! What happened between Gilda and me last night is actually completely unimportant—a sudden flare-up—and although we've been mutually attracted to each other for years, it wasn't even based on deep sexual love ! It was just an unpremeditated roll in the hay and we enjoyed it very much, so there !

OTTO (*furiously*) : Well, one thing that magnificent outburst has done for me is this : I don't feel shut out any more. Do you hear ? Not any more ! And I'm extremely grateful to you. You were right about me being hurt and grieved. I was. But that's over, too. I've seen something in you that I've never seen before; in all these years I've never noticed it—I never realized that, deep down underneath your superficial charm and wit, you're nothing but a cheap, second-rate little opportunist, ready to sacrifice anything, however sacred, to the excitement of the moment——

GILDA : Otto ! Otto—listen a minute ; please listen——

OTTO (*turning to her*) : Listen to what ? A few garbled explanations and excuses, fully charged with a hundred-per-cent feminine emotionalism, appealing to me to hold on to reason and intelligence as it's " our only chance." I don't want an " only chance "—I don't want a chance to do anything but say what I have to say and leave you both to your own god-damned devices ! Where was this much vaunted reason and intelligence last night ? Working overtime, I'm sure.

Working in a hundred small female ways. I expect your reason and intelligence prompted you to wear your green dress, didn't it? With the emerald earrings? And your green shoes, too, although they hurt you when you dance. Reason must have whispered kindly in your ear on your way back here in the taxi. It must have said, " Otto's in Bordeaux, and Bordeaux is a long way away, so everything will be quite safe ! " That's reason, all right—pure reason——

GILDA (*collapsing at the table*): Stop it ! Stop it ! How can you be so cruel ! How can you say such vile things ?

OTTO (*without a break*): I hope "intelligence" gave you a little extra jab and suggested that you lock the door ? In furtive underhand affairs doors are always locked——

LEO : Shut up, Otto. What's the use of going on like that ?

OTTO : Don't speak to me—old, old Loyal Friend that you are ! Don't speak to me, even if you have the courage, and keep out of my sight from now onwards—

LEO : Bravo, Deathless Drama !

OTTO : Wrong again. Lifeless Comedy. You've set me free from a stale affection that must have died ages ago without my realizing it. Go ahead, my boy, and do great things ! You've already achieved a Hôtel de Luxe, a few smart suits, and the woman I loved. Go ahead, maybe there are still higher peaks for you to climb. Good luck, both of you ! Wonderful luck ! I wish you were dead and in hell ! (*He slams out of the room as the curtain falls.*)

END OF ACT I

ACT II : Scene I

The Scene is Leo's *flat in London. It is only a rented flat, but very comfortably furnished. Two French windows at the back open on to a small balcony, which, in turn, overlooks a square. It is several floors up, so only the tops of trees can be seen; these are brown and losing their leaves, as it is autumn. Down stage, on the Right, are double doors leading to the hall. Above these, a small door leads to the kitchen. On the Left, up stage, another door leads to the bedroom and bathroom. There is a large picture of* Gilda, *painted by* Otto, *hanging on the wall. The furniture may be left to the producer's discrimination.*

Discovered : When the curtain rises, it is about ten-thirty in the morning. Eighteen months have passed since Act I. *The room is strewn with newspapers.* Gilda *is lying on the sofa, reading one;* Leo *is lying face downwards on the floor, reading another one.*

Leo (*rolling over on his back and flinging the paper in the air*): It's a knockout! It's magnificent! It'll run a year.

Gilda : Two years.

Leo : Three years.

Gilda : Four years, five years, six years ! It'll run for ever. Old ladies will be trampled to death struggling to get into the pit. Women will have babies regularly in the upper circle bar during the big scene at the end of the second act——

LEO (*complacently*) :   Regularly as clockwork.

GILDA :   The *Daily Mail* says it's daring and dramatic and witty.

LEO :   The *Daily Express* says it's disgusting.

GILDA :   I should be cut to the quick if it said anything else.

LEO :   The *Daily Mirror*, I regret to say, is a trifle carping.

GILDA :   Getting uppish, I see.   Naughty little thing !

LEO (*reading the "Daily Mirror"*) :   " *Change and Decay* is gripping throughout.   The characterization falters here and there, but the dialogue is polished and sustains a high level from first to last and is frequently witty, nay, even brilliant——"

GILDA :   I love " Nay."

LEO (*still reading*):   " But "—here we go, dear !— " But the play, on the whole, is decidedly thin."

GILDA :   My God !   They've noticed it.

LEO (*jumping up*) :   Thin—thin !   What do they mean, " thin " ?

GILDA :   Just thin, darling.   Thin's thin all the world over and you can't get away from it.

LEO :   Would you call it thin ?

GILDA :   Emaciated.

LEO :   I shall write fat plays from now onwards. Fat plays filled with very fat people !

GILDA :   You mustn't let your vibrations be upset by the *Daily Mirror*.   It means to be kind.   That's why one only looks at the pictures.

LEO :   The *Daily Sketch* is just as bad.

GILDA (*gently*) :   Just as good, dear—just as good.

LEO :   Let's have another look at Old Father *Times*.

GILDA :   It's there, behind the *Telegraph*.

LEO (*glancing through it*) : Non-committal, but amiable. A minute, if slightly inaccurate, description of the plot.

GILDA (*rising and looking over his shoulder*) :   Only a few of the names wrong.

LEO :   They seem to have missed the main idea of the play.

GILDA :   You mustn't grumble ; they say the lines are provocative.

LEO :   What *could* they mean by that ?

GILDA :   Anyhow, you can't expect a paper like the *Times* to be really interested in your petty little excursions in the theatre.   After all, it is the organ of the nation.

LEO :   That sounds vaguely pornographic to me.

       The telephone rings.

LEO (*answering it*) : Hallow ! Hallow—'oo is it speaking ?—H'if—if you will kaindly 'old the line for a moment, h'I will ascertain. (*He places his hand over the receiver.*) Lady Brevell !

GILDA :   Tell her to go to hell.

LEO :   It's the third time she's rung up this morning.

GILDA :   No restraint.   That's what's wrong with Society nowadays.

LEO (*at telephone again*) :   Hallow, hallow !—I am seu very sorry but Mr. Mercuré is not awake yet. 'E 'ad a very tiring night what with one thing and another. H'is there any message ?—Lunch on the third—or dinner on the seventh.—Yes, I'll write it daown—not at all !—Thenk you.

GILDA (*seriously*) :   How do you feel about all that ?

LEO :   Amused.

GILDA :   I'm not sure that I do.

LEO : It's only funny, really.

GILDA : Yes, but dangerous.

LEO : Are you frightened that my silly fluffy little head will be turned ?

GILDA : No, not exactly, but it makes me uncomfortable, this snatching that goes on. Success is far more perilous than failure, isn't it ? You've got to be doubly strong and watchful and wary.

LEO : Perhaps I shall survive.

GILDA : You'll survive all right, in the long run—I don't doubt that for a moment. It's me I was worrying about.

LEO : Why ?

GILDA : Not me, alone. Us.

LEO : Oh, I see.

GILDA : Maybe I'm jealous of you. I never thought of that.

LEO : Darling, don't be silly !

GILDA : Last year was bad enough. This is going to be far worse.

LEO : Why be scared ?

GILDA : Where do we go from here ? That's what I want to know.

LEO : How would you feel about getting married ?

GILDA (*laughing*) : It's not that, dear !

LEO : I know it isn't, but——

GILDA : But what ?

LEO : It might be rather fun. We'd get a lot more presents now than if we'd done it before.

GILDA : A very grand marriage. St. Margaret's, Westminster ?

LEO : Yes, with a tremendous " do " at Claridge's afterwards.

GILDA : The honeymoon would be thrilling, wouldn't it ? Just you and me, alone, finding out about each other.

LEO : I'd be very gentle with you, very tender.

GILDA : You'd get a sock in the jaw, if you were !

LEO (*shocked*): Oh, how volgar ! How inexpressibly volgar !

GILDA : It's an enjoyable idea to play with, isn't it ?

LEO : Let's do it.

GILDA : Stop ! Stop, stop—you're rushing me off my feet !

LEO : No, but seriously, it's a much better plan than you think. It would ease small social situations enormously. The more successful I become, the more complicated everything's going to get. Let's do it, Gilda.

GILDA : No.

LEO : Why not ?

GILDA : It wouldn't do. Really it wouldn't.

LEO : I think you're wrong.

GILDA : It doesn't matter enough about the small social situations, those don't concern me much, anyway. They never have and they never will. I shouldn't feel cosy, married ! It would upset my moral principles.

LEO : Doesn't the Eye of Heaven mean anything to you ?

GILDA : Only when it winks !

LEO : God knows, it ought to wink enough at our marriage.

GILDA : Also, there's another thing.

LEO : What ?

GILDA : Otto.

Leo :   Otto !

Gilda :   Yes.   I think he'd hate it.

Leo :   I wonder if he would.

Gilda :   I believe so.   There'd be no reason for him to, really ;   but I believe he would.

Leo :   If only he'd appear again we could ask him.

Gilda :   He will, sooner or later ;   he can't go on being cross for ever.

Leo :   Funny, about Otto.

Gilda :   Screamingly funny.

Leo :   Do you love him still ?

Gilda :   Of course.   Don't you ?

Leo (*sighing*) :   Yes.

Gilda :   We couldn't *not* love Otto, really.

Leo :   Could you live with him again ?

Gilda :   No, I don't think so ;   that part of it's dead.

Leo :   We were right, weren't we ?   Unconditionally right.

Gilda :   Yes.   I wish it hadn't been so drastic, though, and violent and horrid.   I hated him being made so unhappy.

Leo :   We weren't any too joyful ourselves, at first.

Gilda :   Conscience gnawing at our vitals.

Leo :   Do you think—do you think he'll ever get over it, enough for us all to be together again ?

Gilda (*with sudden vehemence*) :   I don't want all to be together again.

The telephone rings.

Leo :   Damn !

Gilda (*humming*) :   Oh, Death, where is thy sting-a-ling-a-ling——

LEO (*at telephone*) :   Hallow !   Hallow—Neo,   I'm afraid he's eout.   (*He hangs up.*)

GILDA :   Why don't you let Miss Hodge answer the telephone ?   It would save you an awful lot of trouble.

LEO :   Do you think she could ?

GILDA :   I don't see why not ;   she seems in full possession of most of her faculties.

LEO :   Where is she ?

GILDA :   She's what's known as " doing the bed-room."

LEO (*calling*) :   Miss Hodge—Miss Hodge——

GILDA :   We ought to have a valet in a white coat, really.   Think if television came in suddenly, and everyone who rang up was faced with Miss Hodge !

> MISS HODGE *enters.   She is dusty and extremely untidy.*

MISS HODGE :   Did you call ?

LEO :   Yes, Miss Hodge.

MISS HODGE :   I was doing the bedroom.

LEO :   Yes, I know you were and I'm sorry to disturb you, but I have a favour to ask you.

MISS HODGE (*suspiciously*) :   Favour ?

LEO :   Yes.   Every time the telephone rings, will you answer it for me ?

MISS HODGE (*with dignity*) :   If I 'appen to be where I can 'ear it, I will with pleasure.

LEO :   Thank you very much.   Just ask who it is speaking and tell them to hold the line.

MISS HODGE :   'Ow long for ?

LEO :   Until you've told me.

MISS HODGE :   All right.

> *She goes back into the bedroom.*

LEO :   I fear no good will come of that.

GILDA :   Do you think while I am here alone in the evenings, when you are rushing madly from party to party, I might find out about Miss Hodge's inner life ?

The telephone rings.

Leo :   There now !

They both wait while the telephone continues to ring.

GILDA (*sadly*) :   Two valets in two white coats, that's what we need, and a secretary and an upper housemaid !

The telephone continues to ring.

LEO :   Perhaps I'd better answer it, after all.

GILDA :   No, let it ring.   I love the tone.

MISS HODGE comes flying in breathlessly, and rushes to the telephone.

MISS HODGE (*at telephone*) :   'Allo ! 'Allo ! 'Allo-'allo-'allo-'allo !——

GILDA :   This is getting monotonous.

MISS HODGE (*continuing*): 'Allo, 'allo—'allo! 'Allo——

GILDA (*conversationally*) :   Tell me, Mr. Mercuré, what do you think of the modern girl ?

LEO (*politely*) :   A silly bitch.

GILDA :   How cynical !

MISS HODGE :   . . . 'allo, 'allo, 'allo, 'allo—'Allo ! 'Allo—— (*She turns to them despondently.*)   There don't seem to be anyone there.

LEO :   Never mind, Miss Hodge.   We mustn't hope for too much, at first.   Thank you very much.

MISS HODGE :   Not at all, sir.

She goes out again.

GILDA :   I feel suddenly irritated.

LEO :   Why ?

GILDA :   I don't know.   Reaction, I expect, after the anxiety of the last few days.   Now it's all over and everything seems rather blank.   How happy are you, really ?

LEO :   Very, I think.

GILDA :   I don't work hard enough, not nearly hard enough ; I've only done four houses for four silly women since we've been in England.

LEO :   Monica Jevon wants you to do hers the moment she comes back.

GILDA :   That'll make the fifth silly woman.

LEO :   She's not so particularly silly.

GILDA :   She's nice, really, nicer than most of them, I suppose.   Oh, dear !

LEO :   Cigarette ?   (*He throws her one.*)

GILDA :   Ernest was right.

LEO :   How do you mean ?   When ?

GILDA :   Ages ago.   He said my life was untidy. And it is untidy.   At this moment it's untidier than ever.   Perhaps you're wise about our marrying ; perhaps it would be a good thing.   I'm developing into one of those tedious unoccupied women who batten on men and spoil everything for them.   I'm spoiling the excitement of your success for you now by being tiresome and gloomy.

LEO :   Do you think marriage would automatically transform you into a busy, high-spirited Peg-o'-My-Heart ?

GILDA :   Something's missing, and I don't know what it is.

LEO :   Don't you ?

GILDA :   No.   Do you ?

LEO :   Yes, I do.   I know perfectly well what's missing——

The telephone rings again.

GILDA : I'll do it this time. (*She goes to the telephone.*) Hallo ! Yes.—Oh, yes, of course ! How do you do ? —-Yes, he's here, I'll call him.—What ?—I'm sure he'd love to.—That's terribly sweet of you, but I'm afraid I can't.—No, I've got to go to Paris.—No, only for a few days.

LEO : Who is it ?

GILDA (*with her hand over the receiver*) : Mrs. Borrowdale. She wants you for the week-end.—(*Into telephone again*) : Here he is.

LEO (*taking telephone*) : Hallo, Marion.—Yes, wasn't it marvellous ?—Terrified out of my seven senses.—What ?—Well, I'm not sure——

GILDA (*hissing at him*) : Yes, you are—quite sure !

LEO : Just hold on one minute while I look at my book.—(*He puts his hand over the receiver.*) What will you do if I go ?

GILDA : Commit suicide immediately; don't be so silly——

LEO : Why didn't you accept, too ? She asked you.

GILDA : Because I don't want to go.

LEO (*at telephone*) : No, there isn't a thing down for Saturday. I'd love to come.—Yes, that'll be grand. —Good-bye. (*He comes over to* GILDA.) Why don't you want to come ? She's awfully amusing, and the house is lovely.

GILDA : It's much better for you to go alone.

LEO : All right. Have it your own way.

GILDA : Don't think I'm being tiresome again, there's a darling ! I just couldn't make the effort— that's the honest-to-God reason. I'm no good at house parties ; I never was.

LEO: Marion's house parties are different. You can do what you like and nobody worries you.

GILDA: I can never find what I like in other people's houses, and everybody worries me.

LEO: I suppose I must be more gregarious than you. I enjoy meeting new people.

GILDA: I enjoy meeting new people, too, but not second-hand ones.

LEO: As I said before, Marion's house parties are extremely amusing. She doesn't like " second-hand " people, as you call them, any more than you do. Incidentally, she's a very intelligent woman herself and exceedingly good company.

GILDA: I never said she wasn't intelligent, and I'm sure she's excellent company. She has to be. It's her job.

LEO: That was a cheap gibe—thoroughly cheap——
  The telephone rings again. MISS HODGE *sur-prisingly appears almost at once. They sit silent while she answers it.*

MISS HODGE (*at telephone*): 'Allo! 'Allo—yes—— (*She holds out the telephone to* LEO.) 'Ere, it's for you.

LEO (*hopelessly*): Dear God! (*He takes it and* MISS HODGE *goes out.*) Hallo!—Yes, speaking—*Evening Standard?*—Oh, all right, send him up.

GILDA: This is a horrible morning.

LEO: I'm sorry.

GILDA: You needn't be. It isn't your fault.

LEO: Yes, it is, I'm afraid. I happen to have written a successful play.

GILDA (*exasperated*): Oh, really—— (*She turns away.*)

LEO: Well, it's true, isn't it? That's what's upsetting you?

43

GILDA :   Do you honestly think that ?

LEO :   I don't know.   I don't know what to think.
This looks like a row, but it hasn't even the virtue of
being a new row.   We've had it before several times,
and just lately more than ever.   It's inevitable that the
more successful I become, the more people will run
after me.   I don't believe in their friendship, and I
don't take them seriously, but I enjoy them.   Probably
a damn sight more than they enjoy me !   I enjoy the
whole thing.   I've worked hard for it all my life.   Let
them all come !   They'll drop me, all right, when they're
tired of me ; but maybe I shall get tired first.

GILDA :   I hope you will.

LEO :   What does it matter, anyhow ?

GILDA :   It matters a lot.

LEO :   I don't see why.

GILDA :   They waste your time, these ridiculous
celebrity-hunters, and they sap your vitality.

LEO :   Let them !   I've got lots of time and lots of
vitality.

GILDA :   That's bravado.   You're far too much of
an artist to mean that, really.

LEO :   I'm far too much of an artist to be taken in by
the old cliché of shutting out the world and living for
my art alone.   There's just as much bunk in that as
there is in a cocktail party at the Ritz.

GILDA :   Something's gone.   Don't you see ?

LEO :   Of course something's gone.   Something
always goes.   The whole business of living is a process
of readjustments.   What are you mourning for ?   The
dear old careless days of the Quartier Latin, when Laife
was Laife !

GILDA :   Don't be such a fool

LEO : Let's dress up poor, and go back and pretend, shall we ?

GILDA : Why not ? That, at least, would be a definite disillusionment.

LEO : Certainly, it would. Standing over the skeletons of our past delights and trying to kick them to life again. That wouldn't be wasting time, would it ?

GILDA : We needn't go back, or dress up poor, in order to pretend. We can pretend here. Among all this—— (*She kicks the newspapers.*) With the trumpets blowing and the flags flying and the telephone ringing, we can still pretend. We can pretend that we're happy.

> *She goes out of the room as the telephone rings. LEO stands looking after her for a moment, and then goes to the desk.*

LEO (*at telephone*) : Hallo !—What ?—Yes, speaking. —Very well, I'll hold the line——

> MISS HODGE *comes in from the hall.*

MISS HODGE : There's a gentleman to see you. He says he's from the *Evening Standard.*

LEO : Show him in.

> MISS HODGE *goes out.*

LEO (*at telephone*) : Hallo—yes ! Hallo there, how are you ? Of course, for hours, reading the papers.— Yes, all of them marvellous——

> MR. BIRBECK *enters.* LEO *motions him to sit down.*

I'm so glad—it was thrilling, wasn't it ?—Did he really ? That's grand !—Nonsense, it's always nice to hear things like that—of course, I'd love to.—Black tie or white tie ?—no tie at all ! That'll be much more comfortable.—Good-bye.—What ?—No, really ? So soon ? You'll know it by heart.—Yes, rather.— Good-bye !

He hangs up the telephone.

I'm so sorry.

MR. BIRBECK (*shaking hands*): I'm from the *Standard*.

LEO: Yes, I know.

MR. BIRBECK: I've brought a photographer. I hope you don't mind? We thought a little study of you in your own home would be novel and interesting.

LEO (*bitterly*): I'm sure it would.

MR. BIRBECK: First of all, may I ask you a few questions?

LEO: Certainly, go ahead. Cigarette?

MR. BIRBECK: No, thank you. I'm not a smoker myself.

LEO (*taking one and lighting it*): I am.

MR. BIRBECK (*producing notebook*): This is not your first play, is it?

LEO: No, my seventh. Two of them have been produced in London within the last three years.

MR. BIRBECK: What were their names?

LEO: *The Swift River* and *Mrs. Draper*.

MR. BIRBECK: How do you spell " Mrs. Draper "?

LEO: The usual way—m r s d r a p e r.

MR. BIRBECK: Do you care for sport?

LEO: Yes, madly.

MR. BIRBECK: Which particular sport do you like best?

LEO: No particular one. I'm crazy about them all.

MR. BIRBECK: I see.

He writes.

Do you believe the talkies will kill the theatre?

LEO: No. I think they'll kill the talkies.

MR. BIRBECK (*laughing*): That's very good, that is! It really is.

LEO : Not as good as all that.

MR. BIRBECK : There's a question that interests our lady readers very much——

LEO : What's that ?

MR. BIRBECK : What is your opinion of the modern girl ?

LEO (*without flinching*) : Downright ; straightforward : upright.

MR. BIRBECK : You approve of the modern girl, then ?

LEO : I didn't say so.

MR. BIRBECK : What are your ideas on marriage

LEO : Garbled.

MR. BIRBECK : That's good, that is. Very good !

LEO (*rising*) : Don't put it, though—don't write down any of this interview ; come and see me again.

MR. BIRBECK : Why, what's wrong ?

LEO : The whole thing's wrong, Mr.——

MR. BIRBECK : Birbeck.

LEO : Mr. Birbeck. The whole business is grotesque.   Don't you see how grotesque it is ?

MR. BIRBECK : I'm afraid I don't understand.

LEO : Don't you ever feel sick inside when you have to ask those questions ?

MR. BIRBECK : No, why should I ?

LEO : Will you do me a very great favour ?

MR. BIRBECK : What is it ?

LEO : Call in your photographer.   Photograph me— and leave me alone.

MR. BIRBECK (*offended*) : Certainly.

LEO : Don't think me rude.   I'm just rather tired, that's all.

MR. BIRBECK : I quite understand.

*He goes out into the hall and returns in a moment with
the photographer.*

Where do you think would be best?

LEO : Wherever you say.

MR. BIRBECK : Just here?

LEO (*taking his stand just in front of the desk*): All
alight

MR. BIRBECK : Perhaps I could come and see you
again some time when you're not so tired?

LEO : Yes, of course. Telephone me.

MR. BIRBECK : To-morrow?

LEO : Yes, to-morrow.

MR. BIRBECK : About eleven?

LEO : Yes. About eleven.

MR. BIRBECK : Now, then—are you ready?

   GILDA *comes out of the bedroom, dressed for the
street. She goes over to* LEO *and puts her arms round
his neck.*

GILDA : I'm going to do a little shopping——
(*Then softly*) : Sorry, darling——

LEO : All right, sweet.

   GILDA *goes out.*

MR. BIRBECK : Just a little smile!

   LEO *smiles as the curtain falls.*

END OF ACT II : SCENE I

ACT II : SCENE II

The Scene is the same, a few days later.

It is evening, and MISS HODGE *has just finished laying
a cold supper on a bridge table in front of the sofa.
She regards it thoughtfully for a moment, and then goes
to the bedroom door.*

MISS HODGE : Your supper's all ready, ma'am.

GILDA (*in bedroom*) : Thank you, Miss Hodge. I
shan't want you any more to-night, then.

MISS HODGE *goes off into the kitchen.* GILDA
*comes out of the bedroom. She is wearing pyjamas and
a dressing gown. She goes over to the desk, on which
there is a parcel of books. She undoes the parcel and
scrutinizes the books, humming happily to herself as
she does so.* MISS HODGE *re-enters from the kitchen,
this time in her coat and hat.*

GILDA : Hello, Miss Hodge ! I thought you'd
gone.

MISS HODGE : I was just putting on me 'at. I think
you'll find everything you want there.

GILDA : I'm sure I shall. Thank you.

MISS HODGE : Not at all ; it's a pleasure, I'm sure.

GILDA : Oh, Miss Hodge, do you think it would be
a good idea if Mr. Mercuré and I got married ?

MISS HODGE : I thought you was married.

GILDA : Oh, I'd forgotten. We never told you,
did we ?

MISS HODGE : You certainly didn't.

GILDA : Well, we're not.

MISS HODGE (*thoughtfully*) : Oh, I see.

GILDA : Are you shocked ?

MISS HODGE : It's no affair of mine, ma'am—miss.

GILDA : What do you think about marriage ?

MISS HODGE : Not very much, miss, having had a basinful meself, in a manner of speaking.

GILDA (*surprised*) : What !

MISS HODGE : Hodge is my maiden name. I took it back in—in disgust, if you know what I mean.

GILDA : Have you been married much, then ?

MISS HODGE : Twice, all told.

GILDA : Where are your husbands now ?

MISS HODGE : One's dead, and the other's in New-castle.

GILDA (*smiling*) : Oh.

MISS HODGE : Well, I'll be getting 'ome now, if there's nothing else you require ?

GILDA : No, there's nothing else, thank you. Good night.

MISS HODGE : Good night, miss.

> MISS HODGE *goes out.* GILDA *laughs to herself; pours herself out a glass of Sherry from the bottle on the table, and settles on to the sofa with the books.* OTTO *comes in from the hall and stands in the doorway, looking at her.*

OTTO : Hallo, Gilda !

GILDA (*turning sharply and staring at him*) : It's not true !

OTTO (*coming into the room*) : Here we are again !

GILDA : Oh, Otto !

OTTO : Are you pleased ?

GILDA : I don't quite know yet.

OTTO : Make up your mind, there's a dear.

GILDA : I'll try.

OTTO : Where's Leo ?

GILDA : Away. He went away this afternoon.

OTTO : This seems a very nice flat.

GILDA : It is. You can see right across to the other side of the square on a clear day.

OTTO : I've only just arrived.

GILDA : Where from ?

OTTO : New York. I had an exhibition there.

GILDA : Was it successful ?

OTTO : Very, thank you.

GILDA : I've decided quite definitely now : I'm ecstatically pleased to see you.

OTTO : That's lovely.

GILDA : How did you get in ?

OTTO : I met an odd-looking woman going out. She opened the door for me.

GILDA : That was Miss Hodge. She's had two husbands.

OTTO : I once met a woman who'd had four husbands.

GILDA : Aren't you going to take off your hat and coat ?

OTTO : Don't you like them ?

GILDA : Enormously. It was foolish of me to ask whether your exhibition was successful. I can see it was ! Your whole personality reeks of it.

OTTO (*taking off his hat and coat*) : I'm disappointed that Leo isn't here.

GILDA : He'll be back on Monday.

OTTO : How is he, please ?

GILDA : Awfully well.

OTTO : Oh, dear ! Oh, dear, oh, dear—I feel very funny ! I feel as if I were going to cry, and I don't want to cry a bit.

GILDA : Let's both cry, just a little !

OTTO : Darling, darling Gilda !

They rush into each other's arms and hug each other.

OTTO : It's all, all right now, isn't it ?

GILDA : More than all right.

OTTO : I was silly to stay away so long, wasn't I ?

GILDA : That was what Leo meant the other morning when he said he knew what was missing.

OTTO : Me ?

GILDA : Of course.

OTTO : I'm terribly glad he said that.

GILDA : We were having a row, trying to find out why we weren't quite as happy as we should be.

OTTO : Do you have many rows ?

GILDA : Quite a lot, every now and then.

OTTO : As many as we used to ?

GILDA : About the same. There's a bit of trouble on at the moment, really. He's getting too successful and sought after. I'm worried about him.

OTTO : You needn't be. It won't touch him—inside.

GILDA : I'm afraid, all the same ; they're all so shrill and foolish, clacking at him.

OTTO : I read about the play in the train. It's a riot, isn't it ?

GILDA : Capacity—every performance.

OTTO : Is it good ?

GILDA : Yes, I think so.

OTTO : Only think so ?

GILDA : Three scenes are first-rate, especially the last act. The beginning of the second act drags a bit, and most of the first act's too facile—you know what I mean—he flips along with easy swift dialogue, but doesn't go deep enough. It's all very well played.

OTTO : We'll go on Monday night.

GILDA : Will you stay, now that you've come back ?

OTTO : I expect so. It depends on Leo.

GILDA : Oh !

OTTO : He may not want me to.

GILDA : I think he'll want you to, even more than I do !

OTTO : Why do you say that ?

GILDA : I don't know. It came up suddenly, like a hiccup.

OTTO : I feel perfectly cosy about the whole business now, you know—no trailing ends of resentment—I'm clear and clean, a newly-washed lamb, bleating for company !

GILDA : Would you like some Sherry ?

OTTO : Very much indeed.

GILDA : Here, have my glass. I'll get another. We'll need another plate as well and a knife and fork.

OTTO (*looking over the table*) : Cold ham, salad ; what's that blob in the pie-dish ?

GILDA : Cold rice pudding. Delicious ! You can have jam with it and cream.

OTTO (*without enthusiasm*) : How glorious !

> GILDA *runs into the kitchen and returns in a moment with plate and knife and fork, etc.*

GILDA : Here we are !

OTTO : I expected more grandeur.

GILDA : Butlers and footmen ?

OTTO : Yes, just a few. Concealed lighting, too.
There's something a thought sordid about that lamp
over there. Did you decorate this room ?

GILDA : You know perfectly well I didn't.

OTTO : Well, you should.

GILDA : Do you want anything stronger to drink
than Sherry ?

OTTO : No, Sherry's all right. It's gentle and
refined, and imparts a discreet glow. Of course, I'm
used to having biscuits with it.

GILDA : There aren't any biscuits.

OTTO (*magnificently*) : It doesn't matter.

GILDA : Do sit down, darling.

OTTO (*drawing up a chair*) : What delicious-looking
ham ! Where *did* you get it ?

GILDA : I have it specially sent from Scotland.

OTTO : Why Scotland ?

GILDA : It lives there when it's alive.

OTTO : A bonny country, Scotland, if all I've heard
is correct, what with the banshees wailing and the
four-leaved shamrock.

GILDA : That's Ireland, dear.

OTTO : Never mind. The same wistful dampness
distinguishes them both.

GILDA (*helping him to ham*) : I knew you'd arrive soon.

OTTO (*helping her to salad*) : Where's Leo gone,
exactly ?

GILDA : Smart house party in Hampshire. Bridge,
backgammon, several novelists, and a squash court that
nobody uses.

OTTO : The Decoration of Life—-that's what that is.

GILDA : Slightly out of drawing, but terribly amusing.

OTTO : It won't last long. Don't worry.

GILDA : Tell me where you've been, please, and what you've seen and what you've done. Is your painting still good, or has it deteriorated just a little ? I'm suspicious, you see ! Dreadfully suspicious of people liking things too much—things that matter, I mean. There's too much enthusiasm for Art going on nowadays. It smears out the highlights.

OTTO : You're certainly in a state, aren't you ?

GILDA : Yes, I am. And it's getting worse.

OTTO : Turbulent ! Downright turbulent.

GILDA : There isn't any mustard.

OTTO : Never mind : I don't want any, do you ?

GILDA : I don't know, really. I'm always a little undecided about mustard.

OTTO : It might pep up the rice pudding !

GILDA : Strange, isn't it ? This going on where we left off ?

OTTO : Not quite where we left off, thank God.

GILDA : Wasn't it horrible ?

OTTO : I was tortured with regrets for a long while. I felt I ought to have knocked Leo down.

GILDA : I'm awfully glad you didn't. He hates being knocked down.

OTTO : Then, of course, he might have retaliated and knocked me down !

GILDA : You're bigger than he is.

OTTO : He's more wiry. He once held me in the bath for twenty minutes while he poured cold water over me.

GILDA (*laughing*) : Yes, I know !

OTTO (*laughing too*) : Oh, of course—that's what you were both laughing at when I came in that day, wasn't it ?

GILDA (*weakly*) : Yes, it was very, very unfortunate.

OTTO : An unkind trick of Fate's, to have dropped it into your minds just then.

GILDA : It made a picture, you see—an unbearably comic picture—we were both terribly strained and unhappy ; our nerves were stretched like elastic, and that snapped it.

OTTO : I think that upset me more than anything.

GILDA : You might have known it wasn't you we were laughing at.   Not you, yourself.

OTTO : It's exactly a hundred and twenty-seven years ago to-day.

GILDA : A hundred and twenty-eight.

OTTO : We've grown up since then.

GILDA : I do hope so, just a little.

OTTO : I went away on a freight boat, you know. I went for thousands of miles and I was very unhappy indeed.

GILDA : And very sea-sick, I should think.

OTTO : Only the first few days.

GILDA : Not steadily ?

OTTO : As steadily as one can be sea-sick.

GILDA : Do you know a lot about ships now ?

OTTO : Not a thing.   The whole business still puzzles me dreadfully.   I know about starboard and port, of course, and all the different bells ; but no one has yet been able to explain to me satisfactorily why, the first moment a rough sea occurs, the whole thing doesn't turn upside down !

GILDA : Were you frightened ?

OTTO : Petrified, but I got used to it.

GILDA : Was it an English ship ?

OTTO : No, Norwegian.   I can say, " How do you do ? " in Norwegian.

GILDA : We must get to know some Norwegian people immediately, so that you can say " How do you do ? " to them.—Where are your pictures ?

OTTO : Not unpacked yet. They're at the Carlton.

GILDA : The Carlton ! You haven't gone " grand " on me, too, have you ?

OTTO : I have, indeed. I've got several commissions to do portraits here in London. The very best people. I only paint the very best people.

GILDA (*almost snappily*) : They have such interesting faces, haven't they ?

OTTO (*reproachfully*) : I don't paint their faces, Gilda. Fourth dimensional, that's what I am. I paint their souls.

GILDA : You'd have to be eighth dimensional and clairvoyant to find them.

OTTO : I'm grieved to see that Leo has done little or nothing towards taming your proud revolutionary spirit.

GILDA : He's inflamed it.

OTTO : I know what's wrong with you, my sweet. You're just the concentrated essence of " Love Among the Artists."

GILDA : I think that was unkind.

OTTO : If you were creative yourself you'd understand better. As it is, you know a lot. You know an awful lot. Your critical faculty is first-rate. I'd rather have your opinion on paintings or books or plays than anyone else's I know. But you're liable to get sidetracked if you're not careful. Life is for living first and foremost. Even for artists, life is for living. Remember that.

GILDA : You have grown up, haven't you ?

OTTO : In the beginning, when we were all in Paris, everything was really very much easier to manage, even our emotional problems. Leo and I were both struggling, a single line was in both our minds leading to success—that's what we were planning for, working like dogs for ! You helped us both, jostling us on to the line again when we slipped off, and warming us when we were cold in discouragement. You picked on me to love a little bit more, because you decided, rightly then, that I was the weaker. They were very happy, those days, and glamour will always cling to them in our memories. But don't be misled by them ; don't make the mistake of trying to recapture the spirit of them. That's dead, along with our early loves and dreams and quarrels, and all the rest of the foolishness.

GILDA : I think I want to cry again.

OTTO : There's nothing like a good cry.

GILDA : You can't blame me for hating success, when it changes all the—the things I love best.

OTTO : Things would have changed, anyhow. It isn't only success that does it—it's time and experience and new circumstances.

GILDA (*bitterly*) : Was it the Norwegians that taught you this still wisdom ? They must be wonderful people.

OTTO (*gently*) : No, I was alone. I just sat quietly and looked at everything.

GILDA : I see.

OTTO : Would you fancy a little more salad ?

GILDA : No, thank you.

OTTO : Then it's high time we started on the cold rice pudding.

GILDA : I see one thing clearly.

OTTO (*smiling*) : What?

GILDA : I'm not needed any more.

OTTO : I thought you were going to say that.

GILDA : It's what you meant me to say, isn't it?

OTTO : We shall always need each other, all three of us.

GILDA : Nonsense! The survival of the fittest— that's what counts.

OTTO : Do have some rice pudding?

GILDA : To hell with you and the rice pudding!

OTTO (*helping himself*) : Hard words. Hard, cruel words!

GILDA : You're so sure of yourself, aren't you? You're both so sure of yourselves, you and Leo. Getting what you want must be terribly gratifying!

OTTO (*unruffled*) : It is.

GILDA (*suddenly smiling*) : Do you remember how I used to rail and roar against being feminine?

OTTO : Yes, dear. You were very noisy about the whole business.

GILDA : I'm suddenly glad about it for the first time. Do you want some jam with that?

OTTO : What sort of jam is it?

GILDA : Strawberry, I think.

OTTO : Of course, I'm used to having dark plum with rice pudding, but I'll make do with strawberry.

GILDA : I'll get it!

She goes into the kitchen. The telephone rings. OTTO answers it.

OTTO (*at telephone*) : Hallo!—Hallo—yes, speaking.— Didn't you recognize my voice?—How absurd! It must be a bad line.—Dinner on the seventh? Yes, I

should love to.—You don't mind if I come as Marie
Antoinette, do you? I have to go to a fancy dress
ball.—Where? Oh, my aunt is giving it—yes, in a
bad house, she runs a whole chain of them, you know!
—Thank you so much.

He hangs up the telephone.

GILDA (*re-entering*): I put it into a glass dish. Who
was that?

OTTO: Somebody called Brevell, Lady Brevell. She
wants Leo to dine on the seventh. I accepted.

GILDA: Good! You can both go. I'm sure she'd
be delighted.

OTTO (*sitting down again*): What! No cream?

GILDA: It was a delusion about the cream. I
thought there was a lot, but there isn't a drop.

OTTO: I think you've improved in looks really with
the passing of the years.

GILDA: How sweet, Otto! I'm so pleased.

OTTO: Your skin, for instance. Your skin's much
better.

GILDA: It ought to be, I've been taking a lot of
trouble with it.

OTTO: What sort of trouble?

GILDA: Oh, just having it pushed and rubbed and
slapped about.

OTTO: Funny, how much in love with you I was!

GILDA: We'll have a good laugh about it when
you've finished your pudding.

OTTO: What's happened to Ernest?

GILDA: He's been away, too, a long way away:
he went on a world cruise with a lot of old ladies in
straw hats!

OTTO: Dear little Ernest!

GILDA : I saw him a few weeks ago, then he went back to Paris.

OTTO : An odd life.   Sterile, don't you think ?

GILDA : You've certainly emancipated yourself into a grand complacency.

OTTO : If you're unkind to me, I shall go back to the Carlton.

GILDA : Have you got a suite, or just a common bedroom and bath ?

OTTO : Darling, I do love you so very much !

GILDA : A nice comfortable love, without heart throbs.

OTTO : Are you trying to lure me to your wanton bed ?

GILDA : What would you do if I did ?

OTTO : Probably enjoy it very much.

GILDA : I doubt if I should.

OTTO : Have I changed so dreadfully ?

GILDA (*maliciously*) : It isn't you that's changed—it's time and experience and new circumstances !

OTTO (*rising*) : I've finished my supper.   It wasn't very good, but it sufficed.   I should now like a whisky and soda.

GILDA : It's in that thing over there.

OTTO (*getting it out*) : It is a thing, isn't it ?   Do you want one ?

GILDA : No, I don't think so.

OTTO : Just a little one ?

GILDA : All right.

OTTO (*pouring them out*) : If we were bored, we could always go to the pictures, couldn't we ?

GILDA : It's too late ; we shouldn't get in to any-thing that's worth seeing.

OTTO: Oh, how disappointing! How very, very, very disappointing!

GILDA: Personally, I'm enjoying myself here.

OTTO (*handing her her drink*): Are you, indeed?

GILDA: Yes. This measured skirmishing is delightful.

OTTO: Be careful, won't you? I do implore you to be careful!

GILDA: I never was. Why should I start now?

OTTO (*raising his glass*): I salute your spirit of defiance, my dearest.

GILDA (*raising her glass*): Yours, too.

OTTO (*shaking his head*): A bad business; a very bad business.

GILDA: Love among the artists.

OTTO: Love among anybody.

GILDA: Perhaps not love, exactly. Something a little below it and a little above it, but something terribly strong.

OTTO: Meaning this?

GILDA: Of course. What else?

OTTO: We should have principles to hang on to, you know. This floating about without principles is so very dangerous.

GILDA: Life is for living.

OTTO: You accused me of being too sure. It's you who are sure now.

GILDA: Sure of what?

OTTO: Sure that I want you.

GILDA: Don't you?

OTTO: Of course I do.

GILDA: Keep away, then, a minute, and let me look at you all over again.

OTTO : I used to sit on the top deck of that freighter, and shut my eyes and see you standing there, just like you are now.

GILDA : Good old romance, bobbing up again and wrapping up our crudities in a few veils !

OTTO : Shut up ! Don't talk like that.

GILDA : I'm not nearly as afraid as you are.

OTTO : You haven't got so much to lose.

GILDA : How do you know ? You've forgotten everything about me—the real me. That dim figure you conjured up under your damned tropic stars was an illusion, a misty ghost, scratched out of a few memories, inaccurate, untrue—nothing to do with me in any way. This is me, now ! Take a good look and see if you can tell what I have to lose in the game, or to win, either—perhaps you can tell that, too ! Can you ? Can you ?

OTTO : You look so terribly sweet when you're angry.

GILDA : Another illusion. I'm not sweet.

OTTO : Those were only love words. You mustn't be so crushing. How are we to conduct this revivalist meeting without love words ?

GILDA : Let's keep them under control.

OTTO : I warn you it's going to be very difficult. You've worked yourself up into a frenzy of sophistication. You've decided on being calculating and disillusioned and brazen, even slightly coarse over the affair. That's all very well, but how long is it going to last ? That's what I ask myself. How long is it going to last—this old wanton mood of yours ?

GILDA (*breaking down*) : Don't—don't laugh at me.

OTTO : I must—a little.

GILDA : It's an unfair advantage.   You've both got it and you both use it against me mercilessly.

OTTO : Laugh, too ; it's not so serious, really.

GILDA : If I once started, I should never stop. That's a warning.

OTTO : Duly registered.

GILDA : What are we going to do about Leo ?

OTTO : Wait and see what he's going to do about us.

GILDA : Haven't you got any shame at all ?

OTTO : Just about as much as you have.

GILDA : The whole thing's degrading, completely and utterly degrading.

OTTO : Only when measured up against other people's standards.

GILDA : Why should we flatter ourselves that we're so tremendously different ?

OTTO : Flattery doesn't enter into it. We are different. Our lives are diametrically opposed to ordinary social conventions ; and it's no use grabbing at those conventions to hold us up when we find we're in deep water.   We've jilted them and eliminated them, and we've got to find our own solutions for our own peculiar moral problems.

GILDA : Very glib, very glib indeed, and very plausible.

OTTO : It's true. There's no sense in stamping about and saying how degrading it all is.   Of course it's degrading; according to a certain code, the whole situation's degrading and always has been. The Methodists wouldn't approve of us, and the Catholics wouldn't either ; and the Evangelists and the Episcopalians and the Anglicans and the Christian Scientists— I don't suppose even the Polynesian Islanders would think very highly of us, but they wouldn't mind quite so much, being so far away. They could all club together—the whole lot of them—and say with perfect truth, according to their lights, that we were loose-living, irreligious, unmoral degenerates, couldn't they ?

GILDA (*meekly*) : Yes, Otto, I expect so.

OTTO : But the whole point is, it's none of their business. We're not doing any harm to anyone else. We're not peppering the world with illegitimate children. The only people we could possibly mess up are ourselves, and that's our lookout. It's no use you trying to decide which you love best, Leo or me, because you don't know ! At the moment, it's me, because you've been living with Leo for a long time and I've been away. A gay, ironic chance threw the three of us together and tied our lives into a tight knot at the outset. To deny it would be ridiculous, and to unravel it impossible. Therefore, the only thing left is to enjoy it thoroughly, every rich moment of it, every thrilling second——

GILDA : Come off your soap box, and stop ranting !

OTTO : I want to make love to you very badly indeed, please ! I've been lonely for a long time without you ; now I've come back, and I'm not going to be lonely any more. Believe me, loneliness is a mug's game.

GILDA : The whole thing's a mug's game.

OTTO : You're infinitely lovely to me, darling, and so very necessary. The circle has swung round, and it's my turn again—that's only fair, isn't it ?

GILDA : I—I suppose so.

OTTO : If you didn't want me, it would be different, but you do—you do, my dearest dear !—I can see it in your eyes. You want me every bit as much as I want you !

GILDA (*with a little smile*) : Yes, every bit.

OTTO : This is a moment to remember, all right. Scribble it on to your heart ; a flicker of ecstasy sandwiched between yesterday and to-morrow—something to be recaptured in the future without illusion, perfect in itself ! Don't let's forget this—whatever else happens, don't let's forget this.

GILDA : How easy it all seems in this light.

OTTO : What small perverse meanness in you forbids you to walk round the sofa to me ?

GILDA : I couldn't move, if the house was on fire !

OTTO : I believe it is. To hell with the sofa !

He vaults over it and takes her in his arms. They stand holding each other closely and gradually subside on to the sofa.

OTTO (*kissing her*) : Hvordan staar det til !

GILDA (*blissfully*) : What's that, darling ?

OTTO : "How do you do ? " in Norwegian.

The curtain slowly falls.

END OF ACT II : SCENE II

ACT II : Scene III

The Scene is the same. It is about ten-thirty the next
morning.
As the curtain rises, Miss Hodge *shows* Ernest
Friedman *into the room.*

Miss Hodge : I will tell madam—miss—madam
you're here, sir.

Ernest : Why so much confusion, Miss Hodge ?

Miss Hodge : I was only told last night, sir, that—
er, well—that—er——

Ernest : Oh, I see.

Miss Hodge : It's a bit muddling at first, in a manner
of speaking, but I shall get used to it.

Ernest : I'm sure you will.

   Miss Hodge *goes into the bedroom, and returns*
   again in a moment with very pursed-up lips.

Miss Hodge (*coldly*) : She will be in in a moment,
sir.

   Miss Hodge *goes into the kitchen and slams the*
   door. Ernest *looks after her in some astonishment.*
   Gilda *enters. She is fully dressed, wearing a hat*
   and coat.

Gilda (*with tremendous gaiety*) : Ernest ! What a
surprise !

Ernest : What's the matter with Miss Hodge ?

Gilda : The matter with her ? I don't know—I
haven't examined her.

ERNEST: It was foolish of you to tell her you and Leo weren't married.

GILDA: It slipped out; I'd forgotten she didn't know. Have you come from Paris?

ERNEST: Yes, last night. There's been a slight argument going on for weeks.

GILDA: Argument? What kind of an argument?

ERNEST: One of those Holbein arguments.

GILDA: Somebody said it wasn't, I suppose?

ERNEST: Yes, that's it.

GILDA: Was it?

ERNEST: In my humble opinion, yes.

GILDA: Did your humble opinion settle it?

ERNEST: I hope so.

GILDA: Admirable. Quiet, sure, perfect conviction —absolutely admirable.

ERNEST: Thank you, Gilda. Don't imagine that the irony in your tone escaped me.

GILDA: That wasn't irony; it was envy.

ERNEST: It's high time you stopped envying me.

GILDA: I don't think I ever shall.

ERNEST: How's Leo?

GILDA: Not very well.

ERNEST: What's wrong with him?

GILDA: Tummy; he's had an awful night. He didn't close an eye until about five, but he's fast asleep now.

ERNEST: I'm sorry. I wanted to say good-bye to you both.

GILDA: Good-bye?

ERNEST: I'm going back to Paris this afternoon and sailing for America on Wednesday.

GILDA: You do flip about, don't you, Ernest?

ERNEST : Not any more. I've decided to live in New York permanently. I've been angling for a particular penthouse for years and now I've got it.

GILDA : How lovely. Is it very high ?

ERNEST : About thirty floors.

GILDA (*gaily*) : Do you want a housekeeper ?

ERNEST : Yes, badly. Will you come ?

GILDA : Perhaps.

She laughs.

ERNEST : You seem very gay this morning.

GILDA : I'm always gay on Sundays. There's something intoxicating about Sunday in London.

ERNEST : It's excellent about the play. I read all the reviews.

GILDA : Yes, it's grand. It ought to run for years and years and years and years and years !

ERNEST : I suppose Leo's delighted.

GILDA : Absolutely hysterical. I think that's what's upset his stomach. He was always over-sensitive, you know ; even in Paris in the old days he used to roll about in agony at the least encouragement, don't you remember ?

ERNEST : No, I can't say that I do.

GILDA : That's because you're getting a bit " gaga," darling ! You've sold too many pictures and made too much money and travelled too much. That world cruise was a fatal mistake. I thought so at the time, but I didn't say anything about it, because I didn't want to upset you. But going round in a troupe, with all those tatty old girls, must have been very, very bad for you. I expected every day to get a wire from somewhere or other saying you'd died of something or other.

ERNEST : Do stop, you're making me giddy.

GILDA : Perhaps you'd like a little Sherry ?

ERNEST : No, thank you.

GILDA : It's very good Sherry ; dry as a bone !

ERNEST : You seem to me to be in a very strange mood, Gilda.

GILDA : I've never felt better in my life. Ups and downs ! My life is one long convulsive sequence of Ups and Downs. This is an Up—at least, I think it is.

ERNEST : You're sure it's not nervous collapse ?

GILDA : I never thought of that ; it's a very good idea. I shall have a nervous collapse !

ERNEST : Will you ever change, I wonder ? Will you ever change into a quieter, more rational person ?

GILDA : Why should I ?

ERNEST : What's wrong now ?

GILDA : Wrong ! What could be wrong ? Everything's right. Righter than it's ever been before. God's in His heaven, all's right with the world—I always thought that was a remarkably silly statement, didn't you ?

ERNEST : Unreasoning optimism is always slightly silly, but it's a great comfort to, at least, three-quarters of the human race.

GILDA : The human race is a let-down, Ernest ; a bad, bad let-down ! I'm disgusted with it. It thinks it's progressed, but it hasn't ; it thinks it's risen above the primeval slime, but it hasn't—it's still wallowing in it ! It's still clinging to us, clinging to our hair and our eyes and our souls. We've invented a few small things that make noises, but we haven't invented one big thing that creates quiet, endless peaceful quiet— something to pull over us like a gigantic eiderdown ;

70

something to deaden the sound of our emotional yellings and screechings and suffocate our psychological confusions——

ERNEST (*weakly*) : I think, perhaps, I would like a glass of Sherry after all.

GILDA (*going to the " thing "*) : It's all right, Ernest, don't be frightened ! You're always a safety valve for me. I think, during the last few years, I've screamed at you more than anyone else in the world.

She hands him the bottle.

Here you are.

ERNEST (*looking at it*) : This is brandy.

GILDA : So it is. How stupid of me.

She finds the Sherry and two glasses.

Here we are !

ERNEST (*putting the brandy bottle on the desk*) : I'm not sure that I find it very comfortable, being a safety valve !

GILDA : It's the penalty you pay for being sweet and sympathetic, and very old indeed.

ERNEST (*indignantly*) : I'm not very old indeed !

GILDA : Only in wisdom and experience, darling.

She pours out Sherry for them both.

Here's to you, Ernest, and me, too !

They both drink.

ERNEST : Now, then ?

GILDA : Now then, what ?

ERNEST : Out with it !

GILDA : Take my advice, my dear ; run like a stag— be fleet of foot ! Beat it !

ERNEST : Why ?

GILDA : I'm a lone woman. I'm unattached. I'm free.

ERNEST : Oh ! Oh, are you, really !

GILDA : I'm cured. I'm not a prisoner any more.
I've let myself out. This is a day of great exaltation
for me.

ERNEST : I'm sure I'm delighted to hear it.

GILDA (*with the suspicion of a catch in her voice*) : I'm
not needed any more—I'm going.

ERNEST : Where are you going ?

GILDA : I haven't the faintest idea. The world is
wide, far too wide and round, too. I can scamper
round and round it, like a white rat in a cage !

ERNEST : That will be very tiring.

GILDA : Not so tiring as staying still ; at least, I
might preserve the illusion that I'm getting somewhere.

ERNEST (*prosaically*) : Have you had a row with Leo?

GILDA : No, I haven't had a row with anyone. I've
just seen the light suddenly. I saw it last night. The
survival of the fittest, that's the light. Didn't you
know ?

ERNEST : I think, perhaps, I should understand
better if you spoke in Russian.

GILDA : Or Norwegian. There's a fascinating
language for you !

ERNEST : I believe there is a very nice nursing home
in Manchester Street.

GILDA (*taking a note out of her bag*) : You see this ?

ERNEST : Yes.

GILDA : It's for Leo.

ERNEST : To read when he wakes up ?

GILDA : Yes. If he ever wakes up.

ERNEST : You haven't poisoned him, have you ?

GILDA : No, but he's nearly poisoned me ! An
insidious, dreary sort of poison, a lymphatic poison,
turning me slowly into a cow.

ERNEST (*laughing*) : My poor Gilda !

GILDA (*propping it up against the brandy bottle*) : I shall leave it here. (

ERNEST : Pity there isn't a pin cushion.

GILDA : I expect you think I'm being over-dramatic ?

ERNEST : Not any more than usual.

GILDA : Well, I'm not. I'm perfectly calm inside. Cold as steel.

ERNEST : Can one be exalted and cold as steel at the same time ?

GILDA : I can. I can be lots of things at the same time ; it becomes a great bore after a while. In the future, I intend to be only one thing.

ERNEST : That being—— ?

GILDA : Myself, Ernest. My unadulterated self ! Myself, without hangings, without trimmings, unencumbered by the winding tendrils of other people's demands——

ERNEST : That was very nicely put.

GILDA : You can laugh at me as much as you like. I give everybody free permission to laugh at me. I can laugh at myself, too, now—for the first time, and enjoy it.

ERNEST : Can you ?

GILDA : Yes ; isn't it lovely ?

ERNEST : I congratulate you.

GILDA : I'm glad you suddenly appeared this morning to say good-bye—very appropriate ! It's a day of good-byes—the air's thick with them. You have a tremendous sense of the "right moment," Ernest. It's wonderful. You pop up like a genie out of a bottle, just to be in at the death ! You really ought to have been a priest.

ERNEST: Are you really serious? Are you really going?

GILDA: I've never been more serious in my life. Of course I'm going—I've got to learn a few things while there's still time—who knows, I might even learn to be an artist! Just think of that! And even if I can't quite achieve such—such splendour, there are other lessons for me. There's the lesson of paddling my own canoe, for instance—not just weighing down somebody else's and imagining I'm steering it!

ERNEST: Oh, I see. I see it all now.

GILDA: No, you don't—not all; just a little, perhaps, but not all.

ERNEST: Where are you going, really?

GILDA: First, to a hotel, to make a few plans.

ERNEST: You can take over my room at the Carlton, if you like. I'm leaving to-day.

GILDA (*laughing hysterically*): The Carlton! Oh, no, Ernest, not the Carlton!

ERNEST: Why, what's the matter with it?

GILDA: It's too big and pink and grand for me. I want a decayed hotel; gentle and sad and a little bit under the weather.

ERNEST: And afterwards?

GILDA: Paris—no, not Paris—Berlin. I'm very attached to Berlin.

ERNEST: Are you sure you're wise? This is rather —well, rather drastic, isn't it?

GILDA (*quietly*): I'm quite sure.

ERNEST: I won't try to dissuade you, then.

GILDA: No, don't. It wouldn't do any good. I'm quite determined.

ERNEST: I have an instinctive distrust of sudden impulses.

GILDA : I'll fool you yet ! I'll make you eat your damned scepticism !

ERNEST (*smiling*) : Sorry !

GILDA : Good-bye, Ernest. I'm going now.

ERNEST : You'll be very lonely. Aren't you afraid ?

GILDA : I can bear it. I've been lonely before.

ERNEST : Not for a long while.

GILDA : Recently, quite—quite recently. Loneliness doesn't necessarily mean being by yourself.

ERNEST (*gently*) : Very well, dear.

GILDA (*suddenly flinging her arms round his neck*) : You're very tender and very kind and I'm tremendously grateful to you ! Come on, let's go.

ERNEST : Haven't you got any bags or anything ?

GILDA : I've packed a dressing case with all my immediate wants ; I shall get everything else new, brand-new——

> *She goes quietly to the bedroom door and gets a dressing case, which she has left just behind it.*

I'll drop you off at the Carlton, and take your taxi on.

ERNEST : Is he asleep ?

GILDA : Fast asleep. Come on !

> *They go out into the hall. Suddenly* GILDA *is heard to say, " Just a moment, I've forgotten something ! "*
>
> *She comes quickly back into the room, takes another letter out of her bag and props it up on the desk. Then she goes out.*
>
> *The front door is heard to slam very loudly.*
>
> *After a moment or two the telephone rings ; it goes on ringing until* MISS HODGE *comes out of the kitchen and answers it.*

MISS HODGE (*at telephone*) : 'Allo, 'allo !—What ?—

75

No, 'e's not—'e's away.—All right !—Not at all.

> *She slams down the telephone and goes back into the kitchen.* OTTO *comes out of the bedroom. He is wearing a dressing gown and pyjamas belonging to* LEO, *and looks very sleepy. He finds a cigarette and lights it ; then goes to the kitchen door.*

OTTO (*calling*) : Gilda !—Gilda, where are you ?

> MISS HODGE *appears. Her face grim with disapproval.*

MISS HODGE : She's gone h'out.

OTTO (*startled*) : Oh ! Did she say where ?

MISS HODGE : She did not.

OTTO : What's the time ?

MISS HODGE : H'eleven.

OTTO (*pleasantly*) : We met last night on the doorstep ; do you remember ?

MISS HODGE : Yes, I remember all right.

OTTO : It was very kind of you to let me in.

MISS HODGE : I didn't know you was going to stay all night.

OTTO : I wasn't sure, myself.

MISS HODGE : A pretty thing !

OTTO : I beg your pardon ?

MISS HODGE : I said, " A pretty thing " and I meant "A Pretty thing "—nice goings on !

OTTO (*amiably*) : Very nice, thank you.

MISS HODGE : I'm a respectable woman.

OTTO : Never mind.

MISS HODGE : I don't mind a little fun every now and then among friends, but I do draw the line at looseness !

OTTO : You're making a mistake, Miss—Miss—— ?

MISS HODGE : Me name's 'Odge.

OTTO : You're making a mistake, Miss Odge.

MISS HODGE : 'Ow do you mean ?

OTTO : You are making a mistake in daring to disapprove of something that has nothing to do with you whatever.

MISS HODGE (*astounded*) : Well, I never !

OTTO : Please go away, and mind your own business.

> MISS HODGE, *with a gasp of fury, flounces off into the kitchen.* OTTO *comes down to the sofa and lies on it with his back towards the door, blowing smoke rings into the air.*
>
> *The door opens and* LEO *creeps into the room. He can only see the cigarette smoke,* OTTO'S *head being hidden by the cushion.*

LEO : Hallo, darling ! I couldn't bear it any more, so I've come back.

OTTO (*sitting up slowly*) : Hello, Leo.

LEO : You !

OTTO : Yes. I couldn't bear it any longer, either, so I've come back.

LEO : Where have you come from ?

OTTO : New York.

LEO : When—when did you arrive ?

OTTO : Last night.

LEO : Why—why aren't you dressed ?

OTTO : I've only just got up.

LEO : You stayed here ?

OTTO : Yes.

LEO (*slowly*) : With Gilda ?

OTTO : Yes.

LEO : I see.

OTTO : It wouldn't be any use lying would it ? Pretending I didn't ?

LEO : No use at all.

OTTO : I'm not even sorry, Leo, except for hurting you.

LEO : Where is Gilda ?

OTTO : She's gone out.

LEO : Out ! Why ? Where's she gone to ?

OTTO : I don't know.

LEO (*turning away*) : How vile of you ! How unspeakably vile of you both !

OTTO : It was inevitable.

LEO (*contemptuously*) : Inevitable !

OTTO : I arrived unexpectedly ; you were away ; Gilda was alone. I love her ; I've always loved her— I've never stopped for a minute, and she loves me, too.

LEO : What about me ?

OTTO : I told you I was sorry about hurting you.

LEO : Gilda loves me.

OTTO : I never said she didn't.

LEO (*hopelessly*) : What are we to do ? What are we to do now ?

OTTO : Do you know, I really haven't the faintest idea.

LEO : You're laughing inside. You're thoroughly damned well pleased with yourself, aren't you ?

OTTO : I don't know. I don't know that either.

LEO (*savagely*) : You are ! I can see it in your eyes— so much triumph—such a sweet revenge !

OTTO : It wasn't anything to do with revenge.

LEO : It was. Of course it was---secretly thought out, planned for ages—infinitely mean !

OTTO : Shut up ! And don't talk such nonsense.

LEO : Why did you do it, then ? Why did you come back and break everything up for me ?

OTTO: I came back to see you both. It was a surprise.

LEO: A rather cruel surprise, and brilliantly successful. You should be very happy.

OTTO (*sadly*): Should I?

LEO: Perhaps I should be happy, too; you've set me free from something.

OTTO: What?

LEO (*haltingly*): The—feeling I had for you—something very deep, I imagined it was, but it couldn't have been, could it?—now that it has died so easily.

OTTO: I said all that to you in Paris. Do you remember? I thought it was true then, just as you think it's true now.

LEO: It is true.

OTTO: Oh, no, it isn't.

LEO: Do you honestly believe I could ever look at you again, as a real friend?

OTTO: Until the day you die.

LEO: Shut up! It's too utterly beastly—the whole thing.

OTTO: It's certainly very, very uncomfortable.

LEO: Is Gilda going to leave me? To go away with you?

OTTO: Do you want her to?

LEO: Yes, I suppose so, now.

OTTO: We didn't make any arrangement or plans.

LEO: I came back too soon. You could have gone away and left a note for me—that would have been nice and easy for you, wouldn't it?

OTTO: Perhaps it would, really. I don't know that I should have done it, though.

LEO: Why not?

OTTO : If I had, I shouldn't have seen you at all, and I wanted to see you very much.

LEO : You even wanted to see me, hating you like this ? Very touching !

OTTO : You're not hating me nearly as much as you think you are. You're hating the situation : that's quite different.

LEO : You flatter yourself.

OTTO : No. I'm speaking from experience. You forget, I've been through just what you're going through now. I thought I hated you with all my heart and soul, and the force of that hatred swept me away on to the high seas, too far out of reach to be able to come back when I discovered the truth.

LEO : The truth !

OTTO : That no one of us was more to blame than the other. We've made our own circumstances, you and Gilda and me, and we've bloody well got to put up with them !

LEO : I wish I could aspire to such a sublime God's-eye view !

OTTO : You will—in time—when your acids have calmed down.

LEO : I'd like so very much not to be able to feel anything at all for a little. I'm desperately tired.

OTTO : You want a change.

LEO : It seems as if I'm going to get one, whether I want it or not.

OTTO (*laughing*) : Oh, Leo, you really are very, very tender !

LEO : Don't laugh ! How dare you laugh ! How *can* you laugh !

OTTO : It's a good joke. A magnificent joke.

LEO (*bitterly*) : A pity Gilda chose just that moment to go out, we could all have enjoyed it together.

OTTO : Like we did before ?

LEO : Yes, like we did before.

OTTO : And like we shall again.

LEO (*vehemently*) : No, never again—never !

OTTO : I wonder.

> *The telephone rings. LEO goes over mechanically to answer it ; he lifts up the receiver, and as he does so he catches sight of the two letters propped up against the brandy bottle. He stares at them and slowly lets the receiver drop on to the desk.*

LEO (*very quietly*) : Otto.

OTTO : What is it ?

LEO : Look.

> OTTO *comes over to the desk, and they both stand staring at the letters.*

OTTO : Gilda !

LEO : Of course.

OTTO : She's gone ! She's escaped !

LEO : Funny word to use, " escaped."

OTTO : That's what she's done, all the same, escaped.

LEO : The joke is becoming richer.

OTTO : Escaped from both of us.

LEO : We'd better open them, I suppose.

OTTO (*slowly*) : Yes—yes, I suppose we had.

> *They both open the letters, in silence, and read them.*

LEO (*after a pause*) : What does yours say ?

OTTO (*reading*) : " Good-bye, my clever little dear ! Thank you for the keys of the city."

LEO : That's what mine says.

OTTO : I wonder where she's gone ?

LEO : I don't see that that matters much.

OTTO : One up to Gilda !

LEO : What does she mean, " Keys of the city " ?

OTTO : A lot of things.

LEO : I feel rather sick.

OTTO : Have some Sherry ?

LEO : That's brandy.

OTTO : Better still.

> *He pours out a glass and hands it to* LEO.

LEO (*quietly*) : Thank you.

OTTO (*pouring one out for himself*) : I feel a little sick, too.

LEO : Do you think she'll come back ?

OTTO : No.

LEO : She will—she must—she must come back !

OTTO : She won't.   Not for a long time.

LEO (*drinking his brandy*) : It's all my fault, really.

OTTO (*drinking his*) : Is it ?

LEO : Yes.   I've, unfortunately, turned out to be successful.   Gilda doesn't care for successful people.

OTTO : I wonder how much we've lost, with the years ?

LEO : A lot.   I think, practically everything now.

OTTO (*thoughtfully*) : Love among the artists.   Very difficult, too difficult.

LEO : Do you think we could find her ?

OTTO : No.

LEO : We could try.

OTTO : Do you want to ?

LEO : Of course.

OTTO : Why ?   What would be the use ?

LEO : She might explain a little—a little more clearly.

OTTO : What good would that do ?   We know why she's gone perfectly well.

LEO : Because she doesn't want us any more.

OTTO : Because she thinks she doesn't want us any more.

LEO : I suppose that's as good a reason as any.

OTTO : Quite.

LEO : All the same, I should like to see her just once—just to find out, really, in so many words——

OTTO (*with sudden fury*) : So many words !   That's what's wrong with us !   So many words—too many words, masses and masses of words, spewed about until we're choked with them.   We've argued and probed and dragged our entrails out in front of one another for years !   We've explained away the sea and the stars and life and death and our own peace of mind !   I'm sick of this endless game of three-handed, spiritual ping-pong—this battling of our little egos in one another's faces !   Sick to death of it !   Gilda's made a supreme gesture and got out.   Good luck to her, I say !   Good luck to the old girl—she knows her onions !

OTTO *refills his glass and drains it at a gulp.*

LEO : You'll get drunk, swilling down all that brandy on an empty stomach.

OTTO : Why not ?   What else is there to do ?   Here, have some more as well.

He refills LEO's *glass and hands it to him.*

LEO : All right !   Here goes.

He drains his glass.

Now we start fair.

He refills both their glasses.

OTTO (*raising his glass*) : Gilda !   (*He drains it.*)

LEO (*doing the same*): Gilda ! (*He drains it.*)

OTTO: That's better, isn't it ? Much, much better.

LEO: Excellent. We shall be sick as dogs !

OTTO: Good for our livers.

LEO: Good for our immortal souls.

He refills the glasses, and raises his.

Our Immortal Souls !

OTTO (*raising his*): Our Immortal Souls !

They both drain them to the last drop.

LEO: I might have known it !

OTTO: What ?

LEO: That there was going to be a break. Everything was running too smoothly, too well. I was enjoying all the small things too much.

OTTO: There's no harm in enjoying the small things.

LEO: Gilda didn't want me to.

OTTO: I know.

LEO: Did she tell you so ?

OTTO: Yes, she said she was uneasy.

LEO: She might have had a little faith in me, I think. I haven't got this far just to be side-tracked by a few garlands.

OTTO: That's what I said to her; I said you wouldn't be touched, inside.

LEO: How about you ?

OTTO: Catching up, Leo ! Popular portraits at popular prices.

LEO: Good work or bad work ?

OTTO: Good. An occasional compromise, but essentials all right.

LEO (*with a glint in his eye*): Let's make the most of the whole business, shall we ? Let's be photographed and interviewed and pointed at in restaurants ! Let's play the game for what it's worth, secretaries and fur coats and *de luxe* suites on transatlantic liners at minimum rates ! Don't let's allow one shabby perquisite to slip through our fingers ! It's what we dreamed many years ago and now it's within our reach. Let's cash in, Otto, and see how much we lose by it.

He refills both glasses and hands one to OTTO.

Come on, my boy !

He raises his glass.

Success in twenty lessons ! Each one more bitter than the last ! More and better Success ! Louder and funnier Success !

They both drain their glasses.

They put down their glasses, gasping slightly.

OTTO (*agreeably*) : It takes the breath away a bit, doesn't it ?

LEO : How astonished our insides must be—all that brandy hurtling down suddenly !

OTTO : On Sunday, too.

LEO : We ought to know more about our insides, Otto. We ought to know why everything does everything.

OTTO : Machines ! That's what we are, really—all of us ! I can't help feeling a little discouraged about it every now and then.

LEO : Sheer sentimentality ! You shouldn't feel discouraged at all ; you should be proud.

OTTO : I don't see anything to be proud about.

LEO : That's because you don't understand ; because you're still chained to stale illusions. Science dispels illusions ; you ought to be proud to be living in a scientific age. You ought to be proud to know that you're a minute cog in the vast process of human life.

OTTO : I don't like to think I'm only a minute cog—it makes me sort of sad.

LEO : The time for dreaming is over, Otto.

OTTO : Never ! I'll never consent to that. Never, as long as I live ! How do you know that science isn't a dream, too ? A monstrous, gigantic hoax ?

LEO : How could it be ? It proves everything.

OTTO : What does it prove ? Answer me that !

LEO : Don't be silly, Otto. You must try not to be silly.

OTTO (*bitterly*) : A few facts, that's all. A few tawdry facts torn from the universe and dressed up in terminological abstractions !

LEO : Science is our only hope, the only hope for humanity ! We've wallowed in false mysticism for centuries ; we've fought and suffered and died for foolish beliefs, which science has proved to be as ephemeral as smoke. Now is the moment to open our eyes fearlessly and look at the truth !

OTTO : What is the truth ?

LEO (*irritably*) : It's no use talking to you—you just won't try to grasp anything ! You're content to go on being a romantic clod until the end of your days.

OTTO (*incensed*) : What about you ? What about the plays you write ? Turgid with romance ; sodden with true love ; rotten with nostalgia !

LEO (*with dignity*) : There's no necessity to be rude about my work—that's quite separate, and completely beside the point.

OTTO : Well, it oughtn't to be. It ought to be absolutely in accord with your cold, incisive, scientific viewpoint. If you're a writer it's your duty to write what you think. If you don't you're a cheat—a cheat and a hypocrite !

LEO (*loftily*) : Impartial discussion is one thing, Otto. Personal bickering is another. I think you should learn to distinguish between the two.

OTTO : Let's have some more brandy.

LEO : That would be completely idiotic.

OTTO : Let's be completely idiotic !

LEO : Very well.

> *They both refill their glasses and drain them in silence.*

OTTO : There's a certain furtive delight in doing something consciously that you know perfectly well is thoroughly contemptible.

LEO : There is, indeed.

OTTO : There isn't much more left. Shall we finish it ?

LEO : Certainly.

> OTTO *refills both glasses.*

OTTO (*handing* LEO *his*) : Now what ?

LEO : Now what what ?

OTTO (*giggling slightly*) : Don't keep on saying, " what, what, what "—it sounds ridiculous !

LEO : I wanted to know what you meant by " Now what " ?

OTTO : Now what shall we drink to ?

LEO (*also giggling*) : Let's not drink to anything—let's just drink !

OTTO : All right.

> *He drinks.*

LEO (*also drinking*) : Beautiful !

OTTO : If Gilda came in now she'd be surprised all right, wouldn't she ?

LEO: She'd be so surprised, she'd fall right over backwards !

OTTO: So should we.

They both laugh immoderately at this.

LEO (*wiping his eyes*): Oh, dear ! Oh, dear, oh, dear, how silly ! How very, very silly.

OTTO (*with sudden change of mood*): She'll never come back. Never.

LEO: Yes, she will—when we're very, very old, she'll suddenly come in—in a Bath-chair !

OTTO (*sullenly*): Damn fool.

LEO (*with slight belligerence*): Who's a damn fool ?

OTTO: You are. So am I. We both are. We were both damn fools in the first place, ever to have anything to do with her.

LEO (*admiringly*): You're awfully strong, Otto ! Much, much stronger than you used to be.

OTTO: I've been all over the world ; I've roughed it—that's what's made me strong. Every man ought to rough it.

LEO: That's the trouble with civilized life—it makes you soft. I've been thinking that for a long time. I've been watching myself getting softer and softer and softer—it's awful !

OTTO: You'd soon be all right if you got away from all this muck.

LEO: Yes, I know, but how ?

OTTO (*putting his arm around his shoulders*): Get on a ship, Leo—never mind where it's going ! Just get on a ship—a small ship.

LEO: How small ?

OTTO: Very small indeed ; a freighter.

LEO: Is that what you did ?

OTTO : Yes.

LEO : Then I will.   Where do very small ships sail from ?

OTTO : Everywhere—Tilbury, Hamburg, Havre——

LEO : I'm free ! I've suddenly realized it.   I'm free !

OTTO : So am I.

LEO : We ought to drink to that, Otto.   It's something worth drinking to.   Freedom's been lost to us for a long, long time and now we've found it again ! Freedom from people and things and softness !   We really ought to drink to it.

OTTO : There isn't any more brandy.

LEO : What's that over there ?

OTTO : Where ?

LEO : On the thing.

OTTO (*going to it*) : Sherry.

LEO : What's the matter with Sherry ?

OTTO : All right.

He brings over the bottle and fills their glasses.

LEO (*raising his*) : Freedom !

OTTO (*doing the same*) : Freedom !

They both drink.

LEO : Very insipid.

OTTO : Tastes like brown paper.

LEO : I've never tasted brown paper.

OTTO : Neither have I.

They roar with laughter.

LEO : Sherry's a very ludicrous word, isn't it, where you begin to analyse it ?

OTTO : Any word's ludicrous if you stare at it long enough.   Look at "macaroni."

LEO : That's Italian ; that doesn't count.

OTTO : Well, " rigmarole " then, and " neophyte " and " haddock."

LEO : And " wimple "—wimple's the word that gets me down !

OTTO : What is a wimple ?

LEO : A sort of mediæval megaphone, made of linen. Guinevere had one.

OTTO : What did she do with it ?

LEO (*patiently*) : Wore it, of course. What did you think she did with it ?

OTTO : She might have blown down it.

LEO (*with slight irritation*) : Anyhow, it doesn't matter, does it ?

OTTO (*agreeably*) : Not in the least. It couldn't matter less. I always thought Guinevere was tedious, wimple or no wimple.

LEO : I'm beginning to float a little, aren't you ?

OTTO : Just leaving the ground. Give me time ! I'm just leaving the ground——

LEO : Better have some more Sherry.

OTTO : I'm afraid it isn't very good Sherry.

LEO (*scrutinizing the bottle*) : It ought to be good ; it's real old Armadildo.

OTTO : Perhaps we haven't given it a fair chance.

He holds out his glass ; LEO *refills it and his own.*

LEO (*raising his glass*) : Après moi le déluge !

OTTO : Après both of us the deluge !

They drain their glasses.

LEO : I think I shall sit down now. I'm so terribly sick of standing up.

OTTO : Human beings were never meant to stand up, in the first place. It's all been a grave mistake.

They both sit on the sofa.

LEO : All what ?

OTTO : All this stamping about.

LEO : I feel ever so much happier. I don't feel angry with you or with Gilda or with anybody ! I feel sort of at peace, if you know what I mean.

OTTO (*putting his arm around him*) : Yes, I know—I know.

LEO : Keys of the city, indeed !

OTTO : Lot of damned nonsense.

LEO : Too much sense of drama, flouncing off like that——

OTTO : We've all got too much sense of drama, but we won't have any more—from now onwards, reason and realism and clarity of vision.

LEO : What ?

OTTO (*very loudly*) : I said " Clarity of vision."

LEO : I wouldn't have believed I could ever feel like this again—so still and calm, like a deep, deep pool.

OTTO : Me, too—a deep pool, surrounded with cool green rushes, with the wind rustling through them——

This flight of fancy is disturbed by a faint hiccup.

LEO (*resting his head on* OTTO's *shoulder*) : Will you forgive me—for—for everything ?

OTTO (*emotionally*) : It's I who should ask you that !

LEO : I'm glad Gilda's gone, really—she was very wearisome sometimes. I shall miss her, though.

OTTO : We shall both miss her.

LEO : She's the only really intelligent woman I've ever known.

OTTO : Brilliant !

LEO : She's done a tremendous lot for us, Otto. I wonder how much we should have achieved without her ?

OTTO : Very little, I'm afraid.   Terribly little.

LEO : And now she's gone because she doesn't want us any more.

OTTO : I think she thinks we don't want her any more.

LEO : But we do, Otto—we do——

OTTO : We shall always want her, always, always, always——

LEO (*miserably*) : We shall get over it in time, I expect, but it will take years.

OTTO : I'm going to hate those years.   I'm going to hate every minute of them.

LEO : So am I.

OTTO : Thank God for each other, anyhow !

LEO : That's true.   We'll get along, somehow—(*his voice breaks*)—together——

OTTO (*struggling with his tears*) : Together——

LEO (*giving way to his, and breaking down completely*) : But we're going to be awfully—awfully—lonely——

> *They both sob hopelessly on each other's shoulders as the curtain. slowly falls.*

END OF ACT II : SCENE III

ACT III : Scene I

Nearly two years have elapsed since Act II.

The scene is ERNEST FRIEDMAN'S *penthouse in New York. It is an exquisite apartment, luxuriously furnished. Up stage, on the Right, are three windows opening on to a balcony. These are on an angle ; below them are double doors leading into the hall. A staircase climbs up the Left-hand side of the room, leading through a curtained archway to the bedrooms, etc. Below the staircase there is a door leading to the servants' quarters. When the curtain rises it is about eleven-thirty on a summer night. The windows are wide open and beyond the terrace can be seen the many lights of the city. There is a table set with drinks and sandwiches, with, below it, an enormous sofa.*

Voices are heard in the hall, and GILDA *enters with* GRACE TORRENCE *and* HENRY *and* HELEN CARVER. *The* CARVERS *are a comparatively young married couple, wealthy and well dressed.* GRACE TORRENCE *is slightly older, a typical Europeanized New York matron.* GILDA *is elaborately and beautifully gowned. Her manner has changed a good deal. She is much more still and sure than before. A certain amount of vitality has gone from her, but, in its place, there is an aloof poise quite in keeping with her dress and surroundings.*

GILDA : Who'd like a highball ?

93

GRACE : We all would.   We all need it !

GILDA : People are wrong when they say that the opera isn't what it used to be.   It is what it used to be— that's what's wrong with it !

HENRY (*going for the drinks*) : Never again !

GILDA : Is there enough ice there, Henry ?

HENRY : Yes, heaps.

HELEN (*wandering out on to the terrace*) : This is the most wonderful view I've ever seen !

HENRY : Next to ours.

HELEN : I like this better ; you can see more of the river.

GRACE : You did all this, I suppose, Gilda ?

GILDA : Not all of it ; just a few extras.   Ernest laid the foundations.

GRACE : When's he coming back ?

GILDA : To-morrow.

GRACE (*wandering about the room*) : It's lovely.

GILDA : I'd forgotten you hadn't been here before.

HENRY : Here, Grace. (*He gives her a drink.*) Gilda——

GILDA (*taking one*) : Thanks, Henry.

HENRY : Helen, do you want yours out there ?

HELEN : No, I'll come in for it.

She comes in, takes her drink, and sits down on the sofa.

GRACE (*stopping before an antique chair*) : Where did you get this ?

GILDA : Italy.   We were motoring to Siena, and we stopped at a little village for lunch and there it was— just waiting to be grabbed.

GRACE : You ought to open a shop ; with your reputation you'd make a packet !

GILDA : This is my shop, really. I make quite enough, one way and another.

HELEN : But the things in this room aren't for sale, are they ?

GILDA : All except the pictures.   Those are Ernest's.

GRACE (*laughing*) : Then they are for sale !

GILDA : Perhaps.   At a price.

HENRY : And, oh boy, what a price !   (*To* HELEN) : What was the name of that one he sold Dad ?

HELEN : I don't think it had a name.

HENRY : The name of the artist, I mean.

GILDA : Matisse.

HENRY : Well, all I can say is, it ought to have been a double Matisse for that money !

GILDA (*smiling*) : Eleven thousand dollars, wasn't it ?

HENRY : It was.

GILDA (*sweetly*) : Your father was very lucky, but then he always has been, hasn't he ?

GRACE : Bow, Henry !   Or fall down dead—one or the other !

GILDA : Do you want to see over the rest of it, Grace ?

GRACE : I do, indeed !   I'm taking mental notes, and if any of them come out right, I'll send you a handsome gift.

GILDA : Terrace first ?   Very nice line in balcony furniture, swing chairs, striped awnings, shrubs in pots——

GRACE : I'd rather die than go near the terrace—it makes me giddy from here.

GILDA : I love being high up.

HELEN : So do I—the higher the better !

GRACE : What floor is this ?

95

GILDA : Thirtieth.

GRACE : I was caught by fire once on the sixth floor ; I had to be hauled down a ladder in my nightgown— since then I've always lived on the ground level.

HELEN : What about burglars ?

GRACE : I'd rather have fifty burglars than one fire. What would you do here if there was a fire, Gilda ? If it started down below, in the elevator shaft or something ?

GILDA (*pointing towards the servants' door*) : Very nice line in fire escapes just through that door ; perfectly equipped, commodious—there's even a wide enough balustrade to slide down.

GRACE : One day there'll be an earthquake in this city, then all you high livers will come tumbling down !

HENRY : In that case, I'd rather be here than on the ground.

GILDA : Come and see the bedrooms.

GRACE : Higher still ?

GILDA : Yes, higher still. You two will be all right, won't you ?

HELEN : Of course.

GILDA (*leading the way upstairs*) : Help yourself to another drink, Henry.

HENRY : Thanks. I will.

GILDA *and* GRACE *disappear through the archway.*

HENRY (*at table*) : Do you want another ?

HELEN : I haven't finished this one yet.

HENRY : Promise me one thing, Helen ?

HELEN : What ?

HENRY : That you'll never become a professional decorator.

HELEN : Why ?

HENRY : I've never met one yet that wasn't hard as nails, and, my God, I've met hundreds !

HELEN : Do you think Gilda's hard ?

HENRY : Hard ! Look at her eyes. Look at the way she's piloting old Grace round the apartment. Look at the way she snapped me up over Dad's picture !

HELEN : You were rather awful about it.

HENRY : So I should think ! Eleven thousand bucks for that daub ! I've only found three people who could tell me what it was supposed to be, and they all told me different.

HELEN : Art's not in your line, Henry.

HENRY : You bet your sweet life it isn't—not at that price !

HELEN : I like modern painting. I think it's thrilling.

HENRY : Bunk.

HELEN (*with superiority*) : That's what everybody always says about new things. Look at Wagner.

HENRY : What's Wagner got to do with it ?

HELEN : When first his music came out everyone said it was terrible.

HENRY : That's jake with me !

HELEN (*laughing patronizingly*) : It's silly to laugh at things just because you don't understand them.

HENRY : You've been around too much lately, Helen ; you ought to stay home more.

HELEN : If it hadn't been for Gilda, I don't know what I'd have done all winter.

HENRY : If it hadn't been for us, I don't know what she'd have done all winter ! You could have fixed our apartment just as well as she did. What do we

97

want with all that Spanish junk?

HELEN: It isn't junk; it's beautiful! She's got the most wonderful taste, everybody knows she has.

HENRY: It's a racket, Helen! The whole thing is a racket.

HELEN: I don't know what's the matter with you to-night.

HENRY: The evening's been a flop. The opera was lousy, and now we've been dragged up here instead of going to the Casino. Just because Gilda's sniffed a bit of business.

There is a ring at the door bell.

HELEN: Do you really think she only got Grace up here to sell her something?

HENRY: I do.

HELEN: Oh, Henry!

HENRY: Don't you?

HELEN: No, of course I don't. They've got a lot of money; they don't need to go on like that.

HENRY: That's how they made the money. Ernest's been palming off pictures on people for years.

HELEN: I don't see why he shouldn't, if they're willing to buy them. After all, everybody sells something; I mean——

The door bell rings again.

HENRY: Don't they keep any servants?

HELEN: I expect they've gone to bed.

HENRY: I'd better answer the door, I suppose.

HELEN: Yes, I think you had.

> HENRY *goes off.* HELEN *does up her face. There is the sound of voices in the hall.* HENRY *re-enters, followed by* OTTO *and* LEO, *both attired in very faultless evening dress.*

HENRY: Mrs. Friedman's upstairs—I'll call her.

LEO: No, don't trouble to do that; she'll be down soon, won't she?

HENRY: Yes, she's only showing Mrs. Torrence over the apartment.

OTTO: Torrence—Torrence! How very odd! I wonder if that's the same Mrs. Torrence we met in the Yoshiwara?

LEO: Very possibly.

HENRY: This is my wife, Mrs. Carver. I'm afraid I don't know your names.

LEO: My name is Mercuré.

HELEN (*shaking hands*): How do you do, Mr. Mercuré?

OTTO: And mine is Sylvus.

HELEN (*shaking hands again*): How do you do, Mr. Sylvus?

LEO (*turning abruptly to* HENRY *and shaking his hand*): How do you do, Mr. Carver?

OTTO (*doing the same with some violence*): How do you do, Mr. Carver?

HENRY: Would you care for a drink?

LEO: Passionately.

HENRY (*coldly*): They're over there. Help yourself.

HELEN (*while they are helping themselves*): Are you old friends of Mrs. Friedman's?

OTTO (*over his shoulder*): Yes, we lived with her for years.

HELEN (*gasping slightly*): Oh!

> *There is silence for a moment.* OTTO *and* LEO *settle themselves comfortably in chairs.*

LEO (*raising his glass*): Here's to you, Mr. and Mrs. Carver.

OTTO (*also raising his glass*) : Mr. and Mrs. Carver.

HENRY (*automatically raising his glass*) : Here's luck !
There is another silence.

LEO (*conversationally*) : I once knew a man called
Carver in Sumatra.

HELEN : Really ?

LEO : He had one of the longest beards I've ever seen.

OTTO (*quickly*) : That was Mr. Eidelbaum.

LEO : So it was ! How stupid of me.

OTTO (*apologetically*) : We've travelled so much, you
know, we sometimes get a little muddled.

HELEN (*weakly*) : Yes, I expect you do.

LEO : Have you been married long ?

HENRY : Two years.

LEO : Oh dear, Oh dear, Oh dear, Oh dear, Oh dear.

HENRY : Why ? What of it ?

OTTO : There's something strangely and deeply
moving about young love, Mr. and Mrs. Carver.

LEO : Youth at the helm.

OTTO : Guiding the little fragile barque of happiness
down the river of life. Unthinking, unknowing, unaware of the perils that lie in wait for you, the sudden
tempests, the sharp jagged rocks beneath the surface.
Are you never afraid ?

HENRY : I don't see anything to be afraid of.

LEO (*fondly*) : Foolish headstrong boy.

OTTO : Have you any children ?

HENRY (*sharply*) : No, we have not.

LEO : That's what's wrong with this century. If
you were living in Renaissance Italy you'd have been
married at fourteen and by now you'd have masses of
children and they'd be fashioning things of great
beauty. Wouldn't they, Otto ?

OTTO : Yes, Leo, they would.

LEO : There you are, you see !

OTTO : The tragedy of the whole situation lies in the fact that you don't care, you don't care a fig, do you?

HELEN (*stiffly*) : I really don't understand what you mean.

> *Conversation again languishes.*

LEO : You've been to Chuquicamata, I suppose ?

HENRY : Where ?

LEO : Chuquicamata.   It's a copper mine in Chile.

HENRY : No, we haven't.   Why ?

LEO (*loftily*) : It doesn't matter.   It's most unimportant.

HENRY : Why do you ask ?

LEO (*magnanimously*) : Please don't say any more about it—it's perfectly all right.

HENRY (*with irritation*) : What are you talking about ?

LEO : Chuquicamata.

OTTO (*gently*) : A copper mine in Chile.

HELEN (*to relieve the tension*) : It's a very funny name.
> *She giggles nervously.*

LEO (*coldly*) : Do you think so ?

HELEN (*persevering*) : Is it—is it an interesting place ?

LEO : I really don't remember ; I haven't been there since I was two.

OTTO : I've never been there at all.

HELEN (*subsiding*) : Oh !

LEO (*after another pause*) : Is Mrs. Torrence a nice woman ?

HENRY : Nice !   Yes, very nice.

LEO (*with a sigh of relief*) : I'm so glad.

OTTO : One can't be too careful, you know—people are so deceptive.

LEO (*grandiloquently*) : It's all a question of masks, really ; brittle, painted masks. We all wear them as a form of protection ; modern life forces us to. We must have some means of shielding our timid, shrinking souls from the glare of civilization.

OTTO : Be careful, Leo. Remember how you upset yourself in Mombasa !

LEO : That was fish.

> HELEN *and* HENRY *exchange startled glances.* GILDA *and* GRACE *reappear through the archway and come down the stairs.* OTTO *and* LEO *and* HENRY *rise to their feet.*

GILDA (*as they come down*) : . . . and the terrace is lovely in the summer, because, as it goes right round, there's always somewhere cool to sit——

> *She reaches the foot of the stairs and sees* OTTO *and* LEO. *She puts her hand on to the balustrade just for a second, to steady herself ; then she speaks. Her voice is perfectly calm.*

GILDA : Hallo !

LEO : Hallo, Gilda.

OTTO : We've come back.

GILDA (*well under control*) : Yes—yes, I see you have. This is Mrs. Torrence. Grace, these are two old friends of mine—Leo Mercuré and Otto Sylvus.

GRACE (*shaking hands*) : Oh—how do you do?

LEO (*shaking hands*) : You must forgive our clothes, but we've only just come off a freight boat.

OTTO : A Dutch freight boat. The food was delicious.

GILDA : I see you both have drinks. Henry, mix me one, will you ?

HENRY : Certainly.

GILDA (*in an empty voice*) : This is the most delightful surprise.   (*To* GRACE) : Do you know, I haven't seen either of them for nearly two years.

GRACE : Gilda has been showing me this perfectly glorious apartment.   Don't you think it's lovely ?

OTTO (*looking around*) : Artistically too careful, but professionally superb.

GILDA (*laughing lightly*) : Behave yourself, Otto !

LEO : Where's darling little Ernest ?

GILDA : Chicago.

HENRY : Here's your drink, Gilda.
     He hands it to her.

GILDA : Thank you.

GRACE (*sinking into a chair*) : Where did you come from on your freight boat, Mr. Mercuré ?

LEO : Manila.

OTTO : It was very hot in Manila.

LEO : It was also very hot in Singapore.

GILDA (*àrily*) : It always is, I believe.

OTTO : It was cooler in Hong Kong ; and in Vladivostock it was downright cold !

LEO : We had to wear mittens.

HELEN : Was all this a pleasure trip ?

LEO : Life is a pleasure trip, Mrs. Carver ; a Cheap Excursion.

OTTO : That was very beautifully put, Leo.   I shall always remember it.

     HENRY *and* HELEN'S *faces set in disapproval.*
     GRACE *looks slightly bewildered.*

GRACE (*with a little social laugh*) : Well, life certainly hasn't been a cheap excursion for me !   Every day it gets more and more expensive.   Everyone here has had the most dreadful winter.   I was in Europe, of course, but they were feeling it there, too, very badly. Paris, particularly. Paris seemed to have lost its vitality; it used to be much more gay, somehow——

OTTO: I once had a flat in Paris. It was really more a studio than a flat, but I had to leave it.

GRACE: They pulled it down, I suppose. They're pulling down everything in Paris now.

OTTO: They pulled it down to the ground; it was a small edifice and crumbled easily.

GRACE: It's sad, isn't it, to think of places where one has lived not being there any more?

LEO: I remember a friend of mine called Mrs. Purdy being very upset once when her house in Dorset fell into the sea.

GRACE (*startled*): How terrible!

LEO: Fortunately Mr. Purdy happened to be in it at the time.

OTTO: In my case, of course, it was more like an earthquake than anything else, a small but thorough earthquake with the room trembling and the chandelier swinging and the ground opening at my feet.

GRACE: Funny. We were talking about earthquakes just now.

LEO: I've never been able to understand why the Japanese are such a cheerful race. All that hissing and grinning on the brink of destruction.

OTTO: The Japanese don't mind destruction a bit; they like it, it's part of their upbringing. They're delighted with death. Look at the way they kill themselves on the most whimsical of pretexts.

LEO: I always thought Madame Butterfly was over-hasty.

OTTO: She should have gone out into the world

and achieved an austere independence.   Just like you, Gilda.

GILDA : Don't talk nonsense.   (*To* GRACE) : They both talk the most absurd nonsense ; they always have, ever since I've known them.   You mustn't pay any attention to them.

OTTO : Don't undermine our social poise, Gilda, you—who have so much !

GILDA (*sharply*) : Your social poise is non-existent.

LEO : We have a veneer, though ; it's taken us years to acquire ; don't scratch it with your sharp witty nails—*darling !*

Everybody jumps slightly at the word " darling."

GILDA : Have you written any new plays, Leo ? Have you painted any new pictures, Otto ?   You must both come to lunch one day and tell me all about yourselves.

LEO : That would be delightful.   Just the three of us.

OTTO : Should old acquaintance be forgot.

LEO : Close harmony.

GILDA : You'll have to forgive me if I'm not quite as helpful to you as I used to be.   My critical faculties aren't as strong as they once were.   I've grown away, you see.

LEO : How far have you grown away, my dear love ? How lonely are you in your little box so high above the arena ?   Don't you ever feel that you want to come down in the cheap seats again, nearer to the blood and the sand and the warm smells, nearer to Life and Death ?

GILDA : You've changed, Leo.   You used to be more subtle.

OTTO : You've changed, too, but we expected that.

HELEN (*social poise well to the fore*) : It's funny how people alter ; only the other day in the Colony a boy that I used to know when he was at Yale walked up to my table, and I didn't recognize him !

LEO : Just fancy !

OTTO : Do you know, I have an excellent memory for names, but I cannot for the life of me remember faces.   Sometimes I look at Leo suddenly and haven't the faintest idea who he is.

LEO (*quickly*) : I can remember *things*, though, very clearly, and past conversations and small trivial incidents.   Some trick of the light, some slight movement, can cause a whole flock of irrelevant memories to tumble into my mind—just unattached fragments, which might have been significant once but which don't seem to mean anything any more.   Trees in a quiet London square, for instance—a green evening dress, with ear-rings to match—two notes propped up against a brandy bottle—odd, isn't it ?

GILDA : Not particularly odd.   The usual litter of an over-sentimental mind.

OTTO : Be careful, Gilda.   An ugly brawl is imminent.

GILDA : I'm not afraid.

OTTO : That's brave, when you have so much to lose.

> *He glances comprehensively round the room.*

GILDA (*quietly*) : Is that a threat ?

OTTO : We've come back.   That should be threat enough !

GILDA (*rising, with a strange smile*) : There now ! That's what happens when ghosts get into the house.

They try to frighten you with their beckoning fingers and clanking chains, not knowing that they're dead and unable to harm you any more.   That's why one should never be scared of them, only sorry for them.   Poor little ghosts !   It must be so uncomfortable, wandering through empty passages, feeling they're not wanted very much.

LEO (*to* GRACE) : You see, Gilda can talk nonsense too.

OTTO (*reprovingly*) : That wasn't nonsense, Leo ; that was a flight of fancy, tinged with the macabre and reeking with allegory—a truly remarkable achievement !

LEO : It certainly requires a vivid imagination to describe this apartment as an empty passage.

GILDA (*laughing a trifle wildly*) : Stop it, both of you ! You're behaving abominably !

OTTO : We're all behaving abominably.

LEO : The veneer is wearing thin.   Even yours, Gilda.

GRACE : This, really, is the most extraordinary conversation I've ever heard.

OTTO : Fascinating, though, don't you think ? Fascinating to lift the roofs a fraction and look down into the houses.

GILDA : Not when the people inside know you're looking : not when they're acting for you and strutting about and showing off !

LEO : How does it feel to be so secure, Gilda ?   Tell us about it.

GILDA (*ignoring him*) : Another drink, Henry ?

HENRY : No, thanks.

HELEN (*rising*) : We really ought to be going now.

GILDA : Oh, I'm so sorry !

LEO : Watch the smooth wheels going round !

OTTO : Reach for a Murad !

GRACE (*also rising*) : I'm going, too, Gilda.   Can I drop anybody ?

HENRY : No, thanks, our car's outside.

GRACE : Good night, Mr. Mercuré.

LEO (*shaking hands*) : Good night.

GRACE (*shaking hands with* OTTO) : Good night.   Can I drop you anywhere ?

OTTO : No, thank you ; we're staying a little longer.

GILDA : No !   Go now, Otto, please.   Both of you, go with Grace.   I'm terribly tired ; you can telephone me first thing in the morning.

LEO : We want to talk to you.

GILDA : To-morrow, you can talk to me to-morrow ; we can all talk for hours.

LEO : We want to talk now.

GILDA : I know you do, but I tell you, I'm tired— dreadfully tired.   I've had a very hard day——

> *She winks at them violently.*

OTTO (*grinning*) : Oh, I see.

HELEN (*at the door*) : Come on, Henry !   Good night, Gilda darling ; it's been a lovely evening.

> *She bows to* OTTO *and* LEO, *and goes out.*   GRACE
> *looks at* OTTO *and* LEO *and* GILDA, *and then with
> great tact joins* HENRY *at the door.*

GRACE (*to* OTTO) : My car's there, if you are coming now.   Good night, Gilda—ring for the elevator, Henry——

> *She goes out with* HENRY.

GILDA (*hurriedly, in a whisper*) : It was awful of you to behave like that !   Why couldn't you have waited quietly until they'd gone?

LEO (*also in a whisper*): They wouldn't go—they were going to stay for ever and ever and ever!

GILDA *runs over to her bag, which is lying on a chair, and takes a latchkey out of it.*

GILDA: Go, now, both of you! Go with Grace. She'll gossip all over the town if you don't. Here's the key; come back in ten minutes.

OTTO: Intrigue, eh? A nice state of affairs.

LEO: Good old Decameron!

GILDA (*shoving the key into his hand*): Go on, quickly! Get a taxi straight back——

They both kiss her lightly on the lips and go out.

GILDA *stands still, staring after them until she hears the door slam. Her eyes are filled with tears. She strides about the room in great agitation, clasping and unclasping her hands. She stops in front of a table on which is someone's unfinished drink. She drinks it thoughtfully, frowning and tapping her foot nervously on the ground.*

Suddenly, she bangs down the glass, snatches up her cloak and bag, switches off all the lights, and runs out through the door leading to the fire escape.

Curtain.

END OF ACT III: SCENE I

ACT III : SCENE II

The Scene is the same, and it is the next morning.

 The windows are wide open, and sunlight is streaming into the room.

 As the curtain rises, MATTHEW *crosses over from the servants' quarters, door Left, and goes into the hall.* MATTHEW *is black but comely. He wears a snow-white coat and dark trousers and is very smart indeed.*

 ERNEST *enters from the hall, carrying a suitcase.*

 MATTHEW *follows him, staggering under three or four large canvases in a wooden crate.*

ERNEST : Put them down there for the moment, Matthew, and get me some coffee.

MATTHEW : Yes, sir.

 He rests the canvases against the wall.

ERNEST (*taking off his hat and coat*) : Is Mrs. Friedman awake ?

MATTHEW : She hasn't rung yet, sir.

ERNEST : All right. Get me the coffee as quickly as you can.

MATTHEW : It's all ready, sir.

 He goes off Left. ERNEST *wanders out on to the terrace and then in again. He picks up a newspaper off the table, glances at it and throws it down again. He is obviously irritable.* MATTHEW *re-enters with a breakfast tray, which he places on a small table.*

MATTHEW : Perhaps you'd like to have it out on the terrace, sir ?

ERNEST : No. This'll do.

MATTHEW : Did you have a good trip, sir ?

ERNEST (*sitting down at the table*) : No, I did not.

MATTHEW : Very good, sir.

He goes out. ERNEST *pours himself some coffee. While he is doing so,* OTTO *and* LEO *come down the stairs. They are both wearing* ERNEST'S *pyjamas and dressing-gowns, which are considerably small for them. Their feet are bare.*

LEO (*as they reach the bottom of the stairs*) : Good morning, Ernest !

ERNEST (*flabbergasted*) : God bless my soul !

OTTO (*kissing him*) : He will, Ernest. He couldn't fail to !

LEO (*also kissing him*) : Dear little Ernest !

ERNEST : Where—where in heaven's name have you come from ?

OTTO : Manila.

LEO (*grinning*) : It was very hot in Manila.

OTTO : Aren't you pleased to see us ?

ERNEST : Have you been staying here ?

LEO : Of course.

ERNEST : Since when ?

OTTO : Last night.

ERNEST : Where did you sleep ?

LEO : Upstairs.

ERNEST : What ! Where's Gilda ?

OTTO : We don't know. She's disappeared.

ERNEST : Disappeared ! What on earth do you mean ?

OTTO : What I say. She's disappeared.

LEO : Disappeared ! Gone.   She fluttered out into the night like a silly great owl.

OTTO : We arrived when she was entertaining a few smart friends, and she pressed a latch-key into our hands and told us to come back later ; and when we came back later, she wasn't here.   So we waited a little while, and then we went to bed.

LEO : We were very tired.

ERNEST : It's fantastic, the whole thing ! Ridiculous.

LEO : Do you think we could have some coffee ?

ERNEST : Yes, you can have some coffee, if you want it.

> *He rings a little bell on the table and slams it down again irritably.*

OTTO : I do hope you're not going to be disagreeable, Ernest.   After all, you haven't seen us for ages.

ERNEST : Disagreeable ! What do you expect me to be ?   I arrive home after twenty hours in the train to find Gilda gone, and you both staying in the house uninvited and wearing my pyjamas.

LEO : We'll take them off at once, if you like.

ERNEST : You won't do any such thing !

> MATTHEW *enters and stands stricken with astonishment.*

Two more cups, Matthew.

MATTHEW : Yes, sir.

> *He goes out, staring.*

ERNEST : Had you warned Gilda that you were coming ?

OTTO : No.   We just arrived—it was a surprise.

ERNEST (*suddenly*) :   What do you want ?

LEO : Why do you ask that ?

ERNEST : I want to know. Why have you come ? What do you want ?

OTTO : We want Gilda, of course !

ERNEST : Have you gone out of your mind ?

LEO : Not at all. It's quite natural. We've always wanted Gilda.

ERNEST : Are you aware that she is my wife ?

OTTO (*turning away*) : Oh, don't be so silly, Ernest !

ERNEST : Silly ! How dare you !

LEO : You're a dear old pet, Ernest, and we're very, very fond of you and we know perfectly well that Gilda could be married to you fifty times and still not be your wife.

MATTHEW *comes in with two cups.*

MATTHEW : Do you want some fresh coffee, sir ?

ERNEST (*mechanically, staring at them*) : No—no, there's enough here.

MATTHEW (*to* OTTO) : Can I get you some grapefruit, sir ? Or an egg ?

OTTO : No, thank you.

MATTHEW (*to* LEO) : For you, sir ?

LEO : No, thank you.

ERNEST : That will do, Matthew.

MATTHEW : Yes, sir.

He goes out.

ERNEST : Do you seriously imagine that you have the slightest right to walk into my house like this and demand my wife ?

OTTO : Do stop saying " my wife " in that complacent way, Ernest ; it's absurd !

LEO : We know entirely why you married Gilda ; and if we'd both been dead it would have been an exceedingly good arrangement.

ERNEST :   You are dead, as far as she's concerned.

OTTO :   Oh, no, we're not !   We're very much alive.

LEO :   I fear your marriage is on the rocks, Ernest.

ERNEST :   This is one of the most superb exhibitions of brazen impertinence I've ever encountered.

OTTO :   It's inconvenient, I do see that.   It may quite possibly inconvenience you very much.

LEO :   But no more than that ; and you know it as well as we do.

ERNEST (*with admirable control*) :   Aren't you taking rather a lot for granted ?

OTTO :   Only what we know.

ERNEST :   I won't lose my temper with you, because that would be foolish——

OTTO :   And ineffective.

ERNEST :   But I think you had better put on whatever clothes you came in, and go away.   You can come back later, when you're in a more reasonable frame of mind.

LEO :   We're in a perfectly reasonable frame of mind, Ernest.   We've never been more reasonable in our lives ; nor more serenely determined.

ERNEST (*with great calmness*) :   Now look here, you two.   I married Gilda because she was alone, and because for many, many years I have been deeply attached to her.   We discussed it carefully together from every angle, before we decided.   I know the whole circumstances intimately.   I know exactly how much she loved you both ; and also, I'm afraid, exactly how little you both loved her.   You practically ruined her life between you, and you caused her great unhappiness with your egotistical, casual passions.   Now you can leave her alone.   She's worked hard and made a reputation for herself. Her life is fully occupied; and she is completely contented. Leave her alone! Go away! Go back to Manila or wherever you came from—and leave her alone!

LEO: Admirable, Ernest! Admirable, but not strictly accurate. We love her more than anyone else in the world and always shall. She caused us just as much unhappiness in the past as we ever caused her. And although she may have worked hard, and although her life is so fully occupied, she is far from being contented. We saw her last night and we know.

OTTO: She could never be contented without us, because she belongs to us just as much as we belong to her.

ERNEST: She ran away from you.

LEO: She'll come back.

The front-door bell rings.

OTTO: She has come back!

There is silence while MATTHEW *crosses from the servants' door to the hall.*

LEO: Coffee! That's the thing—nice, strong coffee! (*He pours some out for himself.*)

OTTO (*doing the same*): Delicious!

ERNEST (*rising, and flinging down his napkin*): This is insupportable!

LEO: Peculiar and complicated, I grant you, and rather exciting, but not insupportable.

GILDA enters, followed by MATTHEW, who looks utterly bewildered. She is wearing a dark day coat and hat over her evening dress, and carrying a brown paper parcel that is obviously her evening cloak. She sees the three of them and smiles.

GILDA: I might have known it!

MATTHEW: Shall I take your parcel, ma'am?

GILDA : Yes, give it to Nora, Matthew ; it's my evening cloak.

MATTHEW : Yes, ma'am.

He goes off, Left, with it, while GILDA *takes off her hat and coat and fluffs out her hair.*

GILDA : I borrowed this coat and hat from the telephone operator at the Ritz : remind me to return it some time this morning, Ernest. (*She comes over and kisses him absently.*) This is all very awkward, isn't it ? I am so sorry. The very first minute you get home, too. It's a shame ! (*To* OTTO *and* LEO) : Did you stay here all night ?

LEO : Yes, we did.

GILDA : I wondered if you would.

OTTO : Why did you sneak off like that ?

GILDA (*coolly*) : I should have thought the reason was obvious enough.

LEO : It was very weak of you.

GILDA : Not at all. I wanted time to think. Give me some coffee, Ernest—no, don't ring for another cup ; I'll have yours. I couldn't bear to see Matthew's eyes popping out at me any more !

She pours out some coffee and sits down and surveys the three of them.

GILDA (*blandly*) : Now then !

LEO : Now then *indeed!*

GILDA : What's going to happen ?

OTTO : Social poise again. Oh, dear ! Oh, dear, oh, dear !

GILDA : You know you both look figures of fun in those pyjamas !

ERNEST : I don't believe I've ever been so acutely irritated in my whole life.

LEO :   It is annoying for you, Ernest, I do see that !
I'm so sorry.

OTTO :   Yes, we're both sorry.

ERNEST :   I think your arrogance is insufferable.   I
don't know what to say.   I don't know what to do.
I'm very, very angry.   Gilda, for heaven's sake, tell
them to go !

GILDA :   They wouldn't.   Not if I told them until I
was black in the face !

LEO :   Quite right.

OTTO :   Not without you, we wouldn't.

GILDA (*smiling*) :   That's very sweet of you both.

LEO (*looking at her sharply*) :   What are you up to ?

OTTO :   Tell us, my little dear, my clever little dear !
Tell us what you're up to.

GILDA :   What have you been saying to Ernest ?

LEO :   Lots of things.

ERNEST :   They've been extremely offensive, both of
them.

GILDA :   In what way ?

ERNEST :   I'd rather not discuss it any further.

GILDA :   I believe you've got a little fatter, Otto.

LEO :   He eats too much rice.

GILDA :   You look very well, though.

OTTO (*raising his eyebrows slightly*) :   Thank you.

GILDA :   So do you, Leo.   The line in between your
eyes is deeper, but you seem very healthy.

LEO :   I am.

GILDA :   You were always very strong, con-
stitutionally.   Strong as an ox !   Do you remember
that, Ernest ?

ERNEST (*irritably*) :   What ?

GILDA (*smiling*) :   Nothing.   It doesn't matter.

LEO : Stop pulling our ears and stroking us, Gilda, and tell us your secret. Tell us why you're so strange and quiet—tell us what you're up to.

GILDA : Don't you know ? I've given in !

LEO (*quickly*) : What !

GILDA (*quietly and very distinctly*) : I've given in. I've thrown my hand in ! The game's over.

ERNEST : Gilda ! What do you mean ?

GILDA : What I say.

ERNEST : You mean—you can't mean that——

GILDA (*gently*) : I mean I'm going away from you, Ernest. Some things are too strong to fight against ; I've been fighting for two years and it's no use. I'm bored with the battle, sick to death of it ! So I've given in.

ERNEST : You're—you're insane ! You can't be serious.

GILDA : I'm not serious ! That's what's so dreadful. I feel I ought to be, but I'm not—my heart's bobbing up and down inside me like a parrot in a cage ! It's shameful, I know, but I can't help it—— (*She suddenly turns on* OTTO *and* LEO) : And you two—you two sitting there with the light of triumph in your eyes !—Say something, can't you ? Say something, for God's sake, before I slap your smug little faces !

LEO : I knew it. I knew it last night !

OTTO : We both knew it ! We laughed ourselves to sleep.

ERNEST : Gilda, pull yourself together ! Don't be a fool—pull yourself together !

GILDA : Don't get excited, Ernest. It doesn't matter to you as much as all that, you know.

ERNEST : You're crazy ! You're stark staring mad !

GILDA (*ecstatically*) :   I am, I am !   I'm mad with joy !   I'm mad with relief !   I thought they really had forgotten me ;   that they really were free of me.   I thought that they were never coming back, that I should never see them again ;   that my heart would be heavy and sick and lonely for them until I died !

LEO :   Serve you right for leaving us !   Serve you damn well right !

GILDA :   Be quiet !   Shut your trap, my darling !   I've got to explain to Ernest.

ERNEST :   I don't want to hear your explanations.   I don't want to hear any more——

OTTO :   Try and stop her, that's all !   Just try and stop her !   She's off, she's embarked on a scene.   Oh, dear love, this is highly delectable !   The old girl's on the war-path !

GILDA :   Be quiet, I tell you !   Don't crow !   Don't be so mean.

ERNEST :   I don't want to hear any more, I tell you !

GILDA :   You've got to.   You must !   There's so much I have to say.   You must listen.   In fairness to yourself and to all of us, you must listen.

ERNEST :   You're being unbelievably vulgar !   I'm ashamed of you.

GILDA :   I'm ashamed of many things, but not of this !   This is real.   I've made use of you, Ernest, and I'm ashamed of that, and I've lied to you.   I'm ashamed of that, too ;   but at least I didn't know it :   I was too busy lying to myself at the same time.   I took refuge in your gentle, kind friendship, and tried to pretend to myself that it was enough, but it wasn't.   I've talked and laughed and entertained your friends ;   I've been excellent company and very efficient.   I've worked hard and bought things and sold things, all the time pretending that my longing for these two was fading! But it wasn't. They came back last night, looking very sleek and sly in their newly pressed suits, and the moment I saw them, I knew; I knew it was no good pretending any more. I fought against it, honestly I did! I ran away from them, and walked about the streets and sat in Childs weeping into glasses of milk. Oh, Ernest, you've understood such a lot, understand just this much more, and try to forgive me—because I can't possibly live without them, and that's that!

ERNEST (*with icy calm*): I gather that the fact that I'm your husband is not of the faintest importance to you?

GILDA: It's never been anything more than a comfortable sort of arrangement, has it?

ERNEST: Apparently not as comfortable as I imagined.

GILDA: Exquisitely comfortable, Ernest, and easy-going and very, very nice; but those things don't count in a situation like this, you must see that!

ERNEST: I see a ruthless egotism, an utter disregard for anyone's feelings but your own. That's all I can see at the moment.

LEO: You should see more, Ernest, you really should. The years that you've known us should have taught you that it's no use trying to make any one of us toe the line for long.

ERNEST: Gilda is different from you two, she always has been.

GILDA: Not different enough.

ERNEST: You let her down utterly. You threw

away everything she gave you. It was painful to watch her writhing in the throes of her own foolish love for you. I used to love you both too. You were young and gay, and your assurance wasn't set and unbecoming as it is now. But I don't love you any more. I'm not even fond of you. You set every instinct that I have on edge. You offend my taste. When Gilda escaped from you I tried to make her happy and contented, quietly, without fuss.

OTTO : She could never be happy without fuss. She revels in it.

ERNEST : Superficially, perhaps, but not really. Not deep down in her heart.

LEO :   What do you know of her heart ?

GILDA :   Cruel little cat.

OTTO :   Shut up !

LEO :   She's chosen to come back to us. She just said so. How do you account for that ?

ERNEST : The sight of you has revived her old idiotic infatuation for you, but only for a little. It won't last. She knows too much now to be taken in by you again.

GILDA :   You're wrong, Ernest. You're wrong.

ERNEST :   Your lack of balance verges on insanity.

OTTO :   Do you know that was downright rude !

GILDA :   Why go on talking ? Talking isn't any good. Look at me, Ernest. Look at me ! Can't you see what's happened ?

ERNEST :   You're a mad woman again.

GILDA :   Why shouldn't I be a mad woman ? I've been sane and still for two years. You were deceived by my dead behaviour because you wanted to be. It's silly to go on saying to yourself that I'm different from

Otto and Leo just because you want to believe it. I'm not different from them. We're all of a piece, the three of us. Those early years made us so. From now on we shall have to live and die our own way. No one else's way is any good, we don't fit.

ERNEST : No, you don't, you don't and you never will. Your values are false and distorted.

GILDA : Only from your point of view.

ERNEST : From the point of view of anyone who has the slightest sense of decency.

LEO : We have our own decencies. We have our own ethics. Our lives are a different shape from yours. Wave us good-bye, Little Ernest, we're together again.

GILDA : Ernest, Ernest, be friendly. It can't hurt you much.

ERNEST : Not any more. I've wasted too much friendship on all of you, you're not worth it.

OTTO : There's a lot of vanity in your anger, Ernest, which isn't really worthy of your intelligence.

ERNEST (*turning on him*) : Don't speak to me, please !

LEO : Otto's perfectly right. This behaviour isn't worthy of your intelligence. If you were twisted up inside and really unhappy it would be different; but you're not, you're no more than offended and resentful that your smooth habits should be tampered with——

ERNEST (*losing control*) : Hold your tongue !—I've had too much of your effrontery already !

GILDA (*peaceably*) : Once and for all, Ernest, don't be bitter and so dreadfully outraged ! Please, please calm down and you'll find it much easier to understand.

ERNEST : You overrate my capacity for understanding ! I don't understand ; the whole situation is revolting to me. I never shall understand ; I never could understand this disgusting three-sided erotic hotch-potch !

GILDA : Ernest !

LEO : Why, good heavens ! King Solomon had a hundred wives and was thought very highly of. I can't see why Gilda shouldn't be allowed a couple or gentlemen friends.

ERNEST (*furiously*) : Your ill-timed flippancy is only in keeping with the rest of your execrable taste !

OTTO : Certain emotions transcend even taste, Ernest. Take anger, for example. Look what anger's doing to you ! You're blowing yourself out like a frog !

ERNEST (*beside himself*) : Be quiet ! Be quiet !

LEO (*violently*) : Why should we be quiet ? You're making enough row to blast the roof off ! Why should you have the monopoly of noise ? Why should your pompous moral pretensions be allowed to hurtle across the city without any competition ? We've all got lungs ; let's use them ! Let's shriek like mad ! Let's enjoy ourselves !

GILDA (*beginning to laugh*) : Stop it, Leo ! I implore you !—This is ludicrous ! Stop it—stop it——

ERNEST (*in a frenzy*) : It is ludicrous ! It's ludicrous to think that I was ever taken in by any of you—that I ever mistook you for anything but the unscrupulous, worthless degenerates that you are ! There isn't a decent instinct among the lot of you. You're shifty and irresponsible and abominable, and I don't wish to set eyes on you again—as long as I live ! Never ! Do you hear me ? Never—never—never !

He stamps out of the room, quite beside himself with fury ; on his way into the hall he falls over the package of canvases.

This is too much for GILDA *and* OTTO *and* LEO ; *they break down utterly and roar with laughter. They groan and weep with laughter ; their laughter is still echoing from the walls as—*

THE CURTAIN FALLS

CAVALCADE

PART ONE

PART TWO

PART THREE

PART ONE: SCENE I

Principals: JANE MARRYOT (aged 31), ROBERT MARRYOT (aged 35), ELLEN (aged 25), BRIDGES (aged 40).

SCENE : *The drawing-room of a London house. The room is charmingly furnished in the taste of the period. There are two windows at the back with a small balcony in front of each of them; apart from this structural necessity the decoration and furniture, etc., can be left to the discretion of the designer.*

TIME : *About 11.45 p.m. Sunday, December 31st, 1899.*

When the curtain rises, ELLEN, the parlourmaid, is discovered setting the table with a light supper consisting of sandwiches and cake. She is a pleasant-looking woman of twenty-five.

Enter BRIDGES, the butler, with a bottle of champagne in a bucket of ice. He is older than ELLEN, about forty, with iron-grey hair.

ELLEN : They won't need champagne if they've got 'ot punch, will they?

BRIDGES : You never know; best to be on the safe side.

ELLEN : How was Cook when you come up?

BRIDGES : Running round that kitchen like a cat on a griddle; New Year's Eve's gone to 'er 'ead, and no mistake.

ELLEN : She's been queer all day, she says she feel

like as if it was the end of everything. So do I, for that matter.

BRIDGES :   Don't start all that over again.

ELLEN :   Oh, Alfred !

BRIDGES :   What ?

ELLEN :   I can't bear to think what it's going to be like when you've gone.

BRIDGES :   Well, don't.

ELLEN :   I can't 'elp it.

BRIDGES :   It's no use upsetting yourself ; think of the missus, think of all the other soldiers' wives. You're in the same boat as wot they are.

ELLEN :   You was never cut out for a soldier.

BRIDGES :   Never mind what I was cut out for. I am one now.

ELLEN :   What's going to 'appen to me and Fanny if anything 'appens to you ?

BRIDGES (*putting his hands on* ELLEN'S *shoulders*) : Look 'ere, old girl, you married me for better or for worse, didn't you ?

ELLEN :   Yes, but——

BRIDGES :   Well, if this turns out to be worse, so much the worse, see ? And if it turns out to be better——

ELLEN :   So much the better—yes, a fat lot of comfort that is.

BRIDGES :   Look at the Missus, with a brother out there ever since the beginning, and now 'er 'usband going, and two growing boys to look after.

ELLEN :   What's the war for, anyhow ? Nobody wanted to 'ave a war.

BRIDGES :   We've got to 'ave wars every now and then to prove we're top-dog——

ELLEN : This one don't seem to be proving much.

BRIDGES : 'Ow can you tell sitting at 'ome 'ere safe and sound ? 'Ow can you tell what our brave boys are suffering out there in darkest Africa, giving their life's blood for their Queen and country ?

ELLEN : Africa looks very sunny and nice in the *Illustrated London News.*

BRIDGES : If this wasn't New Year's Eve, I'd lose my temper, and that's a fact.

ELLEN : Well, it wouldn't be the first time. You'd better go and get the 'ot punch, they'll be in in a minute.

BRIDGES : You mark my words, Ellen, if we didn't go out and give them Boers wot for, they'd be over 'ere wreakin' 'avoc and carnage before you could say Jack Robinson.

ELLEN : Oh, get along with you.

BRIDGES *goes out.*

ELLEN *puts the finishing touches to the table and then, going to the windows, she pulls back the curtains.*

Enter JANE MARRYOT. *She is a handsome woman of about thirty-one. She is wearing an evening gown and cloak.*

Enter ROBERT, JANE'S *husband, following her. He is older, about thirty-five, also in evening dress.*

JANE (*throwing off her cloak*) : I thought we should never get here in time. I'm sure that cabby was tipsy, Robert. How nice the table looks, Ellen. Where did those flowers come from ?

ELLEN : They're from Bridges and me, ma'am, with our very best wishes, I'm sure.

JANE : Thank you, Ellen, very much indeed.

ROBERT : A charming thought, Ellen. Thank you both.

ELLEN : Not at all, sir—it's—it's a pleasure indeed.

ELLEN *withdraws from the room covered with respectful embarrassment.*

JANE *smiles at* ROBERT.

JANE : Small things are so infinitely touching, aren't they ? I feel I want to cry. Just a few gentle tears to usher in the new century.

ROBERT : Do, by all means, dearest : this evening was planned sentimentally.

JANE : Just the two of us saying, " Hail and Farewell."

ROBERT : Not farewell quite yet.

JANE : Soon—dreadfully soon.

ROBERT : You looked so beautiful at dinner.

JANE : Did I, Robert ?

ROBERT : You look so beautiful now.

JANE : Do I, Robert ?

ROBERT : I expect it's only that dress, really. Very deceiving.

JANE : Yes, Robert.

ROBERT : And that ornament in your hair.

JANE : Yes, Robert.

ROBERT : And the fact that I love you so dearly.

JANE : After so long. How can you ?

ROBERT : Perhaps you're hideous and ill-dispositioned and tedious, really, and I never knew.

JANE : Perhaps.

ROBERT : Well, it's too late now. I'm set in the habit of loving you. I shall never know the truth.

JANE : I wonder if the boys are asleep.

ROBERT : Snoring, I expect.

JANE : Oh, no, Robert; not snoring. They both have perfect tonsils. Doctor Harrison said so.

ROBERT : Inherited from their mother, dear. You have the most exquisite tonsils in the world.

JANE : You're in a very facetious mood, Robert. It shocks me a little. This should be a solemn occasion. Your bow is crooked, too, and you look raffish.

ROBERT : Raffish ?

JANE (*suddenly running into his arms*) : Oh, my darling, my darling, why must you leave me ? I shall miss you so.

ROBERT (*smiling and holding her tenderly*) : The Bugle Call, dear, the Red, White and Blue——

Britons never, never, never shall be slaves.

JANE : Don't tease me—not about that. What does it matter about the Boers—it can't matter, really.

ROBERT (*seriously*) : It matters about Jim, doesn't it ? He's out there.

JANE : Yes, I know, I know, but——

ROBERT : But what ?

JANE (*leaving his embrace*) : I'm sorry dear. I was nearly behaving badly.

ROBERT : You couldn't behave badly.

JANE (*lightly*) : Give him my love if you ever see him, if he's alive.

ROBERT : Of course he's alive. They're all alive. They're bound to be relieved soon.

JANE : Everyone has been saying that for weeks.

ROBERT : Baden Powell's a fine man.

JANE : How long will it last, the war, I mean ?

ROBERT : It can't last more than a few months.

JANE : Perhaps it will be over before you get there.

ROBERT : Perhaps.

131

JANE : I suppose you'd hate that. Wouldn't you ?

ROBERT : Bitterly.

JANE : Thank Heaven for one thing. The boys are too young. They won't have to fight ; Peace and Happiness for them. Oh, please God, Peace and Happiness for them, always. (*She leans against the window and looks out.*)

> *Enter* BRIDGES *with a bowl of punch, followed by :*
> ELLEN *entering, carrying a tray of punch glasses and almonds and raisins.*

BRIDGES : It's started, sir. Just twelve o'clock now.

ROBERT : Open the windows quick.

> ROBERT *takes the punch from* BRIDGES *and fills two glasses.*
> BRIDGES *opens the windows wide.*
> *Outside can be heard the growing noise of sirens and chimes of bells.*
> ELLEN *and* BRIDGES *are about to go.*

JANE (*suddenly*) : Stay and drink with us, won't you ? Robert, two more glasses.

BRIDGES : Thank you very much, ma'am.

ELLEN : Thank you, ma'am.

ROBERT (*pouring them two glasses of punch*) : Here you are, Jane, Ellen, Bridges. 1900—1900.

JANE : 1900.

ELLEN and BRIDGES (*together*) : 1900.

> *Suddenly* JANE *hears a sound upstairs. She puts down her glass hurriedly and :*
> JANE *runs out of the room.*

ELLEN : It sounded like Master Joe.

ROBERT (*going to the door and calling after* JANE) : Dearest, bring them down here. Bring them both down.   (*Coming slowly back into the room, smiling.*)   How very impolite of the twentieth century to waken the children.

> *The lights fade as the noise of chimes and sirens grows louder.*

PART ONE : SCENE II

Principals : ROBERT, JANE, ELLEN, BRIDGES.

SCENE :   *A Dockside.*
TIME :   *About twelve noon, Saturday, January 27th, 1900.*

> *Before the stage becomes visible to the audience, down stage on the left* BRIDGES *and* ELLEN *appear in a pool of light.* BRIDGES *is wearing the uniform of a Private in the C.I.V.* ELLEN *is gaily dressed, but weeping.*

BRIDGES :   Be brave, old woman.

ELLEN :   Oh, Alfred, Alfred, my 'eart's breaking.

BRIDGES :   There, there—I'll soon be back—you see.

ELLEN :   I can't bear it.

BRIDGES :   Think of the missus—you'll 'ave to look after 'er, you know.

ELLEN :   I can't think of anything but you going out among all them awful Boers and lying bleeding yer 'eart out on the battlefield.

BRIDGES :   That's a cheerful outlook, I will say.

ELLEN :   And Fanny 'aving no father and me being widowed for life.

BRIDGES :   You're getting morbid, you know.

Fanny'll be all right, and so will you and so will I.
She was right as rain when I kissed her good-bye.
See her laugh, eh?

ELLEN: She didn't mean to laugh; she's too
young to understand.

BRIDGES: All the better, I say. I could do with a
bit of a smile from you, now you mention it.

ELLEN: All right—I'll try.

BRIDGES: That's a girl—— (*He kisses her as*):

> *The lights fade on them and a steamer siren sounds
> loudly.*
>
> *Down stage on the right* ROBERT *and* JANE *appear
> in a pool of light.*
>
> ROBERT *is in the uniform of a C.I.V. officer.*
>
> JANE *is quietly dressed.*

ROBERT: I think I'd better be getting aboard.

JANE: It's come at last, hasn't it—this moment?

ROBERT: You'll be very brave, won't you?

JANE: Take care of yourself, my dearest.

ROBERT: I shall probably be seasick.

JANE: Lie down flat on every possible occasion.

ROBERT: I'll try to remember.

JANE: Bridges will look after you.

ROBERT: Perhaps he'll be lying down flat, too.

JANE: You mustn't worry about me being unhappy
when you've gone. I'm going to keep myself very busy.
Lady Brandon is organizing an enormous relief fund
matinée in February. She asked me to help her, and
there'll be lots of other things, too. I shan't give
myself time to feel anything except just very proud.

ROBERT: I'll write and telegraph whenever it's
possible.

> *Pause.*

JANE : This is horrid, isn't it ?

ROBERT : I really must go.

JANE : Not just for a minute.

ROBERT : I'm going to kiss you once more now, and then I want you to turn away and go on talking, so that you won't see me actually leave you.

JANE (*In a stifled voice*) : Very well, my darling.

ROBERT *kisses her lingeringly.*

(*Turning away and talking rapidly.*) Edward and Joe were terribly anxious to come, too, but I'm glad I didn't bring them really. Joe gets over-excited so easily, and he's had a very bad cold, anyhow. Edward could have come, I suppose, really, but that would have upset Joe so dreadfully, being left alone. Take care of yourself, my own dear—you're not here any more, so I can break down a little—I felt you go when I said about Joe being over-excited—Robert—Robert——

ROBERT *has disappeared into the surrounding darkness. As she turns the lights go up and* ROBERT *is seen threading his way through the crowd to the ship's gangway.* BRIDGES *is waiting for him, and they go aboard together.* JANE *walks over to* ELLEN, *who is sobbing bitterly, and puts her arms round her. The crowd is cheering wildly, although several mothers and sweethearts and wives are weeping.*

The steamer gives a short blast on its siren.

A band strikes up " Soldiers of the Queen."

The decks of the ship are lined with waving soldiers.

The gangway is pulled away. Slowly the ship begins to move as :

The lights fade.

PART ONE : SCENE III

Principals: JANE MARRYOT, MARGARET HARRIS,
EDITH HARRIS (aged 10), EDWARD (aged 12),
JOE (aged 8), ELLEN.

SCENE : *The same as* SCENE I.
TIME : *About five o'clock on the afternoon of Friday, May
18th, 1900.*

> *When the lights go up* EDWARD *and* JOE MARRYOT
> *and* EDITH HARRIS *are discovered playing soldiers on
> the floor.* EDWARD *is aged twelve,* JOE *eight, and*
> EDITH HARRIS *about ten.*

JOE (*shooting off a cannon*) :   Bang—bang, bang, bang.
EDITH (*giving a little squeak*) :   Oh—oh, dear !
EDWARD :   How many ?
EDITH :   Seven.
EDWARD (*curtly*) :   Good !   You'd better retreat.
EDITH :   I don't know how.
JOE :   I'm going to shoot again.
EDITH :   I do wish you wouldn't.   I've only got
fourteen left.
JOE (*yelling*) :   Bang, bang, bang !   Dirty old Kruger
—dirty old Kruger——
EDWARD :   Shut up ! How dare you fire without orders.
JOE (*saluting*) :   I'm sorry, Bobs.
EDITH :   Edward.
EDWARD :   What ?
EDITH :   Need I always be the Boers ?
EDWARD :   Yes.

136

EDITH :   Why ?

JOE :   Because you're a girl—only a girl. Bang, bang, bang !

EDITH (*struggling with her cannon and ammunition*): I'll teach you, you mean little pig !   Bang, bang, bang ! There !   Bang——

> The cannon sticks, so EDITH *throws it at* JOE'S *battalion, annihilating about fifty soldiers.*

JOE (*yelling*):   It's not fair.

EDWARD :   Be quiet.   Edith, that was cheating.

EDITH (*in tears*):   I'm sick of being the Boers—I'll never be the Boers again, never as long as I live !

> The door opens.
>
> Enter JANE, *looking obviously worried and nervy.*
>
> Enter MARGARET HARRIS, *following* JANE.   *She is a nicely dressed woman of about thirty.*

JANE :   Children, why on earth are you making such an awful noise ?   I heard you right down in the hall. Edith, what's the matter ?   Joe be quiet.

EDWARD :   Edith doesn't like being the Boers— she's mutinied.

JANE :   So I should think.

JOE :   Bang, bang, bang !

> JOE *throws* EDITH'S *cannon back at her and hits her on the knee.*
>
> EDITH *screams.*
>
> JANE *slaps* JOE *sharply.*

JANE :   You're a naughty, wicked, little boy. You go upstairs this minute.

> MARGARET *rushes to* EDITH *and proceeds to comfort her.*

MARGARET :   Edith, don't cry—it couldn't have hurt you so very much.

JANE : I can't bear it. Go away, all of you.
Edward, take Joe away.

EDWARD : Sorry, mum.

JANE : Can't you play any other game but soldiers,
soldiers—soldiers hurting each other—killing each
other ? Go away from me—go away—go away—go
away——

> MARGARET, *seeing that* JANE *is in a bad state of
> nerves, bustles all three children out of the room.*

MARGARET : Go along, all of you. Edith, I'm
ashamed of you, making such a fuss. It's only a tiny
little scratch. Go upstairs and ask nurse to put some
Pommade Devigne on it. Go along, now.

> *Exeunt* EDITH, EDWARD *and* JOE.

> MARGARET *shuts the door after the children and
> comes back to* JANE.

> JANE *is wearily removing her hat in front of a mirror.*

> *A barrel organ in the street strikes up "Soldiers of
> the Queen."*

JANE : There's no escape anywhere, is there ?

MARGARET : Shall I throw him something ?

JANE : Make him go away.

> MARGARET *goes to the window and out on to the
> balcony.*

MARGARET : Hi ! Hi !

> *The organ stops.*

Will you please go away further down the street ?
(*Throwing some money out and returning into the room.*)
He's moving off. Do sit down, Jane dear, you've been
standing up all the afternoon.

JANE (*sitting down*) : Will these days never end ?

> *The barrel organ starts again, but much further off.*

MARGARET : News will come soon.

JANE :   I don't believe I shall see either of them ever again.

MARGARET :   Don't give way to despair, Jane. It's foolish.   You must have courage.

JANE :   It's much easier to be brave when there's something to hear, something definite; this long suspense, these dragging, dragging weeks of waiting are horrible.   The two people I love best in the world, so remote from me, beyond reach of my love, probably suffering—it's dreadful, dreadful——

MARGARET :   Mafeking is bound to be relieved within the next few days, all the papers say so.

JANE :   They've been saying so for months—meanwhile Jim is dying there slowly, by inches, starvation and disease and horror.   I can't bear to think of it and yet I can't stop thinking.   I wake at night and see his face, as he was when he was a little boy.   He was always awfully plucky, my little brother, and so very, very dear to me.   (*She breaks down.*)

> *Enter* ELLEN *with tea.   She places it on the table and looks enquiringly at* MARGARET.

> MARGARET *shakes her head.*

MARGARET :   No news, yet, Ellen.   We've been standing outside the Mansion House for hours, and then we went to Fleet Street to the newspaper offices.

ELLEN (*to* JANE) :   Have a nice cup of tea, ma'am, it'll make you feel better.

JANE :   Thank you, Ellen.

ELLEN :   There ain't no cause to worry about the master, ma'am ; he's all right.   I feel it in me bones. You see, he's got my Alfred with 'im, and if anything appened to either of them we'd be bound to 'ear from one of them, if you know what I mean.

JANE: You must be fearfully worried, too, Ellen.

ELLEN: Well, on and off, I am, but I say to myself—no news is good news, and what must be must be, and you'd never believe how it cheers me up.

> ELLEN *goes out.*

MARGARET: Poor Ellen!

> *A newsboy runs by, shouting.*

JANE (*jumping up*): Quick! Quick! Give me a halfpenny.

> JANE *rushes on to the balcony and leans over.*

What is it, Ellen—what is it?

> ELLEN *apparently answers " nothing much," and* JANE *returns wearily.*

Ellen's up those area steps like lightning every time a paper boy passes. No news is good news. What must be must be. Oh, God!

> MARGARET *gets up with an air of determination.*

MARGARET: Now, look here, Jane. I'm going now, and I shall be back at a quarter to seven.

JANE: A quarter to seven—why?

MARGARET: We're going out to dine at a restaurant and we're going to a theatre.

JANE: A restaurant! A theatre! I couldn't!

MARGARET: You could and you will—it's senseless sitting at home all by yourself fretting and worrying, and it doesn't do any good. I'll get Ronnie James to take us, and if he can't, we'll go by ourselves, and I don't care what people say. We'll go to something gay—they say " Mirabelle " is very good.

JANE: I can't Margaret—it's very sweet of you, but I really can't.

MARGARET: I am now going home to have a bath

and put on my new Redfern model, and I shall be back at a quarter to seven.

JANE : Margaret—no, really, I——

MARGARET (*kissing* JANE) : Don't argue—just do what you're told.

JANE : I haven't anything to wear.

MARGARET : Nonsense ! You have your blue " Worth " and if that won't do, put on your presentation gown, feathers and all !

JANE : Margaret, don't be so silly.

MARGARET : I mean it—it's a gesture. Robert and Jim would hate to think of you weeping and wailing. They're being gallant enough. We'd better try and be gallant, too. We'll dine at the Café Royal.

JANE : Margaret !

MARGARET : Be ready at a quarter to seven.

MARGARET *goes out.*

JANE *makes a movement to call* MARGARET *back and then subsides into her chair.*

Suddenly directly under the window another barrel organ strikes up " Soldiers of the Queen."

JANE *jumps up and runs to the window.*

JANE (*on balcony*) : Go on, then—play louder—play louder ! Soldiers of the Queen—wounded and dying and suffering for the Queen ! Play louder, play louder !

She comes back into the room laughing hysterically and proceeds to kick the children's toy soldiers all over the room ; finally collapsing on to the sofa in a storm of tears as :

The lights fade.

PART ONE : SCENE IV

Principals : JANE, MARGARET, MIRABELLE, ADA, EDGAR, TOM JOLLY, SIX C.I.V. GIRLS, CHORUS, STAGE MANAGER.

SCENE : *A theatre.*
TIME : *About 9 p.m. Friday, May 18th, 1900.*

Before the lights go up, a spotlight illuminates JANE *and* MARGARET *in evening cloaks and gowns sitting in a stage box left. When the lights go up, it is seen that they are watching a typical musical comedy of the period. A Sextette of ample girls are singing a song called " The Girls of the C.I.V.", dressed rakishly in C.I.V. uniforms.*

> We're the girls of the C.I.V.
> Form fours, get in line, one two three.
> For our bravery is such
> That the Boers won't like it much
> When we chase them across the veldt and teach
>   them double Dutch
> We're the girls of the C.I.V.
> And we're out for a lark and a spree
> In our uniforms so stunning
> We shall soon have Kruger running
> From the girls of the C.I.V.

The Scene on the stage is excessively rural, with apple blossom predominating. When the girls have finished their number, they bounce off and :

The leading lady, MIRABELLE, *enters.* **She is in**
reality a Princess, but has disguised herself as a farm
girl in order that she might conceivably find a young
man to love her for herself alone. Her costume is
charming but slightly inappropriate for manual labour.
She is met down stage by LIEUT. EDGAR TYRELL,
R.N., *a wooden young man with an excellent tenor voice.*

EDGAR (*saluting*) :   We meet again.

MIRABELLE (*curtseying*) :   Yes, indeed.

EDGAR :   It seems a sin that beauty so rare should be
hidden for ever in this small country village.

MIRABELLE :   Flatterer !

EDGAR :   No, no, I mean it.

MIRABELLE :   You are a sailor, sir, and I have been
warned about sailors.

EDGAR :   What have they told you ?

MIRABELLE :   That sailors are fickle, and that when
they have loved a maid they sail away and leave her
lonely.

EDGAR :   Do you believe that ?

MIRABELLE :   I hardly know.

EDGAR :   Dearest, dearest Mirabelle—my heart is at
your feet.

MIRABELLE (*gaily*) :   Pick it up, sir, pick it up.

EDGAR :   Ah, do not tease me.   Look into my eyes
—can you not see the lovelight shining there ?

MIRABELLE :   I know nothing of love.

EDGAR :   Let me teach you.

MIRABELLE :   I know nothing of life.

MIRABELLE WALTZ

LOVER OF MY DREAMS

SHE :   A simple country maid am I,
          As innocent as any flower.
          The great big world has pass'd me by,
          No lover comes my way to greet me shyly in
             my bower.

HE :   Oh, say not so !
          Such modesty enchants me :
          Could I but stay to while away with you a
             happy hour.

SHE :   It must be Spring that fills my heart to over-
             flowing,
          Ah, whither am I going ?
          What is the voice that seems to say :
          Be kind to love, don't let him call to you
             unknowing.

HE :   If true love comes to you don't turn your face
             away.

SHE: Maybe 'tis something in the air ;
          For Spring is made for lovers only.

HE :   Live for the moment and take care
          Lest love should fly and leave us lonely.

BOTH.   Ah, if love should leave us lonely.

REFRAIN

SHE :   All my life I have been waiting
          Dreaming ages through ;
          Until to-day I suddenly discover
          The form and face of he who is my lover.

No more tears and hesitating ;
Fate has sent me you
Time and tide can never sever
Those whom love has bound forever,
Dear Lover of my Dreams come true.

HE :   All my life I have been waiting,
SHE :   All my life I have been waiting,
HE :   Dreaming ages through ;
SHE :   Dreaming ages through ;
HE :   Until to-day I suddenly discover
SHE :   Until to-day I suddenly discover
HE :   The form and face of she who is my lover.
SHE :   The form and face of he who is my lover.
HE :   No more tears and hesitating ;
SHE :   No more tears and hesitating ;
HE :   Fate has sent me you—Time and tide can never
              sever
SHE :   Fate has sent me you and tide can never sever
HE :   Those whom love has bound for ever,
SHE :   Those whom love has bound for ever,
HE :   Dear lover of my Dreams come true,
SHE :   Dear lover of my Dreams come true,
BOTH :   Dear lover of my
         Dreams come true,
         Dear lover of my Dreams come true,
         Dear lover of my Dreams come true.

Enter TOM JOLLY, *comedian.   He is dressed as a
common sailor.*

Enter ADA *with* TOM (*soubrette*).   *She is dressed as
a dairymaid.*

TOM :   If I make a noise like a cow—would you kiss
me ?

ADA (*laughing*):   Perhaps.

Tom :   Moo—moo. (*He tries to kiss her.*)

ADA :   No, no ! I'm frightened of bulls.

Tom :   If I make a noise like a sheep—then ?

ADA :   Who knows !

Tom :   Baa, baa, baa——

ADA :   No, no—no good at all.

Tom :   I'll sing, then. Sailing, sailing, over the bounding main !

ADA :   I'll kiss you now.   I love donkeys !

FUN OF THE FARM

VERSE

ADA :   Tho' sailors are so brave and bold,
It really must be dreadfully cold
        To sail across the sea.

Tom :   I quite agree,
             I quite agree,
I'm sick of the ocean wild and free,
Heigho, heigho, this is the place for me.

ADA :   Now I am weary of the town
And feel inclined to settle down
        A milk pail on my arm.

Tom :   I feel afraid,
             A London maid
Would never know how the eggs are laid.

ADA :   I'd find a cow
        And milk 'til the pail was full.

Tom :   I'd shear the sow
        And probably milk the bull.

BOTH :   You must agree
             That it would be

The height of true rusticity
If you and I should settle on a farm.

REFRAIN

BOTH : Oh, the Fun of the Farmyard,
        The roosters are crowing,
        The cattle are lowing,
  The turkeys go gobbly gobbly goo
  This really is an alarm yard.

ADA :   Like little Bo-Peep,
        I lose my sheep,
  And cannot find them anywhere.

TOM :   I ought to be shot,
        For I forgot
  To coax the horse to meet the mare.

BOTH :   Who left the canary
        Locked up in the dairy ?

ADA :   Cheep, cheep, cheep, cheep,

TOM : Snort, snort, snort, snort,

ADA :   Moo, moo, moo, moo,

TOM :   Cock a doodle doodle do !

BOTH : Oh, dear, far from being a calm yard,
        Quack, quack, quack, quack,
        All the fun of the farm.

TOM : Tell me something, Ada.

ADA : What ?

TOM : You're no dairymaid, are you ?

ADA : Mr. Inquisitive.

TOM : What are you ?

ADA (*curtseying*) : Lady's maid to the Princess
Mirabelle.

    MIRABELLE *enters unobserved at the back.*

147

TOM :   The Princess ! Then he'll win his bet, after all.
ADA :   Who ?   What bet ?
TOM :   Lieutenant Edgar.   All the officers of the
ship wagered him that he would not win the hand of the
Princess Mirabelle.   He said he'd marry her if she was
ugly as sin ; he needs the money.

   EDGAR *enters*.

EDGAR :   What are you doing here, Tom ?
TOM :   Just farming ! (*Laugh.*)
MIRABELLE :   Stop !
   Enter full CHORUS

FINALE

CHORUS :   What is—what is the matter here ?
MIRABELLE :   Kind friends, you heard my call,
       And so I thank you all
       For while you chatter here
       My heart has been betrayed.
EDGAR :   Ah, no—not so.
       What foolish words you scatter here.
       'Tis naught but your pride that's hurt
       I am afraid.
CHORUS :   Who can he be,
       'Tis plain to see,
        He seems to know her well.
       Who is this man
       Who dares offend
        The Princess Mirabelle ?
MIRABELLE :   You've lied to me and cheated me.
ADA :   Madame, don't let him see
       Your poor heart breaking.
EDGAR :   What ere the future be,
       True love you are mistaking.

WALTZ REFRAIN FINALE

> All my life I have been dreaming,
> Now my dreams must die.
> Within my heart I felt a song awaken,
> And now I find a melody forsaken.
> All your vows were base and scheming,
> All our Love's a lie.
> Cruelly you would deceive me,
> All I say to you is . . .

Enter STAGE MANAGER, *who raises his hand for silence.*

STAGE MANAGER: Ladies and gentlemen—Mafeking has been relieved.

JANE in her box utters a cry of relief.

The players on the stage cheer wildly and the lights fade.

The cheering is heard through the darkness ; when the lights come up the audience is discovered cheering, waving hats and handker chiefs, and programmes are fluttering from the crowded balconies ; some of the audience join hands and sing " Auld Lang Syne." The lights fade.

PART ONE : SCENE V

Principals : MRS. SNAPPER, COOK, ANNIE, ELLEN, BRIDGES, CABBY.

SCENE : *The kitchen of a London house. It is a typical basement kitchen. There is a door at the back opening on to the area steps, also two windows. Another door communicating with the upper parts of the house, and a small door leading into the scullery.*

TIME :   *About 5 p.m. Monday, January 21st, 1901.*

When the lights go up COOK *is making toast in front of the range.*

MRS. SNAPPER (ELLEN'S *Mother*) *is sitting on a chair beside a mail-cart in which reposes (mercifully invisible to the audience) the infant* FANNY.

ANNIE, *a scullery-maid, stands about with her mouth open, obviously in a state of considerable excitement, occasionally putting ineffective finishing touches to the table.*

COOK : 'Ere, Annie, 'old this fork a minute, or we'll have to call the Fire Brigade to put my face out.

ANNIE *takes the fork.*

COOK *fans herself with her apron.*

MRS. S. : I once knew a woman whose front 'air caught fire when she was making toast, and before you could count ten the 'ole room was ablaze. They'd never 'ave been able to recognize her remains if it 'adn't been for 'er cameo brooch.

COOK : They must 'ave known who she was. (*Coming over to the mail-cart*)   And 'ow's her ladyship— who's a lovely girl, eh ?   Don't burn that toast, Annie. (*She clicks her tongue at the infant* FANNY.)   Yer dad's comin' 'ome, ducks, safe and sound.   (*She chants in order to entertain* FANNY.)   Safe and sound, safe and sound.

MRS. S. : I only 'ope 'e is safe and sound, I'm sure.

COOK : The telegram said 'e was.

MRS. S. : Maybe it was a lie to spare Ellen's feelings.

COOK : You're a cheerful one, I must say.

MRS. S. : When I was a girl a friend of mine's

'usband come back unexpected from the Crimea with no legs at all.

> *This is too much for* ANNIE, *who drops the toast and goes off into snuffles of laughter.*

COOK : Stop it, Annie—now look what you've done—cut another piece, quick, they'll be 'ere in a minute.

MRS. S. : I do 'ope Ellen didn't cry at the station, it does make her nose so red.

COOK : Alfred will be so pleased to see 'er 'e won't mind if it's red or blue.   Come on, Annie, 'urry.

ANNIE : 'Ere they are.

COOK : 'Ere, quick ! The rosette for baby. (*She rushes to the dresser and snatches up a red, white and blue rosette.*) You pin it on 'er, Mrs. Snapper, while I tidy me 'air.

ANNIE (*at window*) : They've come in a cab.   Oo-er !

> *There is a great air of tension and excitement in the kitchen, while* ELLEN'S *and* BRIDGES' *legs appear down the area steps.*

> *The* CABBY *follows with* BRIDGES' *kit-bag, which is dumped in the passage.*

> BRIDGES *enters first, looking very hale and hearty.*

BRIDGES (*entering*) : You settle the cab, Ellen, I want to see my love-a-duck.   'Allo, Cook—'allo, Ma—where's my girl ?

> *He kisses* COOK *and* MRS. SNAPPER, *and then puts his head nside the pram.*

'Allo, Fanny. Coo, 'aven't you grown. Ma, you 'aven't 'arf bin feedin' 'er up. (*He makes delighted ourgling noises and prods the baby with his finger.*) See 'er laugh—she knows 'er dad.

> *He puts his head inside again apparently kissing her heartily.*

ELLEN *comes in flushed and happy.*

ELLEN : I thought that train would never come—an whole hour I waited—an' all the people yellin' and screamin'. 'Ere, Alfred, take yer great 'ead out of that pram, you'll frighten 'er.

BRIDGES (*withdrawing*) : She knows me, that's wot—she knows 'er old dad. Look at 'er rosette and all, smart as my eye. (*He turns and sees* ANNIE.) 'Ere, who's this ? We 'aven't 'ad the pleasure.

ELLEN : This is Annie.

BRIDGES : 'Ullo, Annie.

ANNIE (*giggling*) : Welcome 'ome, Mr. Bridges.

ANNIE *and* BRIDGES *shake hands.*

BRIDGES (*putting his arm round* MRS. SNAPPER) : Well, Ma, 'ow's everything ?

MRS. S. : I mustn't grumble.

BRIDGES : So I should just think not. I got a surprise for you.

MRS. S. : What is it ?

BRIDGES : Ellen knows ; I told 'er in the cab. Tell 'er, Ellen.

ELLEN : No, you. Go on.

BRIDGES : Well, you know I said in my letters about a lad called Smart—'Erbert Smart.

COOK : Yes. Ellen read your letters aloud.

BRIDGES : Not all of 'em, I 'ope.

ELLEN : Get on with you, you never let yourself go further than a P.S. and a couple of crosses.

BRIDGES : Well, 'Erbert Smart's got a pub, see, and he's staying out in Africa, and I've bought it from 'im cheap, see ? So much a year until it's paid off. We always wanted to 'ave somewhere of our own, and you can come and live with us, Ma—'ow's that suit ?

MRS. S. :   A pub—is it a respectable pub ?

BRIDGES :   All depends 'ow you behave, Ma, you know what you are when you've 'ad a couple.

MRS. S. (*sniggering*) :   Oh, Alfred, 'ow can you ?

BRIDGES :   Well, what d'you think about it ?

MRS. S. :   It sounds lovely—but 'ow about them upstairs ?

BRIDGES :   That's all right.   I took the master into me confidence.   He wished me luck.

MRS. S. (*breaking down*) :   Oh, dear, I can 'ardly believe it, not 'aving to live alone any more—oh, dear !

BRIDGES :   'Ere, cheer up, Ma.   Come on, 'ave a cup of tea.   There ain't nothing to cry about.   Let's all 'ave tea, for God's sake.   Come on, Cook, me old girl— 'ow'd you like to be a barmaid, eh ?

> *They all sit down to tea, a grand tea with eggs and shrimps.   Everybody is talking at once.*
>
> *Suddenly the cry of a* NEWSBOY *outside cuts through their conversation.*

BRIDGES :   What's 'e yelling about ?

COOK (*giving* ANNIE *a halfpenny*) :   'Ere, Annie, go and get one, quick.

> ANNIE *runs out of the area steps.*
>
> *There is silence in the kitchen.*

BRIDGES :   What's up ?   What's the matter ?

ELLEN :   It isn't anything to concern us.

COOK :   Ellen, 'ow can you—it concerns the whole country.

> ANNIE *comes clattering back with the paper.*
>
> BRIDGES *snatches paper from* ANNIE *and reads it.*

BRIDGES (*reading*) :   Whew !   The Queen—it says she's sinking !

MRS. S. :   There now—I told you so.

COOK (*taking paper*) : Let's 'ave a look.

ANNIE : She's very old, ain't she ?

COOK : Be quiet, Annie. What's that got to do with it ?

ANNIE : Well, I never seen 'er.

BRIDGES : I 'ave—driving along Birdcage Walk once—years ago. Coo ! England won't 'arf seem funny without the Queen !

The lights fade out.

PART ONE : SCENE VI

Principals : ROBERT, JANE, MARGARET, EDITH, EDWARD, JOE

SCENE : *Kensington Gardens. There is a row of high rail-ings down stage so that the audience can see through them the trees and shrubs and seats and people and dogs.*

TIME : *About noon, Sunday, January 27th, 1901.*

During the course of this scene there should be no word spoken. Everyone is in black and they walk slowly as though perpetually conscious of the country's mourning. Even the children are in black and one WOMAN leading a large brown dog has tied an enormous black crepe bow on to his collar.

ROBERT and JANE walk slowly from the left, followed by EDWARD and JOE.

MARGARET HARRIS and EDITH come from right.

They all meet and carry on a subdued conversation for a moment centre, and then part and go their different ways as : The lights fade on the scene.

PART ONE : SCENE VII

Principals : JANE, MARGARET, EDWARD, JOE, EDITH,
ELLEN, BRIDGES, COOK, ANNIE.

SCENE : *Drawing-room of a London House.*
TIME : *About noon, Saturday, February 2nd, 1901.*

*When the lights go up, the children, EDWARD, JOE and
EDITH, all in black, are discovered out on the balcony.
MARGARET and JANE are seated on the sofa.
There is a small table beside MARGARET and JANE
on which there is hot cocoa and cake.*

JOE (*on balcony*) : Mum, mum, there's a policeman on
a lovely white horse !

JANE : Don't jump about, darling, and get hot and
excited.   Edward, keep Joe as quiet as possible.

EDWARD : All right, mum.

JANE : More cocoa, Margaret ?

MARGARET : No, thank you, dear.

JANE : I feel listless and sad, as though her death
were a personal grief.   Strange, isn't it ?

MARGARET : I think everyone feels that.   (*She rises
and goes to the window.*)   All those crowds and crowds of
people ; they've been waiting for hours so patient and
quiet.   There's hardly a sound.

JOE (*running in*) : Mum, could I ever be a policeman ?

JANE : Perhaps, darling—if you're good.

JOE : Are all policemen good ?

JANE : Yes, dear, as good as gold.

JOE : Why did Queen Victoria die, mum .

JANE : Because she was a very old lady, and very tired.

JOE : Could I have another piece of cake ?

JANE : You won't be able to eat any luncheon.

JOE : I'd rather have the cake.

JANE (*smiling*): Very well, then—a small piece. Take some out to Edward and Edith.

JOE : Thanks, mum.

> JOE *dashes out on to the balcony with the cake*.

MARGARET : How proud you must feel, Jane. All your troubles are over—Robert's home, Jim's home. Robert has a V.C.

JANE : Jim ought to have a V.C. too. All those dreadful months.

EDWARD (*rushing in*): They're coming ! They're coming ! Quick—quick !

JANE (*rising*): Run and fetch Ellen and Bridges and Cook.

> EDWARD *tears out of the room*.
>
> JOE *rushes in*.

JOE : Mum, please come out. I dropped a bit of cake. I couldn't help it—Edward pushed me.

> JANE *goes out and looks over*.
>
> *An intelligible voice is heard below*.

JANE (*leaning over*): I'm very sorry, it was an accident.

> *The voice mumbles something*.

He didn't throw it—he dropped it. It was an accident. (*She comes in again*.) Did you throw it, Joe, on purpose ?

> JOE *hangs his head*.

You're a very naughty little boy indeed, and I've a very good mind not to let you see the procession at all.

> EDITH *comes in*.

Following EDITH *are* EDWARD, ELLEN, BRIDGES,
COOK *and* ANNIE, *very smartened up.*

EDWARD :   Mum, will father be riding in the beginning part or the end part ?

JANE :   The beginning, I think. Cook, you'd
better come out here, Annie, too. Ellen, look after
them, will you ?   Bridges, oughtn't you to be wearing
a coat, it's very cold ?

BRIDGES :   I'm all right, thank you, ma'am.   Warm
as toast.

EDWARD (*on balcony*) :   Here they come—quickly,
mum !

> *Everybody crowds out on to the two balconies.*
>
> *There is dead silence and then far away the solemn
> music of the Dead March is heard. As it draws
> nearer the children jump about excitedly.*

JOE (*suddenly*) :   Look, look—there's father—there's
father !

JANE :   Shhh !   Joe, be quiet—keep still.

> *The procession continues. Suddenly there is an
> outburst of cheering from the crowd which is instantly
> subdued.*

That's Lord Roberts.   He held up his hand to stop
them cheering.

JOE :   Is that Bobs, mum—is that Bobs ?

EDWARD :   Look, look—one-armed Giffard.   Oh,
mother, look——

JANE :   Shhh !   Now then, Joe, Edward, stand
absolutely still—to attention, like father showed
you.

> *The* BOYS *stand rigid with their hands to their
> sides.*
>
> BRIDGES *stands rigid with his hands to his*

side, on the other balcony.

The music swells as the band passes directly underneath them.   As it begins to die away COOK *bursts into tears.*

JANE :   Five kings riding behind her.

JOE :   Mum, she must have been a very little lady.
The lights fade.

PART ONE :   SCENE VIII

Principals :   ROBERT, JANE, DUCHESS OF CHURT, MAJOR
DOMO

SCENE :   *The Grand Staircase of a London house.   The head of the staircase is down stage.   The stairs descending downwards and out of sight.   Behind the well of the staircase, can be seen between columns, the beautifully decorated ballroom in which an orchestra is playing the popular waltzes of the day and people are dancing.   The Ball is in full swing.*

TIME :   *About 11 p.m. Thursday, May 14th, 1903.*

When the lights go up, the full splendour of a typical Edwardian Ball should, if possible, burst upon the audience.

On the right and left of the staircase a balustraded balcony leads to the ballroom at the entrance of which FOOTMEN *stand with programmes to hand to the guests.*

The DUCHESS OF CHURT *stands near the head of stairs.*

Near the DUCHESS OF CHURT *stands the* MAJOR
DOMO, *who announces each guest in stentorian
tones.*

*There is a steady babel of conversation and music,
but above it all can be heard the names of guests as
they are announced. One by one, or sometimes escorted,
come the great beauties of the day. They are all
received by the* DUCHESS *and then make their way
towards the ballroom. Finally the* MAJOR DOMO
announces : " SIR ROBERT *and* LADY MARRYOT " *and* :
ROBERT *and* JANE *appear*, ROBERT *with full decora-
tions, and* JANE *in an elaborate ball gown. As they
are received by their hostess* :

The lights fade and the curtain falls.

END OF PART I

PART TWO : SCENE I

Principals : JANE, EDWARD (aged 18), ELLEN, FANNY (aged 7), MRS. SNAPPER, GEORGE, FLO, BRIDGES.

SCENE : *The Bar Parlour of a London pub.*
TIME : *About 5 p.m. Saturday, June 16th, 1906.*

> *When the curtain rises High Tea is just over.* *Seated round the table are* JANE, EDWARD, MRS. SNAPPER, FLO *and* GEORGE GRAINGER. *FLO and GEORGE are very smartly got up.* ELLEN *is seated at the piano with her back to the room.* FANNY (aged 7) *is dancing. When the dance is finished everyone applauds.*

JANE: She dances beautifully, Ellen. Come here, dear.
> FANNY *goes to her.*

I knew you when you were a little tiny baby.

FLO : She's a born dancer, if you ask me—haighly talented, haighly.

ELLEN (*leaving the piano*) : She certainly does love it. On the go all day she is, jigging about.

MRS. S. : Can I press you to another cup, your ladyship ?

JANE : No, thank you, we really must be going in a moment.

FLO (*to* EDWARD) : 'Ow was Hoxford when you left it, Mr. Marryott ?

EDWARD : Awfully nice.

FLO : I've never been there mayself, but George 'as, haven't you, George ?

GEORGE : Oh, yes, nice place, Oxford. Very antique—if you know what I mean.

ELLEN : I'm so glad to 'ear the master, Sir Robert, is well.

JANE : He was so sorry not to be able to come down, but as you know, he's a very busy man these days. He wished very specially to be remembered to you and your husband. He'll be sorry to hear that he's ill.

GEORGE : Ill I Alf ill I What's wrong with him ?
          MRS. SNAPPER *nudges* GEORGE *violently.*
          ELLEN *speaks hurriedly.*

ELLEN : Before you and Flo come, George, I was explaining to 'er Ladyship about poor Alfred's bad leg.

GEORGE : Bad leg ?

MRS. S. (*frowning at* GEORGE) : Yes, very bad—'e's been in 'orrible agony since Sunday.

GEORGE : Where is 'e ?

ELLEN : Upstairs in bed.

GEORGE : I'll pop up and see 'im.

ELLEN : He's asleep now.

FLO : 'Ow did 'e come to 'ave the haccident ?

MRS. S. (*firmly and with great emphasis*) : Cycling, Flo. He was cycling and 'e fell orf.

FLO : I didn't know 'e 'ad a cycle.

MRS. S. : 'E 'asn't any more.

JANE (*rising*) : Well, you will tell him how sorry we were not to have seen him, won't you ? And I do hope he'll soon be quite well again. Come along, Edward. We really must go now.

EDWARD (*rising*) : All right, Mother.

ELLEN : It was so kind of you, ma'am, to come all

this way to see us and to bring Fanny that lovely doll, and everything. Fanny, come and say good-bye to 'er ladyship.

> FANNY *makes an abortive effort at a curtsey.*
>
> JANE *bends down and kisses* FANNY.

JANE : Good-bye, Fanny. (*To* MRS. SNAPPER) Good-bye, Mrs. Snapper. (*She shakes hands.*) Good-bye. (*She bows to* FLO *and* GEORGE.)

FLO : Pleased to 'ave made your acquaintance, I'm sure.

JANE (*to* ELLEN) : Good-bye, Ellen, it's been delightful seeing you again, and to find you well and happy. Don't fail to remember me to Bridges ; my husband and I miss you both still, it seems only yesterday that you were with us.

ELLEN : We miss you, too, ma'am.

JANE : Time changes many things, but it can't change old friends, can it ?

ELLEN (*emotionally*) : No, ma'am. Oh, no, ma'am

> EDWARD, *who has been saying his good-bye to* MRS
> SNAPPER *and* FLO *and* GEORGE, *joins* JANE.

EDWARD : Good-bye, Ellen. Good luck.

ELLEN : Good-bye, Master Edward. Thank you for coming——

> JANE *and* EDWARD *are about to leave when the*
> *street door bursts open and :*
>
> BRIDGES *staggers into the room. He looks unkempt*
> *and unshaven, and is obviously drunk.*
>
> *There is a moment of horrible silence.*
>
> BRIDGES *sees* JANE *and* EDWARD *and pulls up short.*

ELLEN (*in agonised tones*) : Oh, Alfred !

BRIDGES : Ow ! So that's why you wash trying to get me out of the way——

MRS. S. :   Alfred Bridges, be'ave yourself and take yer 'at orf.

BRIDGES (*bowing low to* JANE) :   Pleashed to see you again, milady, I'm shure—welcome to our 'ovel.   (*He lurches towards* JANE.)

> JANE *makes an instinctive movement away from* BRIDGES.
> BRIDGES *draws himself up unsteadily.*

Ow !   I shee—proud and 'aughty, are we——

ELLEN (*wildly*) :   Alfred, stop it !   Stop it !

JANE (*suddenly coming forward and taking both* ELLEN's *hands in hers*) :   Ellen—dear Ellen—I'm so very, very, sorry, and I quite understand.   Please don't be upset and let me come and see you again soon.

> JANE *goes out with* EDWARD.
> *Again there is silence.*
> ELLEN *bursts into hopeless sobbing.*

MRS. S. :   You drunken great brute !

BRIDGES :   Shut yer mouth.   You mind yours and I'll mind mine.

GEORGE :   Look 'ere, 'ole man, you'd better come up and 'ave a lie down.   (*He takes* BRIDGES' *arm.*)

BRIDGES (*pushing* GEORGE *away*) :   Leave me alone. Lot of shnobs—that's wot—lot of bloody shnobs.   I'm not good enough to be 'ome when the quality comes. Ow, no—we'll see who'sh good enough.

ELLEN (*wailing*) :   Oh, oh, oh !   I'll never be able to raise me 'ead again—never—never——

BRIDGES :   'Oo give Fanny that doll ?   'Er noble ladyship ?

MRS. S. (*stepping forward*) :   You let the child alone.

BRIDGES (*pushing* MRS. SNAPPER *so hard that she falls against the table*) :   I can buy me own child a doll, can't

I ? Don't want any bloody charity 'ere. (*He snatches the doll from* FANNY *and pitches it into the fire.*)

> FANNY *screams.*
>
> FLO *makes a dart at the fireplace and finally gets the doll out.*
>
> FANNY *continues to scream.*
>
> ELLEN *goes for* BRIDGES.
>
> BRIDGES *hits* ELLEN.
>
> FLO *and* GEORGE *grab* BRIDGES *and push him out of the room.*
>
> ELLEN, *sobbing, takes* FANNY *in her arms.*
>
> MRS. SNAPPER *sinks into a chair.*

ELLEN : She was right—she was right. Time changes many things——

> *The lights fade.*

PART TWO: SCENE II

Principals : FANNY, FLO.

SCENE : *A London street. The exterior of the public house—the bar parlour of which was the preceding scene—is down stage left. There is a street leading away into darkness up left, and another turning a corner up right. A wedge of houses separates the two streets. There are people at most of the windows of the houses. Down stage right are more houses.*

TIME : *About 10 p.m. Saturday, June 16th, 1906.*

> *The centre of the stage is crowded with people and barrows lit by naphtha flares. There is another pub up*

right from which comes the sound of a penny-in-the-slot
piano and the sound of singing and laughter. Everyone is
moving about and talking. Women with caps and
shawls and string bags are shopping at the booths.   Some
sailors come out of the left pub with two flashily-dressed
girls and roll across to the pub opposite, into which they
disappear. A policeman walks through the crowd and
goes off. A German band assembles down stage left
and begins to play, effectively drowning the noise of three
Coster youths playing mouth-organs. A few Costers in
pearlies start dancing, a ring is made round them, and
people applaud and yell from the windows. A Salvation
Army Band marches on right and proceeds to play and
sing hymns, against the German band. A few people
make a ring round them and begin singing.

    FANNY comes out of the pub left and begins to dance by
herself.

    Some of the crowd laugh and those who are dancing stop
and applaud her. A Coster darts forward and puts
his pearly cap on FANNY'S head.
BRIDGES comes reeling out of the pub—sees FANNY,
and tries to grab hold of her. He is prevented by the
crowd and
BRIDGES is pushed off the stage up right.
Suddenly from just where BRIDGES has gone there comes
a shout and then an agonising scream. The policeman runs across in the direction of the noise. All
the crowd, scenting a street accident, surge off, including
the German band.
Exeunt crowd and German Band.
FLO comes flying out of the pub and
FLO disappears with the crowd.
FANNY continues to dance in pool of light shed by a

*street lamp, to the rather dismal music of the Salvation
Army.*
FLO *comes rushing back and hammers on the door of
the pub.*

FLO : Ellen ! Ellen ! It's Alfred—'e's been run
over—'e's dead. Ellen ! Ellen !
    The lights fade.

PART TWO : SCENE III

Principals : EDWARD (aged 21), JOE (aged 17), TIM
BATEMAN, DOUGLAS FINN, LORD MARTLET
(Chubby), MARION CHRISTIE, NETTA LAKE
(pianist), ROSE DARLING (Ada in " Mirabelle "),
CONNIE CRAWSHAY, DAISY DEVON.

SCENE : *Private room in a popular London restaurant. A
supper table set for ten is on one side of the stage.
There is a sofa at the back and another down stage right,
and an upright piano.*
TIME : *About 1 a.m. Wednesday, March 10th, 1909.*

Round the table are seated EDWARD (*twenty-one*),
TIM BATEMAN, DOUGLAS FINN, MARION CHRISTIE,
NETTA LAKE, *and* ROSE DARLING.
*On the sofa up stage in a more or less amorous attitude
are seated* LORD MARTLET (Chubby) *and* DAISY
DEVON.
On the down stage sofa is seated JOE (*aged seventeen*)
with CONNIE CRAWSHAY, *a very fat blonde.*

166

*Everyone is very gay.   They are all in evening dress.
The men in white ties and the women elaborately and
slightly theatrically fashionable.*

JOE *is obviously the youngest present and appears well
on the way to being very drunk.*

ROSE (*rising, with a glass of champagne in her hand*) :   I
want to propose a toast—to our host !

EVERYONE :   Hear, hear !   (*Etc.*)

MARION :   A lovely little toastie to our lovely little
hostie.

ROSE :   Health, wealth and happiness to our Eddie !

EVERYONE (*repeating*) :   Health, wealth and happiness !   Eddie !   (*Etc.*)

> *They clink glasses.*

CONNIE (*to* JOE) :   Here, sit up.   They're drinking
your brother's health.

JOE (*rising unsteadily*) :   Hear, hear—a thousand
times hear, hear !

> *They all sing " For he's a jolly good fellow," which
> tails off into cries for " speech."*

EDWARD (*rising*) :   Ladies and gentlemen——

JOE (*loudly*) :   Hurray !

EDWARD :   Shut up, Joe.

JOE :   I won't shut up.   Connie agrees with me,
don't you, Connie ?

CONNIE :   Yes, dear, completely, dear.   Shut up,
dear.

JOE :   Good old Connie.   (*He subsides on* CONNIE'S *lap.*)

EDWARD (*continuing*) :   First of all, in response to your
charming toast, I want to apologise for the presence
here to-night of my scrubby little brother Joe.

> *Laughter.*

167

JOE : Here—I say !

CONNIE *puts her hand over* JOE's *mouth.*

EDWARD : He is a crawling, loathsome little creature, as you see, and he really ought not to be here at all, but in his little cot at Eton. I felt, however, that as his elder brother, it was my duty to show him how grown-up people behave. Bring him over here, Connie—he must be christened in Clicquot.

CONNIE : He's almost confirmed in it already.

CONNIE *drags* JOE *over to the table where, protesting loudly, he is anointed by* EDWARD *with champagne.*

JOE : I must speak now. I want to speak.

CONNIE : Let him speak, dear, he's having a lovely time.

JOE : Ladies and gentlemen—I have always looked up to my elder brother Edward. He has always been my ideal of what a great big gas-bag should be, and I take this opportunity of asking Connie to marry me.

Laughter.

CONNIE : Oh, isn't he sweet !

ROSE : You can't have Connie, Joe, she's married already ; you'd better choose me. I'm a widow.

Everybody chants " The Merry Widow " waltz for a moment.

JOE : But I love Connie.

CONNIE : Very well, dear, come back to the sofa, dear. (*She leads* JOE *back.*)

EDWARD (*to* LORD MARTLET) : Chubby, come out of that corner, you've been there long enough.

DAISY (*coming down*) : Quite long enough. This takes me back to the old days of private hansoms. (*She fans herself.*) Give me a drink, somebody.

MARION (*gloomily*): I was once sick in a private hansom.

ROSE : That must have been lovely, dear ; tell us about it.

MARION : Well, it was the two hundredth performance of " Floradora."

ROSE : By God, she's going to !

MARION : And they suddenly put me in the sextette without a rehearsal, and I suppose the excitement went to my stomach.

ROSE : I was in " Mirabelle " then, with poor old Laura Marsden.

EDWARD : " Mirabelle " ! I was taken to see that. Mother was there on Mafeking night. She took me a few weeks later to a matinee.

MARION : *Taken* to see it, were you ! That dates us a bit.

EDWARD : I remember now. You were Ada——

ROSE : Yes, I was Ada.

MARION : And Laura Marsden was Mirabelle, and Mikey Banks was Tom. What a cast that was !

TIM : What happened to Laura Marsden ?

ROSE : She died. (*She makes a significant drinking gesture.*)

TIM : Oh, I see.

ROSE : Nine years ago. Give me another drink, or I shall get reminiscent like Marion.

> NETTA *goes over to the piano and starts thumping the* > *Mirabelle waltz*.

Oh, shut up !

EDWARD : Sing it, Rose.

ROSE : I can't—haven't got any voice.

EVERYONE : Come on, Rose—sing it. Come on, you're among friends.

ROSE :   I can't sing it like Laura used to.   (*She sings
the refrain of the waltz, occasionally forgetting a word or two.*)
        Everybody applauds.
   MARION :   They do take you back, don't they, those
old tunes.
        NETTA *strikes up " Keep off the Grass."*
        The girls sing it together.
        None of the men are really old enough to remember it.
   CHUBBY :   Play something we all know.
        NETTA *starts " Mary " from " Miss Gibbs."*
        *Everyone joins in.   They all go into " The Merry
   Widow " waltz and sing it lustily as*
        The lights fade.

PART TWO :   SCENE IV

Principals :   JANE, ROBERT, JOE, MARGARET, ELLEN,
   FANNY, MRS. SNAPPER, FLO, GEORGE, 1ST WOMAN,
   2ND WOMAN, UNCLE GEORGE, UNCLE DICK.

SCENE :   *The beach of a popular seaside resort.*
TIME :   *About 6 p.m. Monday, July 25th, 1910.*

   The Parade runs along the back about 10 *feet above
   stage level.   Down stage left a bandstand on the same
   level as the Parade juts out on to the beach.   On the right
   the high supports of a swimming enclosure.*
   *There are bathing machines and huts and deck chairs—
   in fact all the paraphernalia of a popular seaside town
   in July.*
   The beach is crowded with people, some paddling

some playing games, and a lot clustered round an open-air stage, listening to UNCLE GEORGE'S *concert party.*

The Concert Party consists of six men : UNCLE DICK, UNCLE BOB, UNCLE HARRY, UNCLE JIM, UNCLE JACK *and* UNCLE GEORGE *himself. They are all dressed in straw hats, coloured blazers and rather grubby white flannel trousers.*

People are constantly passing to and fro along the Parade, and leaning on the railing, looking down on to the beach.

When the curtain rises UNCLE GEORGE *is singing " Put a little bit away for a rainy day." He finishes with a great flourish, then steps forward.*

UNCLE GEORGE : Ladies and gentlemen and kiddies —I am very happy to announce that the winner of this week's Song and Dance Competition is little Miss Fanny Bridges.

  Everyone applauds.

And it gives me great pleasure to present her with this handsome prize as a souvenir of Uncle George and his merry men. Come on up, my dear.

  ELLEN (*in black*) *hoists* FANNY *up from the front row.*

  FANNY *is hoisted up by* ELLEN. *She is wearing a white dress with a black sash.*

  UNCLE GEORGE *kisses* FANNY *and presents her with a box of chocolates.*

  The audience clap and one little girl is led away yelling, apparently an unsuccessful competitor.

UNCLE GEORGE : And now, to conclude this programme Uncle Dick will sing " Take me back to Yorkshire."

UNCLE DICK *rises and sings.*

*All the rest join in the chorus, and then, after
perfunctory applause, the crowd round the booth disperses.*

UNCLE GEORGE *and his* MERRY MEN *pack up
their props and disappear in due course up the steps on to
the Parade.*

Exeunt UNCLE GEORGE *and his* MERRY MEN.

ELLEN *and* FANNY *walk across the beach with* MRS.
SNAPPER, FLO *and* GEORGE. *They meet* MARGARET
HARRIS, JANE *and* JOE.

JANE : Why, it can't be—Ellen—what a surprise !
They shake hands.

ELLEN : Oh, Ma'am—I'd no idea—fancy you being
here !

JANE : Margaret, Joe, you remember Ellen, don't
you ?

MARGARET (*shaking hands*) : Of course ! yes—how
do you do, Ellen ?

JOE : Hullo, Ellen.

ELLEN : You remember mother—Mrs. Snapper—
and Flo and George, my cousins by marriage ?

JANE : Yes, indeed.

MRS. S. : Delighted, I'm sure.
Everyone shakes hands and talks politely.

ELLEN : Well, Master Joe, 'ow you 'ave grown.
Quite the young man about town ! How's Master
Edward ?

JOE : He's here. He and Edith have been to a
concert on the pier. They'll be along soon.

ELLEN (*to* JANE) : I got your letter, ma'am, when
my Alfred died ; it was kind of you to write.

JANE : How is your business going ?

ELLEN : Oh, very well, really. I've managed to

save quite a bit one way and another, and now I've closed the 'ole place for a month so as to give Fanny a holiday. She goes to dancing school now. She's going on the stage.

MARGARET : Surely she's very young.

MRS. S. : She's set on it—plain set on it.

> ROBERT *comes down on to the beach. He has grey hair now and looks very distinguished.*

ROBERT : Jane—there you are—Why, Ellen ! (*He shakes hands.*)

> *All the introductions start all over again.*
>
> *Two elderly women pass in front of them, talking.*

1ST WOMAN : She went on board the ship dressed as a boy, and that's how the Captain recognised them.

2ND WOMAN : 'Er 'air probably come down under 'er cap.

1ST WOMAN : I don't know 'ow she managed at meals. She couldn't wear 'er cap then.

2ND WOMAN : It's Mrs. Crippen that gets on my mind, poor dear, being all chopped up into little tiny pieces——

> *They pass on and up the steps.*
>
> *Meanwhile the* MARRYOTS *and* ELLEN *are parting company.*

ELLEN : It's been lovely seeing you again, ma'am, and you, too, Mrs. Harris. I expect your Edith has grown into a great big girl by now. I remember her when she was ever so small. (*To* ROBERT.) Good-bye, sir—good-bye, Master Joe.

ROBERT : Good-bye, Ellen.

JOE : Good-bye.

JANE : You must come and see us one day—bring Fanny to tea.

ELLEN : Thank you, ma'am—I'd like to see the
'ouse again.   I was very 'appy there——

The MARRYOTS *and* MARGARET *go off.*

MRS. SNAPPER, ELLEN *and* FANNY *rejoin* FLO
and GEORGE, *who have been standing waiting for them
a little way off.*

*The Band, having assembled, breaks into a gay march.
A man walks along with a tray of pink rock, yelling.
All dialogue is drowned in the noise of the band.
Several children dodge in and out, playing Tag. One
child falls down and screams. Suddenly there is the
noise of an aeroplane. Everyone screams and surges
down to the beach, staring upwards. The band stops
abruptly and cranes out of the bandstand. People half
dressed rush out of bathing machines. Somebody starts
cheering—then everyone takes it up. The aeroplane
noise grows fainter. The Band strikes up again. A
troop of Boy Scouts with a very sour six-piece band
march along the Parade. Suddenly there is a roll of
thunder. Everyone looks up apprehensively, people on
the beach begin to collect their children and belongings.
It starts to rain, gently at first, then develops into a down-
pour. People put their coat collars up and run.
Several umbrellas go up, then more, until the whole beach
becomes a sea of umbrellas. Gradually everyone
scurries off. The bandstand has by now let down its
weather blinds. One fat old woman is left asleep in a
deck chair. A tremendous roll of thunder wakes her
abruptly and she struggles to get up, and falls back into
the chair, which collapses.*

PART TWO : SCENE V

Principals : EDWARD, EDITH.

SCENE : *The deck of an Atlantic liner. This is quite a*
small inset scene. The rail of the Promenade Deck
faces the audience. Behind it can be seen the lighted
windows of the lounge. Above can be seen vaguely the
Boat Deck, with ventilators and a funnel silhouetted
against the stars.

TIME : *About 7 p.m. Sunday, April 14th,* 1912.

> EDWARD *and* EDITH, *he in dinner-jacket, she in*
> *evening dress, are leaning on the rail.*

EDITH : It's too big, the Atlantic, isn't it ?

EDWARD : Far too big.

EDITH : And too deep.

EDWARD : Much, much too deep.

EDITH : I don't care a bit, do you ?

EDWARD : Not a scrap.

EDITH : Wouldn't it be awful if a magician came
to us and said : " Unless you count accurately every
single fish in the Atlantic you die to-night ? "

EDWARD : We should die to-night.

EDITH : How much would you mind—dying, I
mean ?

EDWARD : I don't know really—a good deal, I
expect.

EDITH : I don't believe I should mind so very
much now. You see, we could never in our
whole lives be happier than we are now, could
we ?

EDWARD : Darling, there *are* different sorts of happiness.

EDITH : This is the best sort.

EDWARD (*kissing her*) : Sweetheart !

EDITH : Don't darling, we don't want any more of the stewards to know we're on our honeymoon.

EDWARD : Why not ? It gives them so much vicarious pleasure. Most of them have forgotten what it was like.

EDITH : Are all honeymoons like this ?

EDWARD (*firmly*) : Exactly.

EDITH : Oh, Edward—that's rather disheartening, isn't it ? I do so want this to be unique.

EDWARD : It is, for us.

EDITH : Did you ever think when we were children, going to the pantomime, and going to the Zoo, and playing soldiers, that we should ever be married ?

EDWARD : Of course I didn't.

EDITH : Was I nice as a child ?

EDWARD : Horrible !

EDITH : So were you, and so was Joe—vile. You always used to take sides against me.

EDWARD : And yet we all liked one another really.

EDITH : I think I liked Joe better than you, but then he was younger and easier to manage. Dear Joe, he was awfully funny at the wedding, wasn't he ?

EDWARD : Ribald little beast !

EDITH : He has no reverence, I'm afraid.

EDWARD : Absolutely none.

EDITH : He's passing gallantly through the chorus-girl phase now, isn't he ?

EDWARD : Gallantly but not quickly.

EDITH : Well, darling, you took your time over it.

EDWARD : Now then, Edith——

EDITH : You had several affairs before you married me, didn't you ?

EDWARD : Light of my life, shut up !

EDITH : You'd be awfully cross if *I* had, wouldn't you ?

EDWARD : Had what ?

EDITH : Affairs—love affairs—before you.

EDWARD : Did you ?

EDITH : Hundreds.

EDWARD : Liar !

EDITH : I rather wish I had, really. Perhaps I should have learnt some tricks to hold you with when you begin to get tired of me.

EDWARD : I never shall, tricks or no tricks.

EDITH : Yes, you will one day. You're bound to ; people always do. This complete loveliness that we feel together now will fade, so many years and the gilt wears off the gingerbread, and just the same as the stewards, we shall have forgotten what it was like.

EDWARD (*seriously*) : Answer me one thing, truly, dearest. Have you ever seen gingerbread with gilt on it ?

EDITH : Never !

EDWARD : Then the whole argument is disposed of. Anyhow, look at father and mother ; they're perfectly happy and devoted, and they always have been.

EDITH : They had a better chance at the beginning. Things weren't changing so swiftly ; life wasn't so restless.

EDWARD : How long do you give us ?

EDITH : I don't know—and Edward—(*she turns to him*) I don't care. This is our moment—complete and heavenly. I'm not afraid of anything. This is our own, for ever.

> EDWARD *takes* EDITH *in his arms and kisses her.*

EDWARD : Do you think a nice warming glass of sherry would make it any more heavenly ?

EDITH : You have no soul, darling, but I'm very attached to you. Come on——

> EDITH *takes up her cloak which has been hanging over the rail, and they walk away. The cloak has been covering a life-belt, and when it is withdrawn the words " S.S. Titanic " can be seen in black letters on the white.*
>
> *The lights fade into complete darkness, but the letters remain glowing as*
>
> *The orchestra plays very softly and tragically " Nearer My God to Thee."*

PART TWO : SCENE VI

Principals : JANE, ROBERT, JOE, MARGARET.

SCENE : *The drawing-room of a London house. The room is dark ; the blinds are down over the windows.*

TIME : *About 11.16 p.m. Tuesday, August 4th, 1914.*

> *There is the sound of voices outside.*
>
> *Enter* JANE *and* MARGARET, *both in travelling clothes.*
>
> JANE *turns on the lights and the room is seen to be enshrouded in dust-sheets.*

JANE (*shuddering*) :   Why is it that a house that's been shut up for a little while feels so awful ?   (*She goes to the windows, pulls up the blinds, and opens the windows wide.*) There !   That's better.   It's stifling.

MARGARET (*taking off her hat and coat*) :   That was definitely the most uncomfortable journey I've ever experienced.

JOE *rushes in. He still has his hat and coat on.*

JOE :   Mum, have you got any change ?   Father and I have both run out.

MARGARET :   I have—here—(*she fumbles in her bag.*) How much d'you want ?

JOE :   Four bob.

MARGARET :   There's half-a-crown and two shillings.

JOE :   Thanks, Aunt Margaret.

JOE *goes out again.*

JANE :   Help me with these dust-sheets, Margaret. Put them anywhere.   We'll get a char in to-morrow to clean up.

They proceed to pull the dust-sheets off the furniture.
I shall never go on a holiday again, ever.   It's horrid when you're there, and much worse when you come back.

MARGARET :   Still it's better to be here in London if anything's going to happen.

JANE :   It's going to happen all right.   I'm afraid there's no doubt about it, now.

MARGARET (*glancing out of the window*) :   There seem to be lots more people in the streets than usual—where on earth do they all come from ?

JOE *comes in, this time without his hat and coat.*

JOE :   Well, that's that !

JANE :   Where's father ?

JOE : Groping about in the wine cellar like an angry old beetle. He says strong drink is essential in a crisis.

JANE : We must have something to eat, too. I wonder if there is anything.

JOE : There's a strong bit of cold tongue in the larder. I just put my head in and it sang the Marseillaise.

JANE : There must be some biscuits, or something.

JANE *goes out hurriedly.*

JOE (*to* MARGARET) : Cigarette ? (*He offers her his case.*)

MARGARET (*taking one*) : Thank you, Joe.

JOE (*lighting them*) : This is pretty thrilling, isn't it ?

MARGARET : Yes, I suppose so. I must really go and help Jane.

MARGARET *runs out, almost colliding with*

ROBERT, *who is entering with two bottles and some glasses.*

ROBERT : I could only find hock and port, and port's far too heavy at this time of night ; so we'll have to drink to the downfall of Germany in their own damned wine.

JOE : I rather like Germans, don't you, Father ?

ROBERT : Enormously. Move these things off the table, and help me open the bottles.

JOE (*doing so*) : Got a corkscrew ?

ROBERT : In my left pocket.

JOE *gropes for the corkscrew while*

ROBERT *puts the bottles and glasses on the table.*

JOE (*wrestling with a bottle*) : If there is a war, how long do you think it will last ?

ROBERT : Three months, at the outside.

JOE : I suppose we shall win, shan't we ?

ROBERT : Yes—we shall win.

JOE (*hopefully*) : Maybe it will last six months.

ROBERT : Leaving everything else aside, that would be economically quite impossible. Have you any idea of what a war costs, Joe, in actual money ?

JOE : Hell of a lot, I should think.

ROBERT : You're quite right. And the Germans can afford it even less than we can. And then there's Russia.

JOE : Good old Russia !

ROBERT : And France and Italy and America.

JOE : And Japan and China and Finland—why, by God ! we've got 'em licked before we start.

ROBERT : Don't be silly, Joe.

JOE : Are you glad you left the Army, Father, or sorry ?

ROBERT : Absolutely delighted.

JOE : Will you go back again ?

ROBERT : I expect so.

JOE : How will you feel about that ?

ROBERT : Absolutely delighted.

JOE : I suppose I shall have to do something about it, too.

ROBERT : Do you want to ?

JOE : Terribly.

ROBERT : Why ?

JOE : I don't know. It's—it's sort of exciting, isn't it ?

ROBERT : Yes, but don't set your hopes too high, Joey—it takes a lot of training to make a soldier. It will all be over before you get far.

JOE : I wish Edward hadn't been drowned, we could have started off together.

ROBERT (*after a slight pause*) : Don't be too impulsive and patriotic and dashing, Joey. Think of your Mother. Think of me, too, you're all we've got left.

>ROBERT *abruptly puts down the bottle he is holding and*

>ROBERT *goes out on to balcony.*

>JOE *stands staring after* ROBERT *thoughtfully.*

>JANE *enters carrying a tray.*

>MARGARET *enters following* JANE, *with some plates.*

JANE : We found some potted meat and biscuits and Worcester Sauce ; and the tongue doesn't look too bad.

JOE (*taking the tray from* JANE) : It isn't its looks I object to, it's its personality.

>JOE *puts the tray on the table.*

>*A newsboy runs by outside shouting.*

>ROBERT *shouts from the balcony and goes hurriedly from the room.*

>JOE, JANE *and* MARGARET *stand stock still, waiting.*

>ROBERT *returns with the paper.*

ROBERT : We're at war, my dears.

JOE (*grabbing the paper*) : Let me see—let me see——

MARGARET : Listen—listen !

>*From far away comes the sound of cheering.*

>MARGARET *runs out on the balcony for a moment, and then returns.*

>JANE *sinks down on a chair.*

JANE : It's very hot, isn't it ?

JOE : Don't look sad, mum. It won't last long ;

Father says it can't possibly ; and it's terribly exciting.

JANE : I didn't mean to look sad ; I feel rather tired.

JOE (*handing* JANE *a glass of wine*) : Here, mum dear— have a nice sozzle. We ought all to get drunk really, and go roaring about the streets——

JANE : Edward missed this, anyhow. At least he died when he was happy, before the world broke over his head.

ROBERT : Don't take that view, dearest, it's foolish. We've had wars before without the world breaking.

JANE : My world isn't very big.

A group of people pass along under the balcony laughing and cheering. Some of them start singing the Marseillaise and the others drown them with Rule Britannia.

JANE *gets up suddenly.*

JANE : Drink to the war, then, if you want to. I'm not going to. I can't ! Rule Britannia ! Send us victorious, happy and glorious ! Drink, Joey, you're only a baby, still, but you're old enough for war. Drink like the Germans are drinking, to Victory and Defeat, and stupid, tragic sorrow. But leave me out of it, please !

JANE *goes abruptly from the room.*
The lights fade.

PART TWO : SCENE VII

Above the proscenium 1914 *glows in lights. It changes to* 1915–1916, 1917 *and* 1918. *Meanwhile, soldiers march uphill endlessly. Out of darkness into darkness.*

Sometimes they sing gay songs, sometimes they whistle, sometimes they march silently, but the sound of their tramping feet is unceasing. Below, the vision of them brightly-dressed, energetic women appear in pools of light, singing stirring recruiting songs—" Sunday I walk out with a soldier," " We don't want to lose you," etc., etc. With 1918 they fade away, as also does the vision of the soldiers, although the soldiers can still be heard very far off, marching and singing their songs.

PART TWO: SCENE VIII

Principals :   JOE, FANNY.

SCENE :   *A restaurant.*
TIME :   *About 7.30 p.m. Tuesday, October 22nd, 1918.*

JOE *and* FANNY *are seated at a table ; they have just finished dinner.*

JOE *is in officer's uniform.*

FANNY *is in very charming day clothes. She is now nineteen and extremely attractive.*

JOE (*pouring some champagne into* FANNY'S *glass*): Have some more.

FANNY :   Darling, I shall be tight.   You don't want me to fall down during my first number, do you ?

JOE :   How much do you love me ?

FANNY :   Now, then, dear, we've had all this out before.

JOE :   Will you send me a telegram to Dover ?

FANNY :   Of course I will.   I promised, didn't I ?

184

JOE : Once you get into the theatre, with all those changes, you might forget.

FANNY : I'll send Maggie out with it.

JOE : Dear old Maggie. Say good-bye to her for me, won't you ?

FANNY : Aren't you coming down to talk to me while I make up ?

JOE : No, I promised to go home. Mother's waiting for me.

FANNY : I shall have to give it to you now, then.

JOE : What ?

FANNY : Just a little something I had made for you.

JOE : Oh, Fanny—what is it ?

FANNY : Hold on a minute, dear. It's in my bag.

She searches in her bag and produces a small packet.
Here—with my love.

JOE (*opening it*) : Oh, it's lovely.

FANNY : It's nothing really. Just a little souvenir of all the fun we've had.

JOE : You are a darling !

FANNY (*grabbing it from* JOE) : Here, silly, you've missed the whole point. It opens—there.

> FANNY *opens the little locket and discloses a minute*
> *photograph of herself.*

JOE (*taking it*) : It will be with me always, to the end of my days.

FANNY : You won't want it that long.

JOE : I almost wish I didn't love you quite so awfully. It makes going back much worse.

FANNY : I shall miss you dreadfully.

JOE : It has been fun, hasn't it ?

FANNY : Lovely.

JOE : You don't regret it—any of it ?

FANNY :   Not a moment of it.

JOE :   How wonderful you are.   Do you really love me, I wonder, deep down inside, I mean ?

FANNY :   Yes, I think so.

JOE :   Enough to marry me ?

FANNY :   Yes, but I wouldn't.

JOE :   Why not ?

FANNY :   It would be too difficult.   We shouldn't be happy married.   Your Mother wouldn't like it.

JOE :   She'd be all right.

FANNY :   Don't let's talk about it now.   Let's wait until you come back.

JOE :   Very well.

>   *There is silence for a moment.*

FANNY *puts her hand on* JOE's *across the table.*

FANNY :   Listen, dear.   I love you and you love me, and I've got to go now or I shall be late ; and you've got to go, too, but I'm not going to say good-bye. We've had fun, grand fun, and I don't want you to forget me, that's why I gave you the locket.   Please keep it close to you, Joey—darling Joey.

>   FANNY *goes as*
>   *The lights fade.*

PART TWO : SCENE IX

Principals : JANE, JOE.

SCENE :   *A railway station.   The station is foggy and very dimly lit on account of air raids.   The ticket barrier can be vaguely discerned and beyond it, the back of a train.*

Just above the barrier a lamp shines downwards partially illuminating a recruiting poster. On the right is an empty platform, but there are people moving about on it, and several Red Cross orderlies and nurses. There is a crowd of people, mostly women, clustered around the left barrier—occasionally a door in the train opens and a shaft of light falls on to the platform.

TIME: *About 11 p.m. Tuesday, October 22nd, 1918.*

A crowd of soldiers comes on from the left, wearing full equipment. They are greeted by some of the women. Presently a Sergeant enters, and after their good-byes have been said, the Sergeant gets them in line and marches them through on to the platform, where they can be seen getting into the train.

JANE *and* JOE *come on from the left.*

JOE (*breathlessly*): Whew: I thought we were going to miss it, didn't you, mum?

JANE: Yes.

JOE: Not much time for long good-byes, darling.

JANE: I know. I'm glad, really—aren't you?

JOE: Yes. I never know what to say.

JANE: I'm almost hardened to it by now. This has happened so often.

JOE: Dearest mum, you are marvellous. You never make a fuss.

JANE: Don't be too sweet to me, Joey, I don't want to disgrace you, to behave badly.

JOE: You couldn't behave badly.

JANE: How funny! Do you know that Robert said that to me years and years ago. I must be very dull and unimaginative to be so reserved. It was the Boer

187

War, then.   This is very, very different.

> *A whistle blows.*

> Joe *takes* Jane *in his arms.*

JOE :   Good-bye, darling.

JANE :   Good-bye, darling—take care of yourself.

> Joe *rushes through the barrier and jumps into the train just as it starts to move.*

> Jane *stands under the lamp looking after him.*

> *Two or three of the women at the barrier burst into loud sobbing, some soldiers in the train start singing. A big steaming locomotive comes slowly to a standstill at the right hand platform. Almost immediately Red Cross Orderlies begin to walk off the platform carrying wounded men on stretchers.*

> Jane *stands watching them ; her face is quite expressionless. Then with a trembling hand she takes a cigarette out of her bag and lights it.*

> *The lights fade.*

PART TWO : SCENE X

Principals :   JANE, ELLEN, GLADYS (A parlourmaid).

SCENE :   *The drawing-room of a London house. The decoration of the room has changed slightly with the years, but not to any marked extent. It looks very much the same as it has always looked.*

TIME :   *About 11 a.m. Monday, November 11th, 1918.*

> *As the lights go up on the scene, a* PARLOURMAID *shows* ELLEN *into the room.* ELLEN *has certainly*

changed with the years. She is very well dressed,
almost smart.

GLADYS :   Her Ladyship will be down in a moment,
madam.

ELLEN :   Thanks.

GLADYS *goes out.*

ELLEN *wanders about the room. There is a photo-*
graph of EDWARD *on the table, and also one of* JOE.
She looks at them both and sighs.

JANE *enters. She is dressed in street clothes.*

JANE :   Ellen! Gladys said Mrs. Bridges, but I
couldn't believe it was you.

ELLEN :   I just thought I'd call. It's rather important, as a matter of fact.

JANE :   Do sit down. I'm delighted to see you
again.

ELLEN :   Thanks. (*She sits down.*)

JANE :   How's Fanny ?

ELLEN :   Oh, very well. She's in " Over the
Moon," now, you know.

JANE :   Yes. I went the other night. She was
splendid, I felt very proud to know her.

ELLEN :   It's about her I've come to see you, really.

JANE :   Oh! Well ?

ELLEN :   It's—it's—er—rather difficult.

JANE :   What is it ?   What on earth is the matter ?

ELLEN :   About her and Master—her and Joe.

JANE :   Joe ?

ELLEN :   Yes. They've been—well—er—to put it
frankly, if you know what I mean, they've been having
an affair.

JANE :   My Joe ?

ELLEN :   Yes—your Joe.   His last two leaves he

189

spent a lot of time with Fanny.

JANE (*slowly*): Oh, I see.

ELLEN: I wouldn't have come to see you about it at all, only I think Fanny's very upset about it, and now that the war's over—or almost over, that is—and he'll be coming home—I thought——

JANE (*coldly*): What did you think?

ELLEN: Well, I thought they ought to get married.

JANE: Does Fanny want to marry him?

ELLEN: No—er—not exactly. That is—I haven't talked about it to her. She doesn't know I know.

JANE: How do you know?

ELLEN: I found a letter from him——

JANE: And you read it?

ELLEN: Yes—it's here. I've brought it with me. (*She fumbles in her bag.*)

JANE: I don't wish to see it, thank you.

ELLEN: I only brought it because——

JANE (*cutting* ELLEN *short*): Is Fanny in any sort of trouble?

ELLEN: Oh, no. Nothing like that.

JANE (*rising*): Then I think we'd better leave it until Joe comes home. Then he and Fanny can decide what they wish to do.

ELLEN (*also rising*): I—I didn't mean to upset you.

JANE: I'm not in the least upset.

ELLEN: It's been on my mind—it's been worrying me to death.

JANE: I think you should have spoken to Fanny before you came to me. I never interfere with my son's affairs.

ELLEN: Well, I'm sure I'm very sorry.

JANE : Please don't let's discuss it any further. Good-bye, Ellen.

ELLEN : I suppose you imagine my daughter isn't good enough to marry your son ; if that's the case I can assure you you're very much mistaken. Fanny's received everywhere ; she knows all the best people.

JANE : How nice for her ; I wish I did.

ELLEN : Things aren't what they used to be, you know—it's all changing.

JANE : Yes, I see it is.

ELLEN : Fanny's at the top of the tree now ; she's having the most wonderful offers.

JANE : Oh, Ellen !

ELLEN : What is it ?

JANE : I'm so very, very sorry.

ELLEN : I don't know what you mean.

JANE : Yes, you do—inside, you must. Something seems to have gone out of all of us, and I'm not sure I like what's left.   Good-bye, Ellen.

> GLADYS *enters with a telegram.*
>
> JANE *takes telegram.*

Excuse me, will you.   (*She opens it and reads it, and then says in a dead voice.*)   There's no answer, Gladys.

GLADYS (*excitedly*) : It's all over milady—it's eleven o'clock—the maroons are going off.

JANE : Thank you, Gladys, that will do.

GLADYS : Yes, milady.

> GLADYS *goes out.*
>
> JANE *stands holding the telegram. She sways slightly.*

ELLEN : What is it ?   What's happened ?   Oh, my God !

JANE : You needn't worry about Fanny and Joe

any more, Ellen.   He won't be able to come back after all because he's dead.   (*She crumples up and falls to the ground.*)

> Maroons can be heard in the distance and people cheering.

> The lights fade.

PART TWO : SCENE XI

Principal : JANE.

SCENE : *Trafalgar Square.*
TIME : 11 *p.m. Monday, November 11th,* 1918.

> *Before the scene begins* JANE *appears far up stage in a pool of light.   Her hat has been pushed on to one side, her clothes look dishevelled, and her handbag hangs on her arm wide open.   Twined round her neck and over her hat are coloured paper streamers.   She holds in her left hand a large painted wooden rattle, in her right hand a red, white and blue paper squeaker.   Her face is dead white and quite devoid of expression.*

> *The lights go up.*

> JANE *can be seen threading her way like a sleep-walker through dense crowds of cheering, yelling people. They push her and jostle her.   One man blows a long squeaking paper tongue into her face.   There is a motor bus festooned with people and a Rolls Royce and one or two taxis and a hansom cab, all equally burdened with screaming humanity.   They move at a snail's pace. JANE finally arrives down stage under a lamp-post in the*

centre.   She stands there cheering wildly, with the tears rolling down her face.   The lights dim and the yelling crowds fade away. JANE *is left, still cheering and occasionally brandishing the rattle and blowing the squaker.   But she can't be heard at all because the full strength of the orchestra is playing* " Land of Hope and Glory."

END OF PART II

PART THREE : SCENE I

Principals : ROBERT, JANE, MARGARET.

SCENE : *Drawing-room of a London house.*
TIME : 11.45 *p.m. Tuesday, December 31st,* 1929.

> MARGARET *and* JANE, *both old women, are sitting by the fire.* MARGARET *is very made up, with dyed hair.* JANE'S *hair is white.* MARGARET *is wearing a coloured evening gown.* JANE *is in black.*

MARGARET : I assure you he's the most marvellous man I've ever met. I'd never go to another doctor in the world. He has the most wonderful touch—he's completely cured me, and anyhow the hotel is divine. It's really more a Hydro really, although, thank God, not in the English sense. You can eat what you like and do what you like——

JANE : And what do you like ?

MARGARET (*laughing*) : Enjoying myself.

JANE : And you do.

MARGARET : Certainly I do.

JANE : Good !

MARGARET : Jane, dear, you really are hopeless.

JANE : I refuse to be jostled, Margaret. I'm perfectly comfortable where I am, without going gallivanting about the Continent taking cures for ailments I haven't got.

MARGARET : How do you know you haven't got any ailments ?

JANE : Because I'm sane and active, and as strong as a horse. So is Robert. We've both outstayed our welcome, that's the only thing that's wrong with us.

MARGARET : I don't see any sense in sitting waiting for the grave.

JANE : I'm not waiting for anything. I have a perfectly good time. You're not the only one who enjoys yourself. I go to the Opera. I go to theatres, I go to the Zoo, and, I must say, so far I've found the Zoo infinitely the most entertaining.

MARGARET : Dearest Jane—you really are amazing!

    ROBERT *enters. His hair is also white, but he is otherwise hale and hearty.*

ROBERT : It's nearly time.

MARGARET : Good heavens, I must fly. I wouldn't interfere with your little ritual for the world.

JANE : You wouldn't interfere—you're an old friend.

MARGARET (*kissing* JANE): That's very sweet, Jane, but all the same I must go. I promised I'd be at the Embassy at eleven-thirty. Good night, dear. Good night, Robert. No, don't see me down—the car's outside, isn't it ?

ROBERT : Yes, it's been there for a long while.

MARGARET : Happy New Year to you both. Remember you're both dining with me on Thursday.

ROBERT : Good night, Margaret—same to you.

    MARGARET *goes out.*

    ROBERT *goes over to* JANE.

Did Franklin bring the champagne up ?

JANE : Yes, it's by the table.

ROBERT: Good !

JANE: Well, Robert—here we go again.

ROBERT: I believe you laugh at me inside—for my annual sentimental outburst.

JANE: No dear, I don't laugh at you.

ROBERT: One more year behind us.

JANE: One more year before us.

ROBERT: Do you mind ?

JANE: Oh, no—everything passes—even time.

ROBERT: It seems incredible, doesn't it ?   Here we are in this same room !

JANE: Yes.   I've hated it for years.

ROBERT: Do you want to move ?

JANE: Of course not.

ROBERT: We might have some new curtains.

JANE: We have, dear.

ROBERT: Good God, so we have ! I never noticed.

JANE: They've only been up a week.

ROBERT: They look very nice.

JANE: Dear Robert. (*She pats* ROBERT'S *hand.*) What toast have you in mind for to-night—something gay and original, I hope ?

ROBERT: Just our old friend—the future.   The Future of England.

JANE: It's starting—the champagne, quick !

> ROBERT *gets a champagne bottle out of the bucket and struggles with it.*

> JANE *opens the window.*

ROBERT: I can't get the damned thing open.

JANE: Let me try.

ROBERT (*doing it*):   There !

JANE *holds the glasses.*

196

ROBERT *fills the glasses.*

Meanwhile the chimes and sirens are beginning outside.

JANE (*holding up her glass*) : First of all, my dear, I drink to you. Loyal and loving always. (*She drinks.*) Now, then, let's couple the Future of England with the past of England. The glories and victories and triumphs that are over, and the sorrows that are over, too. Let's drink to our sons who made part of the pattern and to our hearts that died with them. Let's drink to the spirit of gallantry and courage that made a strange Heaven out of unbelievable Hell, and let's drink to the hope that one day this country of ours, which we love so much, will find dignity and greatness and peace again.

They both lift their glasses and drink as
The lights fade.

PART THREE : SCENE II

Principals : ROBERT, JANE, FANNY, MARGARET, ELLEN, FULL COMPANY.

SCENE : *A Night Club.*
TIME : *Evening—1930.*

This Scene begins with a night club in which FANNY *is singing, seated on a piano. The decoration is angular and strange, and the song she is singing is oddly discordant.*

197

TWENTIETH CENTURY BLUES

VERSE

Why is it that civilised humanity
Must make the world so wrong ?
In this hurly burly of insanity
Your dreams cannot last long.
We've reached a headline—
The Press headline—every sorrow,
Blues value is News value to-morrow.

REFRAIN

Blues, Twentieth Century Blues, are getting me down.
Who's escaped those weary Twentieth Century Blues.
Why, if there's a God in the sky, why shouldn't he grin ?
High above this dreary Twentieth Century din,
In this strange illusion,
Chaos and confusion,
People seem to lose their way.
What is there to strive for,
Love or keep alive for ?   Say—
Hey, hey, call it a day.
Blues, nothing to win or to lose.
It's getting me down.
Blues, I've got those weary Twentieth Century Blues.

> *When the song is finished, people rise from table
> and dance without apparently any particular enjoy-
> ment ; it is the dull dancing of habit. The lights
> fade away from everything but the dancers, who appear*

to be rising in the air. They disappear and down stage left, six " incurables " in blue hospital uniform are sitting making baskets. They disappear and FANNY is seen singing her song for a moment, then far away up stage a jazz band is seen playing wildly. Then down stage JANE and ROBERT standing with glasses of champagne held aloft, then ELLEN sitting in front of a Radio loud speaker; then MARGARET dancing with a young man. The visions are repeated quicker and quicker, while across the darkness runs a Riley light sign spelling out news. Noise grows louder and louder. Steam rivets, loud speakers, jazz bands, aeroplane propellers, etc., until the general effect is complete chaos.

Suddenly it all fades into darkness and silence and away at the back a Union Jack glows through the blackness.

The lights slowly come up and the whole stage is composed of massive tiers, upon which stand the entire Company. The Union Jack flies over their heads as they sing " God Save the King."

THE END

CONVERSATION PIECE

CHARACTERS:

SOPHIE OTFORD
MARTHA JAMES
MRS. DRAGON
PAUL, DUC DE CHAUCIGNY-VARENNES
MELANIE
ROSE (Her Maid)
THE MARQUIS OF SHEERE
THE EARL OF HARRINGFORD
LORD BRACEWORTH ⎫
LORD DOYNING ⎬ Regency
MR. HAILSHAM ⎭ Rakes
THE DUCHESS OF BENEDEN
THE DUKE OF BENEDEN
LADY JULIA CHARTERIS
HANNAH (Her Maid)
A TIGER
MISS GOSLETT
MISS MENTION
LORD KENYON
LORD ST. MARYS
FISHERMEN
COUNTESS OF HARRINGFORD
LADY BRACEWORTH
MRS. HAILSHAM
HON. JULIAN KANE
MR. AMOS
BUTLER
MR. JONES
COURTESAN
SOLDIERS, GUESTS, etc.
MILLINERS, LADIES OF THE TOWN, VISITORS, etc.
CHILDREN
The whole of the action of the play occurs at Brighton, 1811.

ACT I

SCENE I

PROLOGUE

*At the end of the Overture, the Curtain rises disclosing a
painted curtain, which depicts, in pastel colours, the
Brighton of the Regency.*

    SOPHIE, MARTHA *and* DRAGON *come in, exquisitely
dressed in the fashion of* 1811, *and each carrying a little
mask on an ivory stick. They stand, formally, side by
side, with their masks held before their eyes. They
lower them in order to speak, and retire behind them
again when they are silent.*

BOTH : Ladies and Gentlemen.
SOPHIE : A Prologue to a play is out of date,
      A leisurely technique of past decades,
      So please regard us as two friendly shades
      Returning down the years to indicate,
      More by our presence, than by what we say,
      The atmosphere and tempo of this play.
MARTHA : My friend has explained it most concisely,
      She always was one to put things nicely !
SOPHIE : We represent the fine but faded flower
      Of that old " Demi Monde " that used to be
      At Vauxhall, and at Brighton by the sea
      Before the pure in heart came into power,
      Before a great, but sanctimonious Queen
      Firmly rang down the curtain on our scene.

MARTHA : Please don't suppose *our* flowers were
            faded,
            Others were pushed, *we* were persuaded !
SOPHIE : The interruptions of my friend are meant
            To clarify for you our " Status Quo "
            A social level neither high nor low
            With which we were entirely content
            And which provides the background, may I
            say,
            Of this polite, but faintly raffish play.

   *To music, and with great dignity, they part the
   curtains on the first scene.*

ACT I

SCENE II

*The Scene is part of the Parade at Brighton. There is a
railing running the whole length of the stage and, behind
it, a row of demure Georgian houses. There is room
only for pedestrians to pass between the railing and the
houses.*

*When the curtain rises it is about eleven o'clock on a
sunny spring morning. There are two* FISHERMEN
*leaning against the railing with expressions of static
resignation. Several people pass and re-pass along the
Parade. Two* SOLDIERS *in scarlet coats stop and talk
to a neat little milliner's assistant with a hat box.
A* LITTLE BOY *runs across bowling a hoop, and two*
LITTLE GIRLS *walk along sedately with their* NURSE.

*The whole picture seems fresh and gay and alive, and
the orchestra, which plays continually throughout the
scene, celebrates the entrance of any particular character
with a pleasant little burst of individual melody.
Finally,* SOPHIE OTFORD *and* MARTHA JAMES *walk
on from the left. They are both pretty, and charmingly
dressed, and a certain manner and quality about them
suggest that they are of the superior courtesan class.
They walk languidly and chatter with a vivacity that
one cannot help feeling is just a trifle artificial.* PAUL,
*the Duc de Chaucigny-Varennes, enters from the right.
He is a superbly dressed, neat little man of about
forty-five. He appears to exude an aroma of perfection.
His gestures possess an authentic grace, and although
they are precise they are not in the least overdone. He
turns to the front door of* MELANIE'S *house and rat-
tat-tats briskly on the knocker as the lights fade.*

ACT I

SCENE III

The Scene is the interior of MELANIE'S *house—to be exact,
the living-room. It is charmingly furnished, and the
windows at the back open on to a small balcony which
looks out over the Parade and the sea. There are two
doors. The one up stage right leads into a little hall
and to the rest of the house. The one opposite to it up
stage left leads to* MELANIE'S *bedroom.*

As the lights rise on the scene the rat-tat-tat of the

*knocker can be heard, this rat-tat-tat theme being a
motif in the music which recurs throughout the play.
The music continues, and* ROSE *enters. She is* MELANIE'S
*English maid, a pretty girl in the twenties. She casts
a careful glance over the room to see that everything is
tidy, and then runs downstairs to open the front door.
After a moment she follows* PAUL *into the room. He
walks in with an air of complete authority and hands
her his hat, gloves, and cane.*

PAUL : Chocolate ?

ROSE : All ready, sir.

PAUL : No lumps in it ?

ROSE : Not one, sir.

PAUL : Good.

*He goes over to the desk, and, placing some glasses
upon his nose, seats himself at it. In a methodical
business-like manner he looks through a pile of bills and
papers.* ROSE *goes out to fetch the chocolate. She
returns in a moment with a neatly arranged tray which
she places on the desk.*

ROSE : You're sure you wouldn't like an egg, sir ?

PAUL : Quite sure, thank you.

ROSE : Nor a nice crisp bit of bacon ?

PAUL : It would kill me.

ROSE : I see, sir.

PAUL (*pouring himself some chocolate*) : How is Mademoiselle ?

ROSE : Gay as a lark, sir.

PAUL : Good. How is her English this morning ?

ROSE : I don't know, sir, but my French is improving
by leaps and bounds.

PAUL : Then consider yourself dismissed.

ROSE : You don't really mean that, do you, sir ?

PAUL : No.

ROSE : I didn't think you did really, sir.

PAUL : But I am very displeased with you. The rule of the house is that no one must speak French to Mademoiselle under any circumstances.

ROSE : I only said " Mon Dieu " when I dropped the nail file.

PAUL : Stick to " My God," it's more blasphemous and far more expressive.

ROSE : Very well, sir.

PAUL : This butcher's bill seems very high.

ROSE : It's the veal, I expect. Mademoiselle dearly loves a bit of veal, and I keep telling her it's unreliable.

PAUL : It isn't its integrity I question, but its cost.

ROSE : Yes, sir.

PAUL : In future no more veal except on special occasions. (*He holds out a bill.*) What does this mean ?

ROSE : Humbugs, sir.

PAUL : What are they ?

ROSE : Sort of big bull's eyes.

PAUL (*horrified*) : Bull's eyes ?

ROSE (*laughing*) : Oh, not real ones, sir, they're sweets. You tuck one in your cheek and it keeps you going for hours.

PAUL : Disgusting.

ROSE : Mademoiselle's very partial to them, sir. She saw some in a shop a long time ago, and since then we've 'ad 'em regular.

PAUL : That will be all for the moment, Rose.

ROSE (*curtseying*) : Thank you, sir.

> *She goes out right.* PAUL *continues to check the accounts. After a moment* MELANIE *comes out of her*

207

bedroom. She is wearing a négligé and looks radiant, but her face is slightly distorted by an obvious bulge in the left cheek. PAUL *springs to his feet and bows.*

PAUL : Good morning, Melanie.

MELANIE (*indistinctly*) : My God !

PAUL : What's the matter ?

MELANIE (*gracefully disposing of the humbug in a small handkerchief*) : Mon cher, personne ne m'a dit que——

PAUL (*sternly*) : Anglais.

MELANIE (*demurely*) : I did not know you were here.

PAUL : What were you eating ?

MELANIE : A 'oomboog. Tu veux le voir ?

PAUL : Non. No, certainly not.

MELANIE : They are delicious. Good morning.

PAUL : You slept well ?

MELANIE : Oui.

PAUL : Yes.

MELANIE : Yes, Paul.

PAUL : You have been speaking French to Rose.

MELANIE : Only a little.

PAUL : You have also been eating too much veal. I am very angry with you.

MELANIE : Please, I am sorry.

PAUL : Veal is unreliable and expensive. Those dreadful sweets are bad for your skin, and unless you learn English quickly we shall have to go away, just as we came, without money, without position, without anything.

MELANIE : Ah, ne sois pas fâché, mon cher, it is so difficult, when I awake the morning comes in at the window and makes me gay and I wish to talk very quick to Rose and say how the waves of the sea are pretty and how the sun shines and I learn better every day, I promise I do, but at the very beginning my brain does not wake itself enough and I cannot wait to find the stupid English words.

PAUL : It is so important. So very, very important.

MELANIE : Oui, je sais bien c'est important, mais——

PAUL : Anglais.

MELANIE : Zut ! Je ne peux pas.

PAUL : You must.

MELANIE : Please do not be angry with me this morning. It is my birthday.

PAUL : Again ?

MELANIE : Well, it feels like my birthday.

PAUL : You mean that you feel particularly happy ?

MELANIE : Oui—yes.

PAUL : Why ?

MELANIE : Je ne sais pas.

PAUL : You feel happy to-day without reason, just as yesterday you felt miserable without reason. You are a creature entirely lacking in balance.

MELANIE : I was an acrobat once.

PAUL : Kindly remember that you are my ward, the daughter of my dear friend the Marquis de Tramont, and that you have never even seen an acrobat, let alone been one.

MELANIE : Allez Oop ! (*She performs an acrobat's pose.*)

PAUL : Melanie !

MELANIE : Oh, comme vous êtes fastueux ce matin. Je parie que c'est encore à cause de votre foie.

PAUL : Mon foie est en parfaite santé.

MELANIE : Alors ! Pourquoi cet air de bravache ? C'est affolant. Vous m'accusez d'être heureuse sans raison, mais vous, mon ami, vous êtes âpre et désagréable également sans raison.

PAUL : Vous me désespérez.

MELANIE : Pourquoi ?

PAUL : J'insiste que vous parliez en anglais.

MELANIE : Je ne peux pas et je ne veux pas quand j'ai quelque chose d'important à dire vite, et à ce moment j'ai beaucoup à dire vite. Je travaillerai très fort. Je ferai tout ce que vous dites, mais pas quand vous êtes sévère, pas quand vous refusez de rigoler avec moi. Je vous défie !

PAUL : Soyez raisonnable, ma chère. (*He goes to her, pleading.*)

MELANIE : Riez ! Allez riez !

PAUL : Non.

MELANIE : Allons, un tout petit peu. Allez-y pour me faire plaisir.

PAUL : J'ai dit non.

MELANIE : Bon. Je ne parlerai pas un mot d'anglais jusqu'à ce que vous souriez. (*She sits with decision.*)

PAUL (*without mirth*) : Ha, ha, ha !

MELANIE : That is better.

PAUL : How can I make you realise that Life is serious ?

MELANIE : Because it is not serious.

PAUL : Look at these bills.

MELANIE : I see them.

PAUL : We have been here a month.

MELANIE : Yes, Paul.

PAUL : Nothing has happened at all.

MELANIE (*she rises and walks away*) : We have enough money for three months.

PAUL : Not at this rate.

MELANIE (*turning on him*) : What would you have me do ? Have no food, have no clothes ? Go out into the street in rags and say " Marry me. Marry me " to every man I see ?

PAUL : Don't be ridiculous.

MELANIE : Listen. I will be sensible, even in English I will try to be sensible, but you must not ask me to be serious. This adventure must be gay and funny. We will cheat and lie and pretend to everyone because that is agreed, but there must be truth between us, ourselves.

PAUL (*smiling*) : Entendu !

> *She indicates the sofa. He sits at the end.*

MELANIE : Have you ever had a dear friend called the Marquis de Tramont ?

PAUL : No.

MELANIE : Did he ever have a daughter ?

PAUL : No.

MELANIE : Did you ever by chance visit a café called Le Petit Girondin ?

PAUL : Oui.

MELANIE : Anglais !

PAUL : Yes.

MELANIE : It was very dirty, and there was sand on the floor, and men got drunk and spat on to the sand, sometimes they were sick——

PAUL (*sharply*) : That is enough.

MELANIE : And there was a girl who sang and danced and made acrobatics like this—— (*She does a trick.*) Do you remember ?

PAUL (*admonishing*) : Melanie ! I remember an old grey château with a walled garden, and a sweet fair-haired little girl feeding the swans——

MELANIE : Liar !

PAUL : And there was peace inside the garden, and memories of much happiness, but outside the walls there was horror and bloodshed and revolution, and presently the walls crumbled and the father and mother of the little girl were led away to die——

MELANIE : Stop, please. That is too near your own truth. It has nothing to do with mine.

PAUL : If you insist on truth you shall have it. (*He firmly places her on the sofa.*) You are uneducated, illiterate, a child of the gutter, aren't you ?

MELANIE : Yes.

PAUL : Penniless ?

MELANIE : Yes.

PAUL : I am a ci-devant aristocrat, and old.

MELANIE (*quickly*) : No.

PAUL : Middle-aged then.

MELANIE : Yes.

PAUL : Educated, cultured, and useless.

MELANIE : Yes.

PAUL : And equally penniless.

MELANIE : Yes.

PAUL : But fortunately possessed of an inherent talent for obtaining credit.

MELANIE : Fortunately.

PAUL : You are my only possible business asset.

MELANIE : Let us talk of something else.

PAUL (*continuing*) : Attractive, young, and, surprisingly enough, a virgin.

MELANIE : Please stop now. I will be good, really I will.

PAUL : You are my ward, are you not ? The forsaken daughter of my dear old friend the Marquis de Tramont ?

MELANIE : Yes, Paul.

PAUL : You spent your lisping carefree childhood in an old grey château, didn't you ?

MELANIE : What's " lisping "?

PAUL : Never mind. (*He stalks round the room, engrossed in the story.*) You have never been to Paris in your life, have you ?

MELANIE : No, Paul.

PAUL : What is Le Petit Girondin ?

MELANIE : I suppose it must be a very little man from Bordeaux.

PAUL : Correct. (*He goes to the table, places a chair for her to sit.*) Come ! Business ! Now then, what did Lord Sheere say to you last night ?

MELANIE (*seated*) : Not very much, but he was very ardent.

PAUL : Good. He is coming here this morning.

MELANIE : This morning ?

PAUL : Yes. I wrote him a little note from you. I will receive him and when I have talked to him for a little he will propose marriage.

MELANIE : He seemed last night to wish for something a little less binding.

PAUL : Never mind. When he proposes, you will accept him.

MELANIE : When may I love somebody, please ?

PAUL : Not until you are safely married, and then only with the greatest discretion.

MELANIE (*quietly*) : I see.

PAUL (*after a slight pause*) : What's the matter ?

MELANIE : It doesn't feel like my birthday any more.
(*Singing.*)

> A cloud has passed across the sun,
> The morning seems no longer gay.

PAUL (*speaking*) : I want to get on with these bills.
You had better go and dress.

MELANIE (*listlessly*) : Very well—— (*Singing*.)

> With so much business to be done,
> Even the sea looks grey.

PAUL (*speaking*) : Don't be silly.

MELANIE (*singing*) :

> C'est vrai. C'est vrai.
> It seems that all the joy has faded from the day
> As though the foolish world no longer wants
>   to play.

PAUL (*speaking*) : Go and dress.

MELANIE (*speaking*) : What shall I wear ? A black
crêpe with a little bonnet ?

PAUL : What on earth is the matter with you this
morning ?

MELANIE : White, white for a bride. But the sun
ought to shine on a bride.

PAUL : You're not a bride yet.

MELANIE : But I shall be soon, shall I not ? A very
quiet aristocratic bride with a discreet heart ! (*Singing*.)

> You ask me to have a discreet heart
> Until marriage is out of the way,
> But what if I meet
> With a sweetheart so sweet
> That my wayward heart cannot obey
> A single word that you may say ?

PAUL (*speaking*) : Then we shall have to go away.

MELANIE (*singing*) :
>   No.
>   For there is nowhere we could go
>   Where we could hide from what we know
>   Is true.

PAUL (*speaking*) : Do stop talking nonsense.

MELANIE (*speaking*) : It is not nonsense. You are so sure that everything in life can be arranged just so, like arithmetic.

PAUL : Why not ? Emotion is so very untidy.

MELANIE : The sun has come out again. I feel a little better.

PAUL (*writing something on one of the bills*) : Good.

MELANIE (*goes to the window humming, then returns to the desk and leaning across it she pats* PAUL's *hand*) : I'm sorry. (*Singing.*)

>   Don't be afraid I'll betray you
>   And destroy all the plans you have made,
>   But even your schemes
>   Must leave room for my dreams.
>   So when all I owe to you is paid
>   I'll still have something of my own,
>   A little prize that's mine alone.
>
>   I'll follow my secret heart
>   My whole life through,
>   I'll keep all my dreams apart
>   Till one comes true.
>   No matter what price is paid,
>   What stars may fade
>   Above,
>   I'll follow my secret heart
>   Till I find love.

When she has sung this waltz refrain she goes into her room. PAUL *rings a little bell on the desk.* ROSE *enters.*

PAUL : Rose, prenez le plateau——

ROSE *takes up the tray.*

PAUL : I am expecting the Marquis of Sheere. He should be here at any moment.

ROSE (*raising her eyebrows*) : Oh !

PAUL : Why do you say " Oh " like that ?

ROSE : It seems funny a gentleman of his position calling in the morning.

PAUL : Why funny ?

ROSE : In my last place the gentlemen always called in the evening.

PAUL : I think the sooner you wipe your last place from your mind the better.

ROSE : Yes, sir.

There is a rat-tat-tat on the door downstairs, and ROSE, *with a knowing look in her eye, goes out.* PAUL *rises as* ROSE *re-enters.*

ROSE (*announcing*) : The Marquis of Sheere.

The MARQUIS OF SHEERE (EDWARD) *comes in quickly, wearing an air of expectancy, which changes to slight confusion when he sees* PAUL. *He is a good-looking romantic young man in the twenties.*

PAUL (*going to him*) : Lord Sheere ?

EDWARD : Yes.

ROSE *goes out.*

PAUL : Allow me to introduce myself. I am the Duc de Chaucigny-Varennes.

EDWARD : Oh, how do you do ?

They shake hands.

PAUL : Melanie, my ward, will be here in a moment.

EDWARD (*relieved, but puzzled*): Oh, I'm so glad.

PAUL: In the meantime, can I offer you a little wine?

EDWARD: No, thank you.

PAUL: At least I beg you will be seated. (*He indicates the sofa and draws up a chair for himself.*)

EDWARD (*sitting down*): Thank you.

PAUL: Tell me, do you speak French?

EDWARD: Oui, un peu.

PAUL: I never think that's enough, do you?

EDWARD (*slightly crestfallen*): I suppose not.

PAUL (*charmingly*): Never mind, we will talk English. In the old days before the revolution my mother engaged an English governess for all of us. I remember she had a very pink nose, but her syntax was above reproach.

EDWARD: I'm so glad.

PAUL: It is not a matter for unrestrained jubilation, but we will leave it for the moment as we have things of more importance to discuss.

EDWARD: Have we?

PAUL: I understand that you wish to marry my ward?

EDWARD (*rising, extremely startled*): What! I beg your pardon?

PAUL: You seem embarrassed?

EDWARD (*floundering*): Well—I—er—I——

PAUL (*sententiously*): Ah, Love, Love, that fond foolish ecstasy! It ties the tongue in knots as well as the heart, does it not?

EDWARD: Yes, but you see—I really feel——

PAUL: Come now, there is no need to look so confused. I am a man of the world, old enough to be your father—you can be perfectly frank with me. Please sit down again.

EDWARD *sits.*

EDWARD : I had no idea that Melanie, Mademoiselle de Tramont, had a—a——

PAUL : Guardian.

EDWARD (*gulping*) : Guardian.

PAUL : She is the daughter of my dear old friend the Marquis de Tramont. The whole family was wiped out, father, mother, five sons and four daughters.

EDWARD : A large family.

PAUL : Very large. Melanie alone escaped. She was smuggled out of the château by one of the serving maids, a rude homely girl, who, after many vicissitudes, managed to convey her to me in Amiens, where I was in hiding.

EDWARD : How old was she ?

PAUL : A mere child.

EDWARD : I see.

PAUL (*leaning forward*) : I have watched over her and cared for her all these years. I have seen her grow from childhood to girlhood, from girlhood to womanhood. We have wandered together lonely exiles, through strange countries. Her youth and sweetness have kept my heart alive when everything I loved was dead, and now you come, a stranger, and wish to take her from me——

EDWARD : You misunderstand, sir, I assure you——

PAUL (*holding up his hand*) : No, no, do not protest. I understand only too well. I have known that this would happen. It is the penalty of age to be lonely, and I am quite prepared.

EDWARD (*firmly*) : I have not proposed marriage to Melanie.

PAUL : That does credit both to your upbringing and your personal integrity. I unfortunately am not in a position to put your fears entirely at rest. I cannot tell for certain whether or not she really loves you, but, if you will take the advice of an old man, don't give up hope, don't despair too soon—— (*He rings the bell on the desk.*)

> ROSE *enters very quickly, having obviously been listening at the door.*

ROSE : You rang, sir ?

PAUL : Ask Mademoiselle if she would be kind enough to come here.

ROSE : Yes, sir.

> *She goes into the bedroom.*

PAUL : You understand, her happiness is all that matters to me. I have naturally taken care to make discreet enquiries as to your character and way of life, forgive me being frank, but as a foreigner, such precautions I think may be excused. You may rest assured that at the earliest possible moment, I shall give myself the honour of calling upon your parents.

EDWARD (*terrified*) : For God's sake don't do that !

PAUL (*smiling fondly*) : Foolish boy !

> MELANIE *comes in from the bedroom, very beautifully dressed, and rather pale. She curtseys to* PAUL.

MELANIE : Bonjour, mon oncle.

PAUL (*sweetly*) : Fie donc, Melanie. Anglais, je t'en prie. N'oublie pas ta promesse.

MELANIE : Non. I am sorry. (*She curtseys to* EDWARD.) Good morning, Monsieur le Marquis.

EDWARD : Good morning, Mademoiselle !

PAUL : There is no need to be so formal, my dear. We all understand one another. Lord Sheere and I have had a little talk.

MELANIE (*slightly apprehensive*) : Oh—vraiment ?

PAUL (*taking both her hands*) : My *little* Melanie.

MELANIE (*drawing back—suspiciously*) : Qu'est-ce qu'il y a ?

PAUL : Qu'est-ce qu'il y a ? (*In a very beautiful voice.*) Be gentle with him, my Melanie, gentle and kind. True love is over-sensitive. I will leave you for a while.

MELANIE : No, Paul—please stay——

PAUL : It is better that I should go. (*He places his hand upon* EDWARD'S *shoulder and gazes searchingly into his eyes for a moment.*) My boy !

> PAUL *bows gracefully and goes out, leaving behind him an atmosphere of considerable embarrassment.* MELANIE *and* EDWARD *stand staring at each other until she can bear it no longer, and breaks the strain by going to the window.*

MELANIE (*at window*) : It is a very nice day, is it not ?

EDWARD : Very nice.

MELANIE : So pretty—everything here in England looks so fresh and clean—regardez ce petit bateau à voiles—sail boat ?

EDWARD (*coming also to the window*) : Yes—that's a sailing boat.

MELANIE : Léger sous le soleil, comme un papillon blanc——

EDWARD : Yes. Oh, yes, indeed——

> *A pipe organ begins to play softly in the street below.*

MELANIE : Music too.

EDWARD (*staring at her*): Yes—music too——

MELANIE : Why do you look like that ?

EDWARD : It's true.

MELANIE : What is true ? Je ne comprends pas——

EDWARD : What he said—your guardian—about love.

MELANIE (*turning away*): Oh.

EDWARD : I didn't understand.

MELANIE : The music is too loud.

EDWARD : Why not ? Why shouldn't it be loud ? It plays everywhere, doesn't it—that sort of music— all over the world ?

MELANIE : You speak so quickly—please do not speak so quickly.

EDWARD : Who are you, really ?

MELANIE (*she sits on the sofa, closing her eyes as though repeating a lesson*): I am Melanie de Tramont, the daughter of the Marquis de Tramont, he—my father— was killed in the revolution—my mother also, and my little brother Armand——

EDWARD : And your other brothers and sisters ?

MELANIE : All dead.

EDWARD : What were their names ?

MELANIE : Je ne comprends pas.

EDWARD : How many were there ?

MELANIE : Many—a great many.

EDWARD : You loved them ?

MELANIE : Yes, they were very nice.

EDWARD : And your mother and father ?

MELANIE : Very nice indeed.

EDWARD : Guillotined ?

MELANIE : Please—I cannot bear to speak of it.

EDWARD : I'm sorry.

MELANIE : It is long ago now, but I can never quite forget.

EDWARD : And your guardian—you love him?

MELANIE : Yes.

EDWARD : I see.

MELANIE : As a father.

EDWARD : Who are you—really?

MELANIE : Oh—go away—please go away.

EDWARD : Who are you—really?

MELANIE : I do not know.

EDWARD (*suddenly he sits next to her*) : I love you.

MELANIE (*painfully*) : No.

EDWARD : Before, when I have seen you in the distance, and last night when I talked to you, I wanted you—but now—now I love you——

MELANIE : No, no——

EDWARD : It's true, I know it—it happened suddenly a moment ago—it feels strange, as though I were not quite awake, and yet at the same time more awake than I have ever been before. You see I am not very old, not very experienced yet, and it's—it's the first time.

MELANIE (*she rises, walks away, clasping and unclasping her hands*) : Oh—this is very uneasy.

EDWARD : Why? Didn't you expect it?

MELANIE : No—not like this.

EDWARD : You know—you wanted me to love you, didn't you? Both you and your—your guardian—wanted me to love you——

MELANIE (*retreating from him*) : No, no——

EDWARD : You see I am not quite so young as all that, not quite a fool—my eyes are wide open—there is a lot that I don't understand, a trick, some sort of trick, I feel it with all my instincts, but I don't care—I feel more than that—I feel that you are very lovely, and very sweet too, and that is enough—will you please—please be my wife?

MELANIE (*sinking into a chair and covering her face with her hands*): Laissez-moi, je vous en supplie, laissez-moi——

EDWARD : Look at me.

MELANIE : Non, non——

EDWARD (*gently taking her hands away from her face*): Melanie.

MELANIE (*whispering*): Go away—please, please go away.

EDWARD : Very well. (*He smiles rather tremulously.*) But I shall come back.

MELANIE : Yes, come back—but think a little before you come back—see me once again from the distance——

EDWARD : I am afraid it is too late for that.

MELANIE (*curtseying, with her eyes averted from him*): Thank you, Monsieur le Marquis.

EDWARD (*bowing*): Mademoiselle !

He *looks at her for a moment, and then goes out swiftly. When he has gone she goes to the window and sings very softly, " I'll follow my secret heart " as the lights fade on the scene.*

ACT I

SCENE IV

QUARTETTE : " REGENCY RAKES."

Verse

You may think
Looking at the four of us
Food and drink
Constitute the core of us.
That may be,
But still you'll see
Our names on posterity's page.
You will read
Histories galore of us
Strutting England's stage.
We represent
To a certain extent
The ineffable scent
Of our Age.

Refrain

We're Regency Rakes
And each of us takes
A personal pride
In the thickness of hide
Which prevents us from seeing
How vulgar we're being
Without making us wince.
We're ruthless and rude
And boast of a crude

224

And lordly disdain
Both for mind and for brain.
Tho' obtuse and slow-witted,
We're not to be pitied,
For we follow the Prince,
Every orgy
With our Georgie
Lasts till dawn without a lull.
We can venture
Without censure
To be noisy, drunk, and dull !
We revel in Sport,
Madeira, and Port,
And when we pass out
With Sclerosis and Gout,
All our children will rue our mistakes,
Roystering Regency Rakes.

2nd Refrain

We're Regency Rakes
And each of us makes
A personal issue
Of adipose tissue
But still notwithstanding,
Our stomachs expanding,
We all yearn for romance.
We frequently start
Affairs of the heart,
Sublimely unheeding
That long over-feeding
Has made so disgusting
Our loving or lusting
That girls eye us askance,

Tho' we wonder
As we blunder
Into this or that bordel,
Whom we know there,
Why we go there,
But we're far too drunk to tell,
Tho' over-jocose,
Unfunny and gross,
We don't lose a fraction
Of self-satisfaction.
Complacency never forsakes
Roystering Regency Rakes !

ACT I

SCENE V

The Scene is MELANIE'S *room again. It is about three o'clock in the afternoon.*

When the Curtain rises the room is empty. Presently ROSE *ushers in* SOPHIE OTFORD, MARTHA JAMES *and* MRS. DRAGON. MRS. DRAGON *is an ample lady attired austerely in black, enlivened here and there by an occasional glitter of jet.*

ROSE : Mademoiselle will be with you in a moment.

SOPHIE : Thank you.

ROSE : I will inform Mademoiselle that you are here.

MARTHA : Thank you.

SOPHIE (*conversationally*) : Such a nice little house. Which is the Duc de Varennes' room ?

Rose : Monsieur le Dook don't live here.

Martha (*triumphantly*) : There you are.

She goes up to examine the quality of the wine-glasses on the sideboard.

Sophie : He just visits Mademoiselle, I suppose ?

Rose : Yes, every morning.

Martha : Only in the morning ?

She tests one of the glasses with a snap of her finger— it rings clearly.

Sophie : Don't be crude, Martha.

Rose : Monsieur le Dook is Mademoiselle's guardian.

Sophie : That's right, my dear. You're a very good girl.

Martha : Have you been with Mademoiselle long ?

Rose : Ever since she arrived in England, Madame.

Martha : I seem to know your face. Have I ever seen you before ?

Rose : I don't think you could have, Madame.

Sophie : Where do you come from ?

Rose : I was brought up in Wales, Madame. In a little village by the sea.

Martha : You haven't got a Welsh accent.

Rose : I know. That's what's so funny. My mother and father never 'ave been able to understand it.

Sophie : Well, if they can't, nobody can.

Martha : Were you engaged by Monsieur le Duc, or by Mademoiselle herself ?

Sophie : Martha !

Martha : Well, I want to know.

Rose : I was engaged through a friend.

Sophie : Who ?

Rose (*exasperated*) : Mrs. Edwards, the one who arranged your little affair with Lord Meadowfield.

227

SOPHIE : Don't be impudent.

ROSE : Well, mind your own business, then.

She goes out.

MARTHA : I thought as much. Do sit down, Dragon.

MRS. DRAGON sits down.

SOPHIE : Guardian, indeed !

MARTHA : None of my gentlemen have ever spoken to her alone yet.

SOPHIE : Not even His Grace ?

MARTHA : Not even His Grace.

ROSE returns from the bedroom and the visitors invent charming conversation, until ROSE goes out the other door.

SOPHIE : There's something fishy about it.

MARTHA : There's always something fishy about the French !

MELANIE enters. Everyone curtseys with great enthusiasm.

MELANIE : Ah, chères Mesdames, mes chères Mesdames, comme je suis enchantée de vous voir——

SOPHIE : This is Mrs. Dragon.

MELANIE : 'Ow do you do ?

MRS. DRAGON curtseys, but doesn't say anything.

MARTHA : We've been admiring your charming house.

MELANIE : I am so glad, please sit you down, and the tea will be here soon.

The guests sit on the sofa.

SOPHIE (*with an effort*) : Est-ce que vous trouvez que Brighton est joli ?

MELANIE (*smiling gaily*) : Ah ça, c'est défendu. Monsieur le Duc ne me permet pas de parler un mot de français, parce que, enfin, c'est absolument nécessaire que je fasse des progrès en anglais.

228

SOPHIE : Oh—er oui—je vois, je vois.

They all laugh.

MELANIE : Mais je souffre, ah, mon Dieu, comme je souffre ! Quand je tâche de chercher les phrases, je me sens perdu. C'est idiot !

SOPHIE (*giving up*) : There now.

MELANIE : Mais, vous savez, je fais des progrès, mais quand même je continue à dire des bêtises affreuses, surtout lorsque je me trouve dans une situation délicate. C'est vraiment inouï. Ma langue fourche, et je dis des choses que je ne devrais pas, et Paul, Monsieur le Duc, me regarde d'un petit air narquois, et je veux cacher ma tête comme une autruche.

SOPHIE : I always love the Austrians.

MARTHA : Such charming manners.

ROSE enters with the tea-things which she sets up on a little table.

MELANIE : Please take the tea ?

SOPHIE : Thank you.

They all sit round the table.

MELANIE (*dispensing tea*): It was so kind of you to arrive.

SOPHIE : Martha and I are giving a little party this evening, just cards and conversation and a few friends. His Grace the Duke of Twickenham has promised to honour us, we would be so pleased if you would come too.

MELANIE : It would delight me, but I fear I cannot.

MARTHA : What a shame ! You have another engagement ?

MELANIE : No, I have to work in the evening with Monsieur le Duc.

SOPHIE : As well as the morning ? How tiring !

MELANIE : Another time I should be so glad if you will invite me.

MARTHA : But, of course, we would like to know you better. When we spoke to you the other day on the Steyne we thought you looked so nice and so lonely, with only your maid for company.

SOPHIE: That was a delightful bonnet you were wearing.

MELANIE : The green plush ?

SOPHIE : Yes.

MELANIE : I have two new ones, more pretty, and a cramoisie dress, velvet, for walking—you would like to see ?

MARTHA : Oh yes.

MELANIE : They all came from the little shop of Mrs. Baxter—Rose, please bring the boxes from my room.

ROSE : Yes, Mademoiselle.

She curtseys and goes out.

SOPHIE : Mrs. Baxter is very expensive.

MELANIE : Alas yes, but the line she makes is good.

MARTHA : Are you staying here long ?

MELANIE : I do not really know. My guardian has the business to make, when that is done we will return.

SOPHIE : What is his business ?

MARTHA *and* DRAGON *are* " *all ears.*"

MELANIE : It is financial—I do not know words to explain correctly, but there must be a—a—transaction. That I know very well.

SOPHIE : I see.

MARTHA : Were you born in Paris ?

MELANIE : Oh, no, I lived as a child on the Loire— an old grey château, with a small water where there were swans——

SOPHIE : Very pretty.

MELANIE : Yes, it was pretty; I spent all my early days lisping there.

MARTHA : You haven't got a lisp now.

MELANIE : No, I lost it in the Revolution.

ROSE *enters from bedroom carrying several dress and hat boxes.*

ROSE (*putting them down*) : There, Mademoiselle.

MELANIE : Merci, Rose. (*To* SOPHIE.) You wish to see ? (*To* ROSE.) The mull dress with marabout and the turban——

      ROSE *opens one of the boxes and takes out a turban. Sophie and* MARTHA *give appropriate cries of appreciation.* ROSE *opens another box and takes out a dress. The music, which has been playing softly throughout the scene, falls into a more set rhythm, and* ROSE, MARTHA, SOPHIE *and* MELANIE *sing a quartette while they all try on different garments and hats. In course of this, a fife-and-drum band is heard outside on the Parade, and they all run to the window to wave to the soldiers marching by. Towards the end of the song, there is a rat-tat-tat at the front door. None of them hear except* ROSE, *who runs down to answer it.*

QUARTETTE :

SOPHIE :	Charming ! Charming ! Charming !
ROSE :	This gown is for the morning,
	When Mademoiselle goes out,
	As Madame sees
	In the slightest breeze
	The feathers float about.
SOPHIE . MARTHA :	Charming ! Charming ! Charming !
ROSE :	This jacket is for driving,
	Or strolling beside the sea.

SOPHIE :   Pretty as it seems to be
            It's a little too full in the sleeves for me.
ALL :   Ah la la la—la la—la la.
SOPHIE :   Pretty as it seems to be
            It's a trifle full in the sleeves for me.
MELANIE :   This dress is for the evening,
            To wear when I meet my dear,
            Whenever that may chance to be.
            In the moment that he looks at me
            The skies will suddenly clear.
            I'll know him then for my destiny,
            And so through each changing year
            I shall leave him never, for evermore.
ROSE :   Don't you think these pinks and blues
                are sweet ?
            This stuff is sent especially from France.
MELANIE :   Oh, please, please say you think these
                satin shoes are sweet
            They make me feel I want to dance.

            Danser—Danser—La Vie est gaie,
            Je me sens libre, abandonnée.
            Le chant trouble mon cœur
            Qui donc m'envoie ce doux bonheur,
            Mon corps, mes pieds, ensorcelés
            Légers, ailes, vont s'envoler.
            Tra la la la la—la la la—la la la la la,
            Tra la la la la—la la la—lalalalalala—la—la

SOPHIE : ⎫
MARTHA : ⎬
ROSE :   ⎬ Look for a love that's gay and sweet.
MELANIE : ⎭

232

SOPHIE :
MARTHA :
ROSE :   } Music to guide your dancing feet.
MELANIE :

SOPHIE :
MARTHA :
ROSE :

{ Follow your secret strain
And you won't be living in vain,
Treat your desire by word and deed
Lightly—lightly—
And if at first you don't succeed
Try and try again.

MELANIE :   Mon corps, mes pieds, ensorcelés
Légers, ailes, vont s'envoler.
Tra la la la la—la la la—la la la—la—la
Tra la la la la—la la la——

SOPHIE (*speaking*) : Soldiers !

MARTHA (*rushing to window*) : Quickly—let's see——

ROSE (*also rushing to window*) : I do love soldiers.

MELANIE (*joining them*) : Oh, they are so pretty, so pretty in their red coats.

SOPHIE : They're some of the guards from the Pavilion.

ROSE (*singing*) :   When I see the soldiers marching by
With fife and drum
Beneath a summer sky

SOPHIE :
and
MARTHA :   } Little dears who love to do and die

ROSE :   My spirit sings
And spreads its wings to fly.

SOPHIE (*spoken*) : Nicely put, my girl, but a trifle affected.

ROSE : Well, it's true.

MARTHA : Look at the officer leading them.

SOPHIE : I must admit he could leave his shoes under my bed any time he liked.

ROSE (*singing*) :

> Think of all the battles they have won

MELANIE (*singing*) :

> So brave and strong
> They march along
> Like little boys
> Who play with toys
> For fun.

SOPHIE
and   } Little boys who frolic in the sun.
MARTHA :

ROSE :   Right—right—right left right——

ALL :   Right—right—right left right left——

> March, little soldiers, we all adore
>   you,
> We'd swoon before you
> If we thought that you would care,
> Whate'er befalls you,
> Where duty calls you,
> We should love to be there,
> To share
> All your troubles, but we'd never dare,
> But we're quite prepared to cheer you to
>   victory,
> To joy or despair,
> Joy or despair,
> That's only fair.
> Dear little soldiers,

234

Should you admire us
And feel desirous
On returning from the fray,
We'd soon surrender,
You'd find us tender
And sublimely unresisting
In assisting
You to spend
Your soldiers' pay pay pay.

At the end of the song, when MELANIE, MARTHA,
and SOPHIE *are twirling gaily about the room,* ROSE
*re-enters and announces in rather gloomy tones: The Duke
and Duchess of Beneden. The music stops dead as they
enter. They are elderly; haughty and grim.*

DUCHESS (*stiffly*): Mademoiselle de Tramont?

MELANE (*curtseying*): Oui!

DUCHESS: I am the Duchess of Beneden. Please
forgive us for calling upon you so—so unexpectedly. I
believe you are acquainted with my son, Lord Sheere?

DUKE: A moment, my love, just a moment, do not
rush matters.

MELANIE: I think you do not know Mrs. James and
Mrs. Otford.

DUCHESS (*icily*): I do not.

MELANIE (*charmingly*): Then it is easy that you should
because they are here.

> *She indicates them with a polite gesture; they both
> curtsey low. The* DUCHESS *bows almost imperceptibly.*

SOPHIE: This is Mrs. Dragon.

MARTHA: Of Dorset.

DUCHESS (*without the faintest sign of recognition*): Indeed?

SOPHIE (*after a slight pause*): Nice weather, taken all
in all?

235

MELANIE : Will you not sit yourselves down ?

DUCHESS : No, thank you.

MELANIE : Perhaps you would like the tea ?

DUCHESS (*with an atrocious accent*) : Non merci. Je pense qu'il serait mieux si nous parlons en français.

MELANIE : Au contraire, Madame, my friends do not understand French.

MARTHA (*with great refinement*) : Oh, please don't bother about us, we shall have to go now, anyhow.

MELANIE : Oh, no, please stay a little longer.

SOPHIE : We really must go, we have an appointment with the Duke of Twickenham (*Pertly to the* DUCHESS.) He is your cousin, I believe ?

The DUCHESS *turns away without answering.*

MARTHA : Come on, Dragon. (*She goes to the door.*)

SOPHIE : Good-bye, my dear Duke—it's ages since we last met, isn't it ? Do you remember ? That New Year's party at Mrs. Johnstone's—a very gay evening, wasn't it ? (*She turns to* MELANIE.) Au revoir, Mademoiselle. (*She curtseys.*)

MARTHA (*also curtseying*) : We must meet again very soon.

SOPHIE : Et merci beaucoup !

MELANIE : Au revoir.

> MRS. DRAGON *does a slightly abortive curtsey to everyone and the three of them go out, followed reluctantly by* ROSE. *When the door has closed behind them the* DUCHESS *turns.*

DUCHESS : As I said before, I believe you are acquainted with my son ?

MELANIE : Yes.

DUCHESS : You would be doing my husband and

myself a great service if you discontinued that acquaintance.

MELANIE : You are come here to ask a service ?

DUKE : Yes, Mademoiselle, we have.

MELANIE (*to the* DUCHESS): Then I do not understand how your manner is so unpolite.

DUKE : My wife is upset, naturally upset.

MELANIE : Pourquoi ?

DUKE : Edward is our only son.

MELANIE : Is that not more your fault than mine ?

DUCHESS : It is no use bandying words, Frederick, and wasting time. (*To* MELANIE.) I am a woman of the world, Mademoiselle, and I fully realise your position.

The DUKE *looks appraisingly at* MELANIE, *through his quizzing glass.*

MELANIE : I fear I do not understand.

DUCHESS : Things may be different in France. I am sure I do not know about that since that dreadful Bonaparte has ruined the country, but here in England, there are still two distinct worlds. You belong to one, and my son belongs to the other. Those two worlds do not mix.

MELANIE : I would prefer that you speak to my guardian of these things.

DUCHESS (*sniffing*): Guardian !

MELANIE : Monsieur le Duc de Chaucigny-Varennes.

DUKE : Perhaps, my love, that, after all, would be a better plan.

DUCHESS : Please, Frederick, allow me to deal with this. (*To* MELANIE.) My son is infatuated with you, but he is young and that infatuation will not last. It must not last. I wish you to give me your word that you will never see him again. My husband and I are fully prepared to compensate you within reason.

MELANIE : Compensate ?   Que-ce que c'est ça—compensate ?

DUCHESS (*laconically*) : Money.

MELANIE : Money! You will pay me money ?

DUCHESS : Yes.

MELANIE : To see your son never again ?

DUCHESS : Yes.

MELANIE : If I love him, what then ?

DUCHESS : That is beside the point.

MELANIE : I think you will perhaps go away now.

DUCHESS : Five hundred pounds.

MELANIE : He is very charming, your son, and his eyes are very clear and true. I think he will be angry.

DUCHESS : A thousand pounds.

MELANIE (*ringing the bell on the desk*) : I am tired, Madame. I cannot sit down until you go.

DUKE : Mademoiselle, I beg of you—my wife is distraite——

MELANIE : That is not of interest to me.

DUCHESS (*losing control slightly*) : I would like to make one thing clear to you. My son is not yet of age. If he marries without his parents' consent he will not have a penny. Not a penny ! Do you understand that ?

DUKE : Georgina, Georgina—please——

MELANIE : He would make a very sweet husband, your son, even without a penny, because he is kind.

ROSE *enters, and stands by the door.*

DUKE : Come, Georgina.

The DUCHESS *looks at* MELANIE *furiously for a moment in silence, and then, without a word, turns her back on her and sweeps out of the room followed by the*

238

DUKE. *The* DUKE *turns at the door and bows with the suspicion of a smile.* ROSE *follows them out, and* MELANIE *runs to the window to peep through the curtains at them. In a moment or two* ROSE *returns.*

MELANIE : Ça y est !

ROSE : What's that ?

MELANIE : Some Madeira, quickly, my legs will not stand. (*She sinks down on the sofa.*)

ROSE *runs to a little side table and pours her out a glass of Madeira.*

ROSE : My goodness ! Her face when she went out !

MELANIE : Mon Dieu ! Her face when she came in.

ROSE : That bonnet !

MELANIE (*starting to laugh*) : Like a pheasant.

ROSE : Feathers and all. (*She starts to laugh too.*)

MELANIE (*laughing more wildly*) : The Duke—the poor, poor man——

ROSE : Looked like a corpse, and no wonder——

They are both laughing weakly when PAUL *comes into the room.*

PAUL : Why was the front door open ?

ROSE : Oh, dear !

PAUL : What is the matter ?

MELANIE (*hysterically*) : Five hundred pounds—a thousand pounds—not enough—not quite enough—but better than nothing !

PAUL : That will do, Rose.

ROSE : Yes, sir.

She goes out, wiping her eyes.

PAUL : Now, what has happened ?

MELANIE : Je vous raconterai ce qui vient de passer. On m'a insulté et si cela ne me faisait pas tant rire j'aurais envie de pleurer.

PAUL : Qui vous a insulté ? Que voulez-vous dire ?

MELANIE : La très charmante mère de Monsieur le Marquis, ils sortent d'ici, le Duc et la Duchesse, je ne suis pas encore assez bien élevée—j'avais envie de lui cracher à la figure—c'est un grossier vieux chameau—elle s'est conduite avec moi comme envers une grue !

PAUL : J'espère que vous ne lui avez pas donné de raison pour vous prendre comme telle.

MELANIE : Du reste tout ceci est de votre faute. Je n'avais aucune envie de connaître tous ces gens. J'étais bien plus heureuse là où j'étais.

PAUL : Ça c'est idiot !

MELANIE : Mais c'est vrai ! Vous voulez que je l'épouse votre Marquis? Ah bien, soit: et puis après, vous verrez, il sera sans le sou, et moi, je serai forcée de retourner chanter dans un café—Madame la Marquise au café chantant ! Ça sera du joli, et ça sera bien faire pour vous !

> *There is a rat-tat-tat at the door.* MELANIE *runs to the window.*

C'est le Duc, et tout seul cette fois.

PAUL : I'll talk to him.

MELANIE : No.

PAUL : But, my dear Melanie——

MELANIE : Go into the bedroom.

PAUL : But I——

MELANIE : Go quickly—listen at the door—and do not come out until I say——

PAUL : You will call me ?

MELANIE : I will say, " The sea is so pretty." Go on —quickly——

> PAUL *goes into the bedroom.* MELANIE *pushes the boxes to the back of the room.* ROSE *enters.*

Rose (*with a slight leer*) : The Duke of Beneden.

 Melanie *is now seated, posing for the interview. The* Duke *enters. He bows with almost overdone politeness.* Rose *goes out.*

Duke : Mademoiselle, I—I—have returned.

Melanie : I see you have.

Duke : I ask your forgiveness.

Melanie : Thank you.

Duke : My wife——

Melanie : She is upset ?

Duke : Yes.

Melanie : Distraite ?

Duke : Exactly.

Melanie : Ill-mannered ?

Duke : Yes—er—I mean—well, you understand ?

Melanie : I do not understand.

Duke (*with a charming smile*) : Please try.

Melanie : That is better.

Duke : You are very pretty, Mademoiselle, and very charming.

Melanie : Oh !

Duke : I am sure that you cannot possibly be hard-hearted.

Melanie : It is difficult to have the soft heart when one is insulted.

Duke : My wife does not understand as I understand.

Melanie (*averting her eyes*) : Oh, Monsieur le Duc.

Duke : Do you love my son ?

Melanie (*still looking down*) : I do not know.

Duke : He loves you ?

Melanie : Yes.

Duke : Do you wish to marry him ?

MELANIE : Please—I do not know.

DUKE : All his money is controlled by his mother; if you did become his wife, she would cut him off entirely.

MELANIE : I see.

DUKE : Whereas I——

MELANIE (*looking up sharply*) : You ?

DUKE (*with slight embarrassment*) : I find myself in an extremely awkward position.

MELANIE : Why ?

DUKE : I do not want to bore you with my troubles, but you are so sympathetic.

MELANIE (*going to him*) : What is it you would say ?

DUKE : I have a little house in London, a dear little house very nicely furnished just near Berkeley Square, and it is unhappy because it is not lived in, the pretty furniture is covered up and the blinds are drawn.

MELANIE : How sad !

DUKE : You see, I am an old man now.

MELANIE : Non, Monsieur.

DUKE : Well, elderly.

MELANIE : Perhaps.

DUKE : And my heart, like the house, is covered up, and the blinds are drawn.

MELANIE (*turning away*) : Your wife, does she know about the little house ?

DUKE : No.

MELANIE : And your heart ? Does she know about that ?

DUKE : No.

MELANIE (*resting her hand lightly on his arm*): Poor Monsieur le Duc, life is very difficult, is it not ?

DUKE : I knew you would understand. (*He holds her hand, almost as though he didn't notice it.*)

MELANIE : What is the rent of the little house ?

DUKE : That is all paid.

MELANIE : And is there a little carriage with white horses and a footman on the box ?

DUKE : How did you guess ?

MELANIE : And every month, the bills of the house ? They will be much ?

DUKE (*tentatively*) : Two hundred pounds ?

MELANIE (*firmly*) : Three hundred pounds.

DUKE (*smiling*) : Three hundred pounds.

MELANIE : On the first day of every month ?

DUKE (*pulling her a little towards him*) : On the first day of every month.

MELANIE (*surrendering*) : But I do not yet know about London.

DUKE : It is delightful ! You would love it.

MELANIE : But I love it here in Brighton.

He takes her in his arms.

The sea is so pretty.

> PAUL *enters from the bedroom. The* DUKE *starts back and hurriedly disentangles himself from* MELANIE.

PAUL (*sternly*) : Melanie !

MELANIE (*terrified*) : Ah, mon Dieu !

PAUL : Monsieur, I do not think I have the pleasure of your acquaintance.

DUKE : I am the Duke of Beneden.

PAUL : Melanie, go to your room.

MELANIE : Mais, mon oncle, je——

PAUL : Immediately. Do as I tell you.

MELANIE : Oui, mon oncle.

> *She drops a hurried little curtsey to the* DUKE, *curtseys to* PAUL, *makes a wry face and goes out.*

PAUL : Now then, Monsieur !

DUKE : I see it all now.

PAUL : You are the father of the Marquis of Sheere ?

DUKE : Yes.

PAUL : I see. Good-bye, Monsieur.

DUKE : I would like to explain.

PAUL : There is nothing to explain. It is all depressingly clear. (*He rings the bell.*) I will call upon you and the Duchess later when I have decided what course to take.

DUKE : Look here, sir, I——

PAUL : The Duc de Chaucigny-Varennes. At your service.

ROSE *enters.*

Rose, kindly conduct his Grace downstairs.

ROSE : Yes, sir.

DUKE : I fear you don't quite understand. There is some mistake——

PAUL : There is a very grave mistake, and I understand perfectly. Good-bye. (*He bows abruptly.*)

> The DUKE *still hesitates for a moment, then bows stiffly and goes out followed by* ROSE, *who has the impertinence to wink broadly at* PAUL *over her shoulder.*
>
> The music swells and MELANIE *puts her head round the bedroom door.* PAUL *beckons to her, and they both tiptoe in time to the music to the window, where, shaking with silent laughter, they peep through the curtains as the lights fade.*

ACT I

Scene VI

Trio : Martha, Sophie *and* Dragon.
"There's Always Something Fishy About the
French."

Verse 1

Sophie :   A life of Love is curious
But not injurious
If you are wise,
Martha :   For you get pleasure,
Leisure,
Knowledge to treasure
After the gay life dies ;
Sophie :   Tho' men we seldom bind to us
They're often kind to us,
Martha :   And entre nous
Both :   English Gentlemen,
Spanish Noblemen,
Indian Merchantmen too
Always play the game,
Never cause us shame.

Refrain 1

Both :   But there's always something fishy about
the French !
Whether Prince or Politician
We've a sinister suspicion
That behind their " savoir faire "
They share

245

A common contempt
For every mother's son of us.
Tho' they smile and smirk
We know they're out for dirty work,
So we're most polite
But don't put out the night-light!
Every wise and thoroughly worldly wench
Knows there's always something fishy
about the French!

Refrain 2

BOTH :   Oh, there's always something fishy about
the French!
As a Race, they're conscientious
But undoubtedly licentious,
Tho' the compliments they pay
Are gay
And ever so nice,
We don't believe a word of them.
They may kiss our hands
And talk to us of foreign lands,
We " Toi " and " Moi "
And watch for " Je ne sais quoi."
Every time their fingers begin to clench—
Well, we know there's something fishy
about the French!

After a short dance they go off left as the lights fade.

ACT I

SCENE VII

This Scene is the Public Gardens.

It is evening, and there are lights in the Pavilion windows. Down stage on the left is a stone or wooden seat.

When the curtain rises there is a mixed collection of people on the stage. Residents. Visitors. A few soldiers. A man with a hurdy-gurdy. Several ladies of the town, some with escorts, some without. Everyone has his back turned to the audience, and is obviously craning to see somebody pass by. MISS GOSLETT *and* MISS MENTION, *two elderly maiden ladies, have actually stood upon the seat in order to see better. After a moment or two, the tune that the band is playing comes to an end with a little flourish of brass. Everyone relaxes, and proceeds to stroll about.* MISS GOSLETT *and* MISS MENTION *climb down off the seat and sit on it.*

MISS GOSLETT : He's certainly getting very fat.

MISS MENTION : Perhaps it's dropsy.

MISS GOSLETT : Surely not, at his age.

MISS MENTION : A friend of mine died of dropsy when she was only twenty-three. They kept on tapping her and tapping her, but it was no good.

MISS GOSLETT : That poor Princess Caroline, it does seem a shame.

MISS MENTION : Such a common face.

MISS GOSLETT : She can't help that, to be sure.

MISS MENTION : This place is certainly much more lively than Exeter, although I *do* miss the cathedral.

The man with the hurdy-gurdy approaches them, playing busily.

MISS GOSLETT (*fumbling in her reticule*) : I must give him some pence.

MISS MENTION : It will only encourage him.

MISS GOSLETT hands the man a few pennies, and he goes off. The band starts again, this time playing a slightly more sentimental tune. The DUKE OF BENEDEN strolls across accompanied by the MARQUIS OF SHEERE.

EDWARD : But, Papa, I assure you, she is different——

DUKE : My dear boy, that sort of woman is never so very different.

EDWARD (*hotly*) : You cannot possibly tell what sort of woman she is.

DUKE : I shall make it my business to find out.

They go off. SOPHIE walks on accompanied by LORD KENYON, an immaculately dressed dandy, who is obviously a little the worse for drink.

SOPHIE : Not to-night. I have already told you, I have another engagement.

LORD KENYON : Just a little drive.

SOPHIE : I do not trust your horses.

LORD KENYON : What is wrong with them?

SOPHIE : They make conversation impossible.

They meet MARTHA with LORD ST. MARYS.

MARTHA : My dear, I've been searching for you everywhere.

SOPHIE : I can't think why.

MARTHA : Lord St. Marys wants to be presented to Mademoiselle what's-her-name.

SOPHIE (*raising her eyebrows*) : Oh, does he? (*To* LORD ST. MARYS.) For your own benefit, or somebody else's?

LORD ST. MARYS : I cannot give away State secrets.

SOPHIE : I thought as much.

MARTHA : I hope this—this commission of yours won't prevent you from coming to the Assembly Rooms later on ?

LORD ST. MARYS : That all depends, neither my heart nor my soul is my own these days——

> *They pass out of sight, all four of them, as the* DUKE *OF* BENEDEN *and* EDWARD *come on right, in time to meet* LADY JULIA CHARTERIS *who is strolling down from the back, accompanied only by her maid. She is a handsome authoritative woman, exquisitely gowned middle-aged, and slightly over-made-up.*

DUKE (*bowing*) : My dear Julia ! I thought you were in Spain.

JULIA : I'm grateful even for the thought, Frederick. The last ten years have seemed singularly barren without your attentions.

DUKE (*hurriedly*) : This is my son, Julia.

JULIA (*smiling in response to* EDWARD'S *bow*) : We have met before.

EDWARD : Madame—I——

JULIA : Don't look confused. You couldn't possibly remember. It was years ago, in London. We stopped to converse for a moment, your nurse and I, and you were permitted to bite my glove.

EDWARD : I never tasted a more delicious glove.

JULIA : This has been a strange day, my first in England for a long while. A day of ghosts. Out of the past they come, one after the other, looking almost as real as when they were alive. You are the sixth, Frederick, there really should be seven. Seven is my lucky number.

DUKE : You still gamble as much as ever ?

JULIA : Yes, with the difference that I know now that it is far too late to win.

> *They exchange bows. The* DUKE *and* EDWARD *stroll off up stage.* JULIA *has just reached the seat on her way off, when* PAUL *hurries on. He is obviously searching for someone. He passes* JULIA *without looking at her.*

JULIA (*stopping dead*) : The seventh!

PAUL (*turning*) : I beg your pardon ?

JULIA (*singing softly*) : Au clair de la lune, mon ami Pierrot——

PAUL (*staring at her*) : Julie !

JULIA : I thought you were dead.

PAUL (*warmly kissing her hand*) : Oh, how charming to see you again, how very, very charming.

JULIA : English, too ! Almost without an accent.

PAUL : How long ago is it ?

JULIA : Let us both try *not* to remember.

PAUL : It is so difficult—seeing you again so suddenly, so unexpectedly—conjures up so much of the past.

JULIA : The past is dead—perhaps happily.

> *They sit.*

PAUL (*incredulously*) : It isn't true. Do you remember the salon of Madame de Plessier ?

JULIA : And Father François, and the little pink cakes with seeds in them—— ?

PAUL : And the day you cried over the dead dog !

JULIA : I've cried over many dead dogs since then—

> *At this moment* MELANIE *comes on. She goes swiftly up to* PAUL.

MELANIE : Ah, mon cher, enfin ! J'ai pensé que vous étiez perdu.

PAUL : Julia, I want to present to you my ward, Melanie de Tramont.

> MELANIE *and* JULIA *both curtsey.* JULIA *is palpably very puzzled.*

JULIA : De *Tramont ?*

MELANIE : Oui, Madame. I am the daughter of the dear old Marquis de Tramont.

JULIA : I shouldn't boast of it, my dear, as he was unmarried.

MELANIE (*to* PAUL) : Je ne comprends pas.

PAUL : I will explain later. Lady Julia Charteris and I are very old friends——

> *At this moment,* MARTHA *appears with* LORD ST. MARYS.

MARTHA : Oh, Mademoiselle, will you please allow me to introduce a friend of mine, Lord St. Marys.

> MELANIE *curtseys,* LORD ST. MARYS *bows.*

MELANIE : Enchantée, Monsieur.

LORD ST. MARYS : Please forgive me for imposing myself upon you, Mademoiselle, but I have been commanded to approach you on behalf of His Royal Highness the Prince Regent.

MELANIE : Ah, mon Dieu ! Son Altesse ?

LORD ST. MARYS : His Royal Highness wishes to know whether you would do him the honour of taking supper with him this evening ?

PAUL : Will you please tell His Royal Highness with our most deep thanks that this evening it would not be possible as she is a little ill.

JULIA : This situation seems a trifle delicate. I hope to continue our reminiscences very soon, Paul. Au revoir, Mademoiselle de Tramont. Come, Hannah.

> *She goes off with her maid.*

LORD ST. MARYS : I fear that Mademoiselle does not quite understand. My request, coming from such an exalted quarter, amounts practically to a command.

PAUL : Mademoiselle de Tramont, my ward, has not yet had the honour of being presented to His Royal Highness.

LORD ST. MARYS : The fact, His Royal Highness is the first to deplore——

PAUL : Surely, it is a matter soon remedied ?

LORD ST. MARYS : If Mademoiselle will allow me to escort her now, I, myself, will take great pleasure in presenting her.

PAUL : I fear, Monsieur, there is some mistake. Will you kindly bear my homage to His Royal Highness, and inform him, with all due respect, that I will be honoured to present my ward to him myself, on a more formal occasion.

LORD ST. MARYS (*stiffly*) : My regrets, Monsieur.

PAUL (*amiably*) : And mine.

LORD ST. MARYS *bows abruptly, and goes off with* MARTHA *and* DRAGON *follows.*

MARTHA : Well, really !

PAUL : Come, Melanie.

He crooks his arm, and MELANIE, *after bowing politely to* MARTHA, *takes it. The band strikes up a particularly gay little tune. As they walk away,* MELANIE *turns her head towards* DRAGON, *who winks broadly at her, kicking up the back of her dress, as——*

THE CURTAIN FALLS

ACT II

SCENE I

The painted curtains again.
SOPHIE *and* MARTHA *appear before them as in the Prologue.*

SOPHIE :   This play, or let us say, this pantomime,
          Being too small in scope, too tenuous,
          Too personal to illustrate the strenuous
          And glittering excitements of the time,
          We feel it, in a sense, obligatory
          To hint at what goes on *behind* the story.
MARTHA : My friend, though a trifle too rhetorical,
          Means it should be more historical.
SOPHIE :   We ask you to imagine, if you please,
          That just around the corner of the tale,
          Mrs. Fitzherbert and the Prince inhale
          The selfsame air, the same urbane sea-
                breeze.
          Imagine that this world is living still
          And passing just beneath the window-sill.
MARTHA : You've left out Brummell, the pert
                impostor,
          And what about Pitt ? And the Duke of
                Gloucester ?
SOPHIE :   Picture a little further if you will
          The neat Pavilion Gardens, and the
                Steyne.

The little band that orchestrates the scene.
The Fireworks, the Races, the Quadrille,
And furthermore, the bawdy, merry Hell
Created by our lordly clientèle !
They curtsey, and go off, left and right.

ACT II

SCENE II

The Scene is MELANIE'S *room again.*
When the curtain rises it is early afternoon. MELANIE
*is seated at a table upon which is a pile of books. She is
wearing large horn-rimmed glasses, and an expression of
rather depressed concentration. She is also sucking a
pencil, and there is a paper bag of humbugs on the table
by her side. She sings a song, half in French and half in
English, dealing entirely with the intricacies of language.
English Lesson :* MELANIE.

Verse

The Tree is in the Garden,
The water is in the Pot ;
The Little sheep
On the mountain sleep,
The fire is very hot.

Refrain

Oh ! c'est dur,
Tous ces mots obscurs
Me rendent triste ;

Rien n'existe
Que le malheur qui insiste ;
Dieu, je tâche d'apprendre, mais voilà
Je ne peux pas.

Verse 2

The fire is *not* in the garden,
The tree is not in the pot,
The silly sheep
On the something sleep,
But whether they do or not,
I do not care a jot ;
I don't care if they're cold
Or if they're hot.

The CHILDREN *sing, "* La—la—la*," etc., outside the window. She shuts it, and the* CHILDREN *stop singing.*

Refrain 2

Oh ! c'est dur,
Tous ces mots obscurs
Me rendent triste ;
Rien n'existe
Que le malheur qui insiste ;
Dieu, je tâche d'apprendre, mais voilà
Je ne peux pas.

At the end of it, she rests her head wearily on her hands, and is obviously on the verge of tears. ROSE *enters.*

ROSE : There is a lady downstairs to see you.

MELANIE (*perking up slightly*) : Is it Mrs. James or Mrs. Otford ?

ROSE : No. She said the name was Lady Julia Charteris.

255

MELANIE : Tall, with a painted face ?

ROSE : Yes, and very grandly dressed. She came in a curricle.

MELANIE : I do not wish to see her. I do not wish to see anyone.

ROSE : Shall I say you're out ?

MELANIE : Yes, please—say I am a long way away.

At this moment LADY JULIA *comes into the room.*
MELANIE *jumps to her feet.*

JULIA : Please forgive me, but it was so very draughty in the hall.

MELANIE : I am at my work, Madame.

JULIA : So I see. How interesting.

MELANIE : I fear that Monsieur le Duc is not here.

JULIA : I know. It was you I wished to see.

MELANIE (*making the best of the situation*) : I am very happy, Madame. Perhaps you will sit yourself ?

JULIA (*looking round the room*) : Not just for a moment, thank you. I want to enjoy this charming room. What pretty curtains—and what a lovely view.

MELANIE : Yes, the view is pretty.

JULIA : I believe they are arranging for a new ship to travel between here and Dieppe. That will be so convenient, won't it ?

MELANIE : I do not very much like ships.

JULIA : I have so much to talk to you about. Your guardian and I are old friends, you know. We spent a great deal of our childhood together in France.

MELANIE : That is very nice.

JULIA : Is it entirely necessary for your maid to chaperon us ?

MELANIE : You will bring the tea, please, Rose.

ROSE : Yes, Mademoiselle.

She goes out reluctantly, taking the writing-table.

JULIA : It was such a pleasant surprise to see Paul—
your guardian—again. I had thought he was dead.
(JULIA *sits on the sofa.*)

MELANIE : No, he is alive.

JULIA : I suppose you are too young to remember his
wife, and his mother and father ?

MELANIE : Yes, I was young.

JULIA : I understand that you, too, were bereaved of
your parents during the Terror.

MELANIE : What, please, is " bereaved " ?

JULIA : I mean that they died. That they were
guillotined.

MELANIE : Please, I would rather not speak of
it.

JULIA : I understand that perfectly. I knew your
father many years ago.

MELANIE : Yes ?

JULIA : A most witty and delightful man.

MELANIE : Yes, he was very nice.

JULIA : It was so strange of him to keep his marriage
such a secret. Paul, apparently, was the only one who
knew anything about it.

   MELANIE *sits.*

MELANIE : It was a secret because of the Jesuits.

JULIA : The Jesuits ?

MELANIE : Yes—my father made them a promise,
when he was very little, that he never would take wife
and make marriage with himself.

JULIA : I see.

MELANIE : The Jesuits are very powerful.

JULIA : They must be. Where did you live when you
were a child ?

257

MELANIE : A grey walled château near Bordeaux. It is all very distant in my mind.

JULIA : The Château de Tramont, no doubt ?

MELANIE : Yes. There were swans.

JULIA : Graceful creatures, but disagreeable.

MELANIE : Yes, they were very disagreeable.

JULIA : There was a moat, too, I expect, and tall trees, and I suppose you were brought to Paris by your faithful old nurse ?

MELANIE : Yes.

JULIA : You were not dressed as a boy by any chance, were you ?

MELANIE : No, why should I be boy ?

JULIA : Merely a matter of convention. Perhaps you're really a boy now. Perhaps you're the Dauphin. That's quite an interesting idea.

MELANIE : I think you are laughing.

JULIA : You remember very little about your early life ?

MELANIE : It is so far away.

JULIA : So very far away from the truth !

MELANIE (*rising and drawing herself up with great dignity*) : Madame !

JULIA : My dear child, don't be absurd. The whole story is idiotic. You have been very badly rehearsed. Paul should be ashamed of himself.

MELANIE : I do not understand what you speak, Madame.

JULIA : Nonsense. You understand perfectly well.

MELANIE : And I do not understand why you come here.

JULIA : I came to find out what you were like. To see what sort of mistress Paul had picked out for himself.

MELANIE : Mistress ! I am no mistress.

JULIA : Oh, come, come, you can hardly expect me to believe that.

MELANIE (*furious*) : How dare you speak these words to me.

JULIA (*rising*) : There is no necessity for you to lose your temper, my dear.

MELANIE : Do not please call me " my dear "—do not please call me any name. Go away.

JULIA : Certainly. I have found out all that I wanted to know.

MELANIE : You have found nothing, because what you know is not true.

JULIA : You can hardly blame me for that, as you have been lying steadily to me for the last ten minutes.

MELANIE : You wish to find about me, do you ? You wish to tell all your friends and make a joke. I will explain to you more, very much more. Listen—I am the daughter of a Mandarin in China—he was my first father—my second father was a Russian Jew in Prague —he sold silks, and little jewellery, and furs for your neck—I lived in Spain—I lived in Italy—I was born in the far Indies—my mother was black, black, black ! My brothers and sisters were slaves—no, they were little pigs—they ran about in the fields trying with their big noses to find out things—like you, Madame—I am a cocotte from the streets—I am a singer of songs—I am the new wife of Napoleon Bonaparte—take these tales, Madame—take them for your friends—but take them very quickly—now, at this moment—because if you do not go away and leave me alone I will smack your painted face and pull out your dead hair by the roots !

JULIA (*quietly*) : Obviously a gutter-snipe.

At this moment PAUL *enters.* MELANIE *runs to him.*
PAUL *and* MELANIE *speak to each other from now on-*
wards in French, unless otherwise indicated.

PAUL : My dear Julia, what a charming surprise—

MELANIE : Dites-lui de s'en aller—elle me rend folle.

PAUL : Melanie—je vous prie de vous surveiller.

MELANIE : Non, je ne me surveillerai pas. J'en ai
assez de me surveiller. J'en ai assez de ces vieilles rosses
anglaises. Si elles se regorgent tant, si elles relèvent si
haut le nez, c'est sans doute pour ne pas sentir la
puanteur de leur fausse moralité. . . .

JULIA : I congratulate you, Paul.

PAUL : My dear Julia——

MELANIE : Appelez-la : "ma chère"; appelez-la : "ma
bien-aimée" si vous voulez, mais que je ne la voie plus.

PAUL : Lady Julia est une vieille amie, et je ne
supporterai pas que vous lui parliez sur ce ton.

MELANIE : Je ne me soucie pas de savoir depuis
quand elle est votre amie, mais je sais qu'elle n'a pas le
droit de venir ici, chez moi, pour m'insulter.

PAUL : Alors chaque fois que je tourne le dos
quelqu'un vous insulte—cela devient fatigant.

MELANIE : C'est pourtant vrai—on m'insulte. Cette
vieille bête curieuse m'a jeté à la figure que j'étais votre
maîtresse—Je ne le supporterai plus—Je ne resterai pas
dans ce pays, pas même pour vous—pas même pour
l'amour de Dieu. Je retourne chez les miens—chez les
honnêtes et braves gens de la rue—Je n'ai pas besoin de
leur mentir à eux—Je n'ai pas besoin d'être polie avec
eux, ni de leur faire des sourires, quand j'ai envie de les
étrangler—Je vous dis que je retourne en France—Je
partirai demain, quand je devrais nager jusque-là.

She whirls off into the bedroom and slams the door.

PAUL *and* JULIA *stand looking after her for a moment,*
then JULIA *laughs.*

JULIA : That was all very interesting.

PAUL : I hope, Julia, that since the old days your
French has not improved too much.

JULIA : I could understand the gist of what she was
saying, if not the actual words.

PAUL : How fortunate.

JULIA : I think, if only on account of our early years,
some explanation is required.

PAUL : It was unkind of you to come here and bully
the child.

JULIA : I didn't bully her. I merely wanted to find
out who and what she was. Then she flew into a
strange fury and was extremely rude. I do not like
people being rude to me.

PAUL : She shall apologise later on.

JULIA (*grandly*) : This is quite unnecessary.

ROSE *enters with tea. While she is arranging it upon*
the table, JULIA *and* PAUL *talk of other things.*

PAUL : I suppose you have been to the Pavilion ?

JULIA : Yes. I supped there the other evening. It is
quite hideous.

PAUL : Very informal, I believe ?

JULIA : Oh yes, and very agreeable. One plays cards
and dances a little. Mrs. Fitzherbert plays very high, but
then she always has, hasn't she ?

ROSE *goes out.*

PAUL : It is only by shutting the eyes of my mind
very tight that I can conjure up the school-girl I used
to know.

JULIA : Surely that is quite natural. Twenty-five
years leaves an adequate margin for change--and decay !

PAUL : Decay? (*Sadly.*) Perhaps you are right.

JULIA : Now, tell me, Paul—what does all this mean? Why are you here?

PAUL : It is an odd story, quite fantastic. I think I need you a little.

JULIA : What can I offer you? My heart, my advice, or merely a little tea? (*She goes to the table.*)

PAUL : All three.

JULIA : Surely not the first, when your own is apparently so very much engaged.

PAUL : I fear you misunderstand the situation.

JULIA : I shall be only too pleased to be enlightened. Here is the tea, anyhow. (*She hands him a cup of tea.*)

> *He stands opposite to her.*

PAUL : I feel at a loss—guilty—and yet I have nothing to be guilty about really.

JULIA : I think it was rather unkind of you to take poor Maurice de Tramont's name, and fasten it on to the first little light-of-love you meet.

> PAUL *raps his cup sharply on the saucer.*

PAUL (*icily*) : Melanie is not my light-of-love.

JULIA (*smiling incredulously*) : My dear Paul!

PAUL : It's perfectly true. She has never been anybody's light-of-love. That is her greatest asset.

JULIA : Asset?

PAUL (*he sits*) : Yes. Business asset. She is my plan. My trick to be played upon the world. My livelihood.

JULIA : Have you gone mad?

PAUL : No. I have merely transformed myself, owing to hard circumstances, from an effete aristocrat into a cunning and unscrupulous adventurer.

JULIA : That sounds faintly theatrical.

PAUL (*rising*) : The murder of my wife and child was

theatrical enough—the deaths of my mother and father and sister on the guillotine were equally theatrical. My life from then onwards, as a fugitive, was an endless succession of serio-comic stage effects. I was a baker's assistant—a lawyer's clerk—a tutor to the children of nouveaux riches parvenus. Two years ago I found Melanie singing in a café. She seemed to me to be better material than my snivelling little bourgeois pupils, so I took her away from the café and kept us both on my savings. Every now and then I procured for her an engagement to sing at a private house. Five months ago I had a stroke of luck. I managed to sell two pictures from the old house, which somehow or other had been overlooked by the revolutionaries. With that money I brought her here.

JULIA : Why ?

PAUL : She is to make a rich marriage.

JULIA : And you take commission ?

PAUL : Yes.

JULIA : In England, we describe that as pimping !

PAUL : At that rate every fondly ambitious mother is a pimp.

JULIA : That is hardly the same thing.

PAUL : Well ?

JULIA : Well—I think it is a good joke, in very bad taste.

PAUL : Taste is too expensive a social luxury for a poor man.

JULIA : I suppose the poor little thing is in love with you ?

PAUL (*startled*) : In love with me ! What nonsense ! (*He laughs.*)

JULIA : I should have thought it was inevitable.

PAUL : I appreciate the compliment, Julia, but I think it is a trifle far-fetched. This whole plan has been understood completely between us from the first as a business arrangement.

JULIA : How wise.

PAUL : Will you help me ?

JULIA : With all your worldly experiences, Paul, you have contrived to remain singularly naïf.

PAUL : At any rate, even if you cannot help, please make me a promise that you will not hinder.

JULIA : Of course if it's money you want you could always marry me. I have plenty.

PAUL (*shocked*) : Julia !

JULIA : We could find some employment for Melanie. She might even be my maid.

PAUL : I see I have made a mistake.

JULIA (*rising with decision, and patting his shoulder*) : No, Paul. Don't be afraid. I won't give away your secret, and I'll help you all I can. It should be amusing at least.

PAUL : How much do you despise me for it ?

JULIA : Just a little. If it matters to you.

PAUL : I'm sorry.

JULIA : Cunning, unscrupulous adventurers have no time to waste on conscience. Call her in. We will discuss possibilities.

PAUL : Do you think that is wise ?

JULIA : I can manage her.

PAUL : Very well. (*He goes to the bedroom door.*) Melanie. Venez ici.

 After a moment MELANIE *comes in. She sees that* JULIA *is still there and her face hardens immediately.*

PAUL : Melanie. I wish you to apologise to Lady Julia.

264

MELANIE (*firmly*) : No.

PAUL (*sternly*) : Please do as I tell you.

MELANIE : I have nothing to say.

JULIA : But it is for me to say I am sorry. I was over-inquisitive, and I jumped to conclusions too hastily. Mademoiselle, I ask your forgiveness.

MELANIE (*bowing*) : Merci, Madame.

JULIA : Shall we be friends ?

MELANIE : Je ne comprends pas.

PAUL : You are being very ungracious, Melanie.

MELANIE : I am sorry.

PAUL : I have told Lady Julia everything. She has promised to help us.

MELANIE : You have told her—what ?

JULIA : A story. Just a story, Mademoiselle, but it is a very interesting story, and I should like, as Paul and I are such old friends, to help to bring it to a happy ending.

> MELANIE *looks searchingly from one to the other, and then, with a great effort, smiles.*

MELANIE (*curtseying*) : Merci beaucoup, Madame. I understand now.

> JULIA *also curtseys.*

JULIA (*briskly*) : Come now—to business.

MELANIE (*with great manner*) : Madame will sit ?

JULIA (*sitting down*) : Thank you.

MELANIE (*enquiringly to* PAUL) : What business shall we begin ?

PAUL : We can talk quite freely in front of Lady Julia.

MELANIE : That is very nice.

JULIA : In the first place, whom do you know here ?

MELANIE (*humming softly*) : Even the sea looks grey.

PAUL : Melanie !

MELANIE (*fiercely singing*) : C'est vrai !

JULIA (*politely*) : I beg your pardon ?

MELANIE : It is nothing, Madame, but when business is here to be talked—— (*Singing.*) It seems that all the joy has faded from the day—as though the foolish world no longer wants to play——

JULIA : Really, these vocal outbursts are most disconcerting.

PAUL : Do be good, Melanie.

MELANIE : Very well—I will be good.

PAUL : Lord Sheere is our only definite proposal so far.

JULIA (*to* MELANIE) : Do you like him ?

MELANIE (*singing*) :

> I'll follow my secret heart my whole life
> through.
> I'll keep every dream apart till one comes
> true.
> No matter what price is paid,
> What stars may fade—above
> I'll follow my secret heart
> Till I find—Love.

She rises while she is singing this, and walks over to the window. She finishes with her back turned.

PAUL (*irritably*) : Melanie ! Will you kindly concentrate ?

JULIA : I do see how difficult it must be, for anyone so young and so charming, to banish sentiment entirely.

MELANIE (*turning*) : You are sympathetic, Madame, but it is not so very difficult really. Sentiment is very silly. (*She looks at* PAUL *and her voice hardens.*)

JULIA : How wise.

MELANIE : There is no sentiment in the whole world that is real.

JULIA : Wiser still.

MELANIE : Real enough to waste the time upon—Paul has spoken me that very often.

JULIA : How very sensible of him.

MELANIE : I will be sensible too and make business. (*She puts a chair by the table and sits.*) I have three with which to begin.

JULIA : Three !

MELANIE : Yes, I make the progress. First there is the Prince Regent. He wishes to sleep with me.

PAUL : Melanie !

MELANIE (*quickly*) : Do not be shocked, Paul. That is true, and we are speaking of truth.

JULIA (*laughing*) : Admirable.

MELANIE : If I do that—there is a risk—a risk that I may not stay in the royal heart long enough to gain large money for Paul.

PAUL : I will not have you speaking like that—it is intolerable.

JULIA : She is quite right, Paul. It ill becomes you to be so outraged. Remember how unscrupulous you are.

MELANIE : Then there is the Duke of Beneden. He has a little house with pretty furniture and a coach with brown horses and three hundred pounds on the first day of every month—these things would be useful, would they not ?

JULIA : Hard work, but a little more lasting than the other.

MELANIE : Then there is Lord Sheere.

JULIA : That's better.

MELANIE : He loves me.

JULIA : Excellent.

MELANIE : But if we marry, there is no money at all.

JULIA : That can soon be remedied if your social position is improved. You must first of all be presented—more or less informally, here—at the Pavilion.

PAUL : But how ? Who will present her ?

JULIA : I will, but before that you must give a little supper party. I will arrange it, and invite the guests. Lord St. Marys must come, and the Benedens, and Lord Sheere, and the Harringfords—they are very useful.

MELANIE (*rising sharply*) : Are they rich ? Have they a foolish son ? (*She goes to the window.*)

JULIA (*ignoring her, to* PAUL) : You must have cards, and good wine—Mademoiselle might sing a little—she has such a charming voice, but I should suggest songs more closely allied to the Classics than to the café chantant.

PAUL (*going over to her*) : I can never begin to express my gratitude, Julia——

JULIA : Not at all. Old friends must be kept from starving. If all else fails I shall take up a subscription for you.

PAUL : I am still very low in your eyes, I see.

JULIA : You share that position with almost everyone I know. (*Rising.*) I will leave you now. Call upon me to-morrow and we will discuss the party invitations.

PAUL : I will send for a carriage.

JULIA : My curricle is outside. (*She crosses to* MELANIE *and curtseys.*) Au revoir, Mademoiselle.

MELANIE : Au revoir, Madame.

JULIA : And please accept my admiration. Your common sense is magnificent—(*she laughs*). But you will

be careful, won't you, not to betray too much hardness
of heart. Cynicism in the young is *so* unbecoming.

> *She sweeps out, followed by* PAUL. MELANIE, *when
> they have gone, picks up* JULIA'S *handkerchief from the
> floor, sniffs it contemptuously, and pitches it into the
> waste-paper basket—as the lights fade.*

ACT II

SCENE III

QUARTETTE : FISHERMEN.
        "*There was once a little village.*"

There was once a little village by the sea,
Where we lived our lives in amiable tranquillity.
We were humble in our ways
And we swam through all our days
As little fishes swim—in immobility ;
We watched for gales in the evening sky
And we trimmed our sails till the night went by,
No less, no more,
Than stones on an English shore.

Then whimsical Fate,
Resenting our state,
Decided to break us
And mould and re-make us ;
Our sweet isolation
From civilisation

Has all vanished away.
We're urban and proud,
Supporting a crowd
Of Doxys and Dandys
And Regency Randys,
Who fiddle and faddle
And piddle and paddle
And turn night into day.
The Pavilion
Cost a million
As a monument to Art,
And the wits here
Say it sits here
Like an Oriental tart !
The dashing "beau monde "
Has ruffled our pond,
And even the turbot
Know Mrs. Fitzherbert.
We're richer than ever before
But Brighton is Brighton no more.

ACT II

SCENE IV

The Scene is a larger room on the ground floor of MELANIE'S
*house. It is circular and the ceiling is supported by
pillars. There are two sets of double doors upstage
right and left. Downstage, almost on the footlights,
there are two curved benches. There is a buffet on the*

*left side of the stage upon which are jugs of iced wine
and elaborate cakes and other delicacies. From behind
the right-hand double doors comes the sound of music.
There are candles on the buffet, and in sconces on the
walls. Hanging in the centre is a large crystal chandelier.
Up at the back of the stage between the door there is a
low dais upon which is a clavisan.*

When the Curtain rises the GUESTS *are grouped, with*
JULIA *and* PAUL *in the centre, forming a beautiful
"still" picture. This attitude is held through a phrase
of music, when, at a given point, the "picture" comes
to life, and the party is in progress.*

*Note : Throughout this Scene there are musical "stops"
to allow the dialogue to be heard. All guests, etc., not
actually concerned in dialogue, remain immovable, in
whichever positions they may be.*

*There is the sound of laughter and dancing from
ballroom.* GUESTS *are strolling about and chatting to
one another. There are several people clustered round
the buffet.*

PAUL *and* JULIA *are standing centre. A* BUTLER
flings open the doors left, and announces, in succession :

BUTLER : Lady Mosscrock. The Earl and Countess
of Harringford.

The HARRINGFORDS *enter and* PAUL *goes forward
to receive them. The conversation is too general for
their exact greetings to be heard. They come over to*
JULIA *and talk for a little, meanwhile the* BUTLER
announces in succession : MR. *and* MRS. HAILSHAM,
THE LADY BRACEWORTH, THE HONOURABLE
JULIAN KANE, LORD DOYNING. (*Musical stop.*)

LADY H. (*to* JULIA): What a charming house, and what a lovely party. You must come to tea to-morrow and tell me the name of our host over and over again. I know I shall never remember it.

JULIA : The Duc de Chaucigny-Varennes.

LADY H. : The French do seem to go out of their way to make things hard for us, don't they ? All those hyphens.

LORD H. : Where's the girl you told us about ? The ward or niece or whatever she is.

JULIA : You shall see her soon. She is very lovely.
    Music resumes.
    They pass on to talk to someone else. The BUTLER *announces* THE DUKE *and* DUCHESS OF BENEDEN. *When they enter* PAUL *receives them politely but with a certain hauteur. Presently the* DUCHESS *takes* JULIA'S *arm and walks her downstage left. They sit for a few moments on the curved bench.* (*Musical stop.*)

DUCHESS : Julia. I must tell you frankly. I do not understand at all. I am completely at a loss.

JULIA : Why, Georgina ?

DUCHESS : Frederick made me come, I still don't approve——

JULIA : You have no reason not to approve. You merely jumped to conclusions too hastily. As usual.

DUCHESS : Do you mean to tell me——

JULIA : I don't mean to tell you anything, Georgina, except that I have known the Chaucigny-Varennes family all my life, and that Paul is one of my oldest friends.

DUCHESS : But the girl—I can't believe——

JULIA : You made a grave mistake, and all I can suggest is that you remedy it as soon as possible. Melanie will be down soon.

The DUKE *joins them.*

DUKE : Is Edward here?

JULIA : I haven't seen him yet.

DUCHESS : He hasn't spoken to me for four days.

JULIA : You really can't be surprised. You both of you made a bad blunder.

DUCHESS : But those dreadful women! Trying on each other's hats.

JULIA : Melanie is a stranger here. How was she to know whom to receive and whom not to receive?

DUCHESS : Very well, Julia, I'll take your word for it, for the time being, but I'm still not convinced.

Music resumes—Short phrase—Musical stop.

She moves away to talk to LADY HARRINGFORD.

JULIA : Really, Frederick, Georgina is more disagreeable than ever.

DUKE : She is upset.

JULIA : You've been saying that for twenty years.

DUKE : It's been true for twenty years.

JULIA : I don't know how you've stood it.

DUKE : On the contrary, you should know better than anyone.

JULIA (*laughing*) : Yes, Frederick, perhaps I should. Poor Georgina.

DUKE : The years have changed you very little.

JULIA : Thank you, Frederick.

DUKE : Dear Julia. (*He kisses her hand.*)

JULIA : That gesture was reminiscent—almost painfully so. Fortunately the light is too strong to allow us to deceive ourselves.

DUKE : Deceive ourselves?

JULIA : Into a momentary belief that we were young again.

DUKE : Julia—do you remember——?

JULIA : I remember nothing. That is one of my greatest virtues. Who is your mistress at the moment ?

DUKE : Really, Julia !

JULIA : Or have you retired from public love ?

(*Music resumes.*)

She curtseys to him rather mockingly, and goes over to PAUL. *The* DUKE *moves over to the buffet. There is a general buzz of conversation during which* LORD SHEERE *and* LORD ST. MARYS *are announced and make their entrance.* PAUL *receives them.*

(*Musical stop.*)

MELANIE *comes in quite quietly and unostentatiously, but even so, her entrance is the signal for the conversation to die down. People turn, with elaborate casualness, to scrutinize her. She looks pale, but very lovely.*

MELANIE (*to* PAUL) : My dress would not manage itself. I am so sorry. (*She curtseys to* JULIA.) Madame.

JULIA : You look delicious, my dear.

MELANIE : Merci, Madame.

She curtseys to EDWARD *and* LORD ST. MARYS.

JULIA (*to the* DUCHESS OF BENEDEN) : Georgina—I want to present to you Mademoiselle Melanie de Tramont.

DUCHESS (*stiffly*) : How do you do ?

MELANIE (*curtseying low*) : I am honoured, Madame.

DUCHESS (*with an effort*) : I am delighted to see you again.

MELANIE : Again ? Ah, forgive me, Madame, but I am so quite sure that we have never, never met before.

DUCHESS : That is very charming of you, Mademoiselle.

The DUKE *comes up.*

PAUL : Ah, Monsieur le Duc, I wish to present my ward, Melanie de Tramont.

> *The* DUKE *bows low, and again* MELANIE *curtseys.*

DUKE : I hope you are enjoying yourself in England, Mademoiselle ?

MELANIE : Yes, I love it here. The sea is so pretty !

> (*Music resumes.*)
> (*Musical stop.*)
> *The* BUTLER *flings open the doors and announces :*
> MRS. JAMES, MRS. OTFORD *and* MRS. DRAGON.
> *There is a horrified silence for a moment or two.*

PAUL : Melanie ! Did you invite them ?

MELANIE : Pourquoi pas ? They are my friends.

> SOPHIE *and* MARTHA *enter, followed discreetly by* MRS. DRAGON. *They are extravagantly dressed and over-bejewelled.*

SOPHIE : My dear, what a *lovely* party.

MARTHA : So sweet of you to ask us.

> *They curtsey.* MELANIE *greets them with enthusiasm.*

JULIA (*to* PAUL) : This is idiotic !

PAUL : We must get rid of them.

JULIA : It's too late now. Oh, what an abysmal mistake !

DUCHESS (*to* PAUL, *sweetly*) : Good night, Monsieur. It has been so delightful.

PAUL : But surely, Duchess, you are not leaving ?

DUCHESS : A sudden headache. It will be better in the morning. My husband, I am sure, will be delighted to stay.

> *She bows coldly to* JULIA *and goes out.* LADY HARRINGFORD *comes up to* PAUL.

LADY H. : Good night, Monsieur—I have to drive to London early to-morrow and I am very tired.

(Music resumes.)

PAUL *bows, and she goes off after the* DUCHESS.

Nearly all the women in the room come up in turn to say good-bye to PAUL, *but you do not hear the exact excuses they give because* MELANIE *has led* SOPHIE *and* MARTHA *and* MRS. DRAGON *downstage right to the bench.*

(Musical stop.)

JULIA (*to* PAUL): You see! *(She sits.)*

SOPHIE: We should scold you, Melanie.

MELANIE: What is "scold"?

MARTHA: Be angry.

MELANIE: Angry! Why?

SOPHIE: We didn't know it was this sort of party.

MELANIE: I do not understand.

SOPHIE: We never like meeting these sort of women.

MARTHA: Most of them are the wives of our gentlemen, you know. It's very awkward.

SOPHIE: Don't stand there twiddling your fingers, Dragon. Go and get yourself some claret.

MRS. DRAGON *goes over to the buffet.*

MELANIE (*noticing what is happening*): They have all gone away—all the ladies.

SOPHIE: That's our fault.

MELANIE (*suddenly angry*): I understand now—very, very well—Paul——

PAUL *comes over to her.*

Paul—I do not believe you know Madame Otford and Madame James.

PAUL (*bowing coldly*): Enchanted.

MELANIE: These ladies have been very kind to me —I should like that you know that—they have made me happy——

276

PAUL : That is delightful.

SOPHIE : I think we had better go, Martha. I feel quite faint.

MELANIE : If you go, I will go with you.

PAUL : Don't be ridiculous, Melanie.

MELANIE (*to* SOPHIE) : You must not go—you must stay for me to sing—it is all arranged—Lord Sheere—Lord St. Marys——

> EDWARD *and* LORD ST. MARYS *come over to her.*

PAUL : Melanie !

MELANIE : This is my party, Paul. I wish to enjoy myself. Lord Sheere, Lord St. Marys—I have something to say to you—where is the Duke ?—I have something to say to him also.

JULIA (*rising*) : What is happening ?

MELANIE : Nothing, Madame, except that I am going to sing—it was planned that I should sing—because I sing so charmingly, do I not ? (*To* EDWARD *and* LORD ST. MARYS.) Messieurs, you will sit, please, next to my two friends—ah, Monsieur le Duc de Beneden—I wish that you pay very special favour to a lady much in my esteem—Mrs. Dragon——

> *She darts to the buffet and brings* MRS. DRAGON *over to the* DUKE. MRS. DRAGON *looks slightly flustered owing to having a glass of claret in one hand and a large sandwich in the other. However, she manages to curtsey, a trifle unsteadily.*

Where is Mr. Jones ? He is to play—please find Mr. Jones, Paul——

JULIA (*laughing, none too pleasantly*) : Excellent—the whole situation is most entertaining.

MELANIE : I am glad if you are gay, Madame—I would like that everybody is gay.

PAUL (*to* MELANIE): Melanie—écoutez! Je veux vous dire quelque chose d'importance——

MELANIE: Do not speak in French, Paul—I cannot understand—I can understand only English among my English friends—ah, there is Mr. Jones—please play for me, Mr. Jones—Mr. Jones plays very light, very pretty—everybody will please sit—Monsieur le Marquis —it is from the distance that you see me now—please for me remember that—Monsieur le Duc—when you are in your small house in London, with the shutters drawn—think sweetly of me, because I shall be far away—Lord St. Marys, you have proposed such kind honours, but I am too little in life to say Yes or No— I may only say merci——

MR. JONES *begins to play the clavisan. Everybody sits down, looking faintly bewildered.* PAUL *remains standing, near* JULIA. MELANIE *starts to sing. First she sings to* EDWARD, *briefly, but with very genuine sweetness. Then she turns to the* DUKE OF BENEDEN. *For him, the words she sings are tinged with gentle malice. She sings to* LORD ST. MARYS *smilingly and with a certain mocking deference. Last of all she turns suddenly towards* PAUL. *To him she sings in French, an unmistakable love song. Her whole heart is in her voice.* PAUL *starts back in horrified amazement.* JULIA'S *face hardens into an expression of ill-repressed fury.*

(*Musical Finale.*)

MELANIE: Dear Friends,
              Will you forgive me, pray,
              If many of the words I say
              In English may be wrong.
ALL: She hasn't been in England very long.

278

MELANIE : A stranger in a foreign land,
I beg that you will understand
How gratefully I find
The gentlemen so very kind,
So very kind.

(*To the* DUKE OF BENEDEN.)
The offer of protection
That Monsieur le Duc has made
I set aside,
For my foolish pride
Would feel itself betrayed.

ALL : Charming—Charming—Charming !

MELANIE (*to* LORD ST. MARYS) :
Monsieur, my Lord St. Marys
Has made me an offer too.
Royal though his scheme may be,
It could never be part of a dream for me.

ALL : Ah la la la—la la—la la.

MELANIE : Handsome though your Prince may be,
He is far too broad in the beam for
me.

(*To the* MARQUIS OF SHEERE.)
But there is one, one only,
Who honours me with his heart,
Although I'm not the wife for him
I shall cherish all my life for him
A feeling somehow apart.
I'd suffer sorrow and strife for him.
Though we may be lovers never,
We're friends for ever—for evermore.

(*Spoken.*)
Thank you, my dear, for being so sweet to me.

EDWARD (*kissing her hand*) : Melanie !

279

MELANIE : There is only room for one true love in my heart—my secret heart.

EDWARD : I understand.

MELANIE : I know you do.

JULIA : This is most illuminating.

MELANIE : Paul !

PAUL (*horrified*) : Melanie—please——

MELANIE (*simply*) : It is you I love, I always have, from the very beginning—— (*She sings.*)

> C'est assez de mensonge,
> Le secret qui me ronge,
> Que tout au fond de moi
> J'ai tendrement gardé.
> Enfin avec franchise
> Il faut que je vous dise,
> Avouant mon secret,
> Que tu n'as pas compris
> Plus de cœur discret,
> C'est toi qui par l'amour,
> Toi qui m'as délivrée,
> Je suis à toi toujours.
> Esclave de mon cœur,
> Me rendras-tu la vie.
> Je t'en supplie, crois-moi,
> Lorsque je dis c'est toi
> Plus de cœur discret.
> C'est toi qui par l'amour,
> Toi qui m'as délivrée,
> Je suis à toi toujours.
> Esclave de mon cœur,
> Me rendras-tu la vie.
> Je t'en supplie, crois-moi,
> Je t'en supplie, crois-moi,

C'est Toi.
Parmi le monde entier c'est toi que j'aime.
Je t'en supplie,
Crois-le si même
Tu ne le veux.
Toi,
Parmi le monde entier c'est toi que j'aime,
Je suis à toi Toujours.

At the end of the song MELANIE *swoons. There is an immediate buzz of excited conversation.* SOPHIE *runs forward, followed by* MARTHA. LORD ST. MARYS *hurries forward with a chair.*

SOPHIE : Dragon—fetch some wine—quickly——

MARTHA : Feathers—burn them under her nose—here—— (*She tears some feathers out of her hair.*)

SOPHIE : That's no good.

JULIA : A strange performance.

PAUL (*quivering*) : Please go now—I wish that every-one should go.

All the men start to go.

JULIA : Very well—poor Paul—I am so sorry.

PAUL : To-morrow—we will talk to-morrow.

JULIA : Frederick !—Edward—will you please see me to my carriage ?

JULIA *and the* DUKE *exeunt.*

SOPHIE (*to* MELANIE) : It's all right, dear—we're all going——

MELANIE (*opening her eyes*) : Paul.

MARTHA : Just lie still a minute.

SOPHIE : Come away, Martha.

MARTHA : All right, all right, I'm coming——

They go to the door, call DRAGON *and all go out. During this scene nearly everyone has gone.* MELANIE

is sitting on a chair, very white and quite still. PAUL
sees the last guest, EDWARD, *out, and closes the door.*

PAUL (*in a cold voice*) : Well—I hope you're satisfied.

MELANIE (*pleadingly*) : Paul !

PAUL : Everything is ruined—everything is finished.

MELANIE : Je vous aime.

PAUL : Ne vous moquez pas de moi.

MELANIE : Non, c'est vrai. Je vous ai toujours
aimé.

PAUL : Vous avez d'étranges façons de me témoigner
votre amour ; en me rendant ridicule.

MELANIE : Est-ce si ridicule d'être aimé de moi ?

PAUL : Il ne peut pas y avoir d'amour entre nous ;
une folie—voilà tout.

MELANIE : Non, c'est vrai.

PAUL : Savez-vous seulement ce qui est vrai ? Vous
avez manqué à tous vos engagements, vous m'avez
menti, vous êtes jouée de moi.

Angrily he crosses to the sofa L.

MELANIE : Et pourquoi m'en serais-je privée ? Dans
toutes vos adroites combinaisons avez-vous un seul
instant—pensé—à moi ? Jamais !

PAUL : Pardon—tout était convenu entre nous dès le
début. Vous saviez tout et vous aviez tout accepté.

MELANIE ; Bien sûr, j'avais tout accepté. Une fille
dans la situation où j'étais, aurait été folle de ne pas
tout accepter.

PAUL : C'était un contrat d'affaires, et vous y avez
manqué.

MELANIE : Pouvais-je répondre de mon cœur ?

PAUL : De votre cœur !

MELANIE : Je vous aime, vous entendez. Vous
pouvez dire que je suis folle, vous pouvez vous per-

suader que tout ceci est stupidement romanesque : cela
vous met à votre aise, n'est-ce pas ?

PAUL : Je suis parfaitement à mon aise.

MELANIE : Mais c'est vrai, et mon amour est au fond
de moi, au plus profond de moi. De ma vie, aucun
sentiment n'a poussé en moi des racines si profondes.
Regardez-moi maintenant — regardez-moi bien ! — je
vous en prie, vous qui êtes si sage et si stupidement
cruel—vous—l'homme le plus adroit que je connaisse
et, de loin, le plus imbécile.

PAUL : Merci !

MELANIE : Vous avez pour toujours renoncé à
l'amour, quand votre femme a été tuée, n'est-ce pas ?
Dieu merci, vous me l'avez assez souvent répété.

PAUL : Melanie, je vous en prie !

MELANIE : Et alors vous pensez pouvoir traverser
la vie à l'abri, inaccessible, dans une magnifique
sécurité, n'est-ce pas ?

PAUL : Je me passerai fort bien de vos conseils.

MELANIE : Vous m'avez ramassée dans le ruisseau
et vous m'avez appris la révérence et à faire les manières
et à mentir à la vie.

PAUL : C'était bien nécessaire.

MELANIE : Mais voilà que, tout à coup, la vie a pris
sa revanche, et elle s'est jouée de vous—et elle s'en
jouera toujours. La vie est trop puissante en moi pour
que j'accepte vos combinaisons. C'est vrai la vie—et
c'est important—plus important que votre tranquillité
et que votre cynisme prudent.

PAUL : Vous perdez le sens.

MELANIE : Allez-vous-en, et réfléchissez un peu.
Allez-vous-en, et comprenez brusquement quel mal
infini vous avez essayé de me faire.

PAUL : C'en est trop !

MELANIE : —et à vous aussi——

PAUL : C'en est trop !

MELANIE : —je t'aime—je t'aime—je t'aime—et toi aussi quelque part au fond de toi—tu m'aimes.

> PAUL *starts to go.*

Tout me le crie. Chacun de mes instincts, chaque battement de mon cœur, chaque bouffée d'air que je respire. Vous allez essayer de m'échapper—cela aussi je le sais—mais vous ne le pourrez pas——

> *He is just going out of the door and she breaks down completely.*

—vous ne le pourrez pas——

> *She sinks into the chair, sobbing. The last chords of her love song to him crash out in the orchestra as—*

THE CURTAIN FALLS

ACT III

Scene I

The Scene is " The Steyne " and the time of day is about noon. It is a clear sunny morning and there are a good many people strolling about. As usual, there is an undercurrent of music to the whole scene, and Characters pass as in the First Act.

Miss Goslett and Miss Mention walk slowly across, talking.

MISS GOSLETT : You don't put the nutmeg on until afterwards.

MISS MENTION : I still don't understand. Surely if you leave it too long to cool, it gets lumpy.

MISS GOSLETT : Not if you stir it enough in the first place.

MISS MENTION : And why a *wooden* spoon ?

MISS GOSLETT : It says so in the recipe.

MISS MENTION : Well, personally I prefer to remain faithful to the ordinary tapioca.

They both pass out of sight.

The Lady Braceworth enters right with the Duchess of Beneden. They meet Mrs. Hailsham centre, who has come on from the left.

DUCHESS : Good morning, Amelia.

MRS. HAILSHAM : My dear. (*They kiss.*)

LADY B. : Amelia.

MRS. HAILSHAM : My dear. (*They kiss.*)

DUCHESS : How is Mortimer ?

MRS. HAILSHAM : Worse, I'm afraid. He had a shivering fit at three this morning. I've been up half the night.

LADY B. : How dreadful !

MRS. HAILSHAM : When he crept into my bed at about six he seemed calmer, but his nose was very hot and dry.

DUCHESS : You really should take him to the Vet.

MRS. HAILSHAM : I intend to this afternoon.

   LADY HARRINGFORD *joins them.*

LADY H. : Georgina.

DUCHESS : Ettie. (*They kiss.*)

LADY H. : Amelia !

LADY B. : Good morning, Ettie. (*They kiss.*)

LADY H. : Louisa !

MRS. HAILSHAM : My dear. (*They kiss.*)

LADY H. : I've had a horrible morning. Nono was sick three times at breakfast.

DUCHESS : Perhaps it's an epidemic.

LADY H. : I shall take him to the Vet. this afternoon.

LADY B. : Is he a really good Vet. ?

MRS. HAILSHAM : Charming, my dear, absolutely charming.

LADY B. : Then I shall come with you this afternoon and bring Fifi.

DUCHESS : Is she ill too ?

LADY B. : Well, not exactly ill, but moody.

LADY H. : There's probably something in the air here, it's very strong.

DUCHESS : Funnily enough it seems to suit Boney very well. He's much brighter here than in Shropshire.

MRS. HAILSHAM : Shropshire *is* enervating.

DUCHESS : I can't decide whether it's the sea air or the sulphur tablets, but he's certainly a different dog.

LADY B. : I'm so glad, because I never cared for him very much as he was.

DUCHESS : It betrays a small mind, Louisa, to be offended just because he didn't take to you at the very first moment.

MRS. HAILSHAM : I don't like animals to be too friendly.

DUCHESS : At any rate he is a remarkably good house-dog.

LADY B. : I should say more thorough than good.

DUCHESS : Really, Louisa !

MRS. HAILSHAM : How is Frederick ?

DUCHESS : I really don't know, he didn't come home until four.

LADY H. : Neither did James.

MRS. HAILSHAM : Nor Robert.

LADY B. : Desmond hasn't come home yet.

LADY H. : It's such a bad example for the children. They ask such difficult questions.

DUCHESS : That dreadful party, and those appalling women. I shall never forgive Julia.

LADY B. : She must be mad.

LADY H. : The French Duke seemed polite, I thought, but peculiar.

MRS. HAILSHAM : My dear, (*to music*) there's always something fishy about the French.

DUCHESS : As a race they're erotic.

LADY B. : And completely idiotic.

LADY H. : Still, they have a certain air.

MRS. HAILSHAM : A " flair."

DUCHESS : Whatever you say, I don't believe a word of it.

> *They all talk together.*

MRS. HAILSHAM : I didn't object to the girl so much, of course she was quite obviously common——

LADY B. It's all very fine to excuse them on the grounds of being foreigners, but really——

LADY H. : Never in all my life have I had such a shock as when the door opened and those women came into the room——

DUCHESS : It's entirely Julia's fault. She gave me her solemn promise that she had known the Duke for years——

> *On the last phrase of "Fishy about the French," which the orchestra has been playing softly during this scene, they all sing suddenly together.*

ALL FOUR : There's *always* something fishy about the French !

> *This last line leads them into their quartette, " Mothers and Wives," during which* SOPHIE, MARTHA, MRS. DRAGON *and another courtesan trip gaily across the scene on the arms of the* DUKE OF BENEDEN, MR. HAILSHAM, LORD BRACEWORTH *and* LORD HAR-RINGFORD.

QUARTETTE : " MOTHERS AND WIVES."

> In an atmosphere of bawdy jeu d'esprit
> We contrive to be tenaciously conventional,
> Tho' intelligent, we hope,
> Our imaginative scope
> When all is said and done
> Is one-dimensional.

Our appearance should be ample guarantee
Of our vigorous and rigorous morality,
We regard our husbands' gout
As a proper and devout
And Godly recompense
For sensuality.
But when we look at our greying hairs
We sometimes sigh as we say our prayers,
Dear Lord,
We're bored,
Is virtue enough reward?

*Finally, at the end of the quartette, the mothers and
wives go disconsolately away, leaving the stage comparatively empty save for a few pedestrians who pass
and re-pass from time to time.* JULIA *and* PAUL *enter
from the left. During this scene, characters pass by at
given moments.*

JULIA : My dear Paul, such sentimentality is utterly
ridiculous.

PAUL : That is how I feel.

JULIA : Those feelings may do credit to your heart,
but certainly not to your intelligence.

PAUL : It has nothing to do with my heart.

JULIA : Are you sure?

PAUL (*vehemently*) : Quite sure.

JULIA : Then be sensible. This idiotic charade cannot
go on any further, you must see that.

PAUL : Yes, I see that.

JULIA : She is a nice little thing and, I am sure,
perfectly sincere, but as is only to be expected, when a
girl of her class is suddenly plumped down in an entirely
different milieu, her values have become hopelessly
confused.

PAUL : How can I send her away ? She has done her best.

JULIA : It was a business contract between you, and now it is over.

PAUL : I know, but——

JULIA : She made a fool of you last night. She took your pride from you, and your position from you, and those are all that you have left.

PAUL : Not intentionally.

JULIA : Look at me for a moment, Paul, carefully and clearly. I am middle-aged and lonely and, oddly enough, I love you.

PAUL : Julia !

JULIA : Don't affect such surprise. You must know it perfectly well. You must have known that I would not have taken all this trouble to help you with a scheme of which I heartily disapproved if I had not realised, in the first moment of seeing you again, that over all these years, and through all our strange adventures, you are the one man in the whole world that I love, and that I have always loved.

PAUL : What can I say to you, Julia ?

JULIA : The truth, whatever it may be.

PAUL : I don't believe I know it.

JULIA (*smiling*) : Dear Paul.

PAUL : Are you laughing at me ?

JULIA : Just a little.

PAUL : I am sure you are right to laugh, but please don't, I feel small enough already, and cheap, and of no account.

JULIA : You are worrying about Melanie ?

PAUL : Of course.

JULIA : Listen to me. She is not happy here, she

never has been. We will send her back to Paris with
enough money to keep her in comfort until she finds
a nice husband for herself of her own class.

PAUL : I have no money.

JULIA : I have, a lot.

PAUL : Julia !

JULIA : Please, please, I beseech you to be sensible.
Money cannot matter between us, just as the wild
ecstasies of passion cannot matter between us. I am
rich and, as I said before, lonely. You are poor, and
equally lonely. We have still time for many years of
happiness together—Paul——

She knocks at the door.

PAUL : If only I could have known before.

JULIA : Fate has offered us a wonderful chance. It
would be foolish to allow it to slip away.

PAUL : Perhaps you are right—perhaps this is the
truth.

JULIA : The truth is here, very clear and simple.
Two very old friends have suddenly, unaccountably,
found each other again——

*She holds out her hand to him and he kisses it. During
this scene all the lights have faded except on the exact
spot where they are standing. As JULIA turns to go into
the house, this light also fades.*

ACT III

Scene II

The Scene is Melanie's *room again.*

When the Curtain rises Melanie *and* Edward *are discovered clasped tightly in each other's arms. They do not move until* Rose *enters.*

Rose : Mademoiselle.

Melanie (*over* Edward's *shoulder*) : Yes ?

Rose : It was only the milkman.

Melanie (*irritably*) : Oh—— (*To* Edward.) Then we will sit down again.

Rose : Do you want some fresh chocolate ?

Melanie (*feeling the chocolate pot on the table*) : No, this is still quite hot.

Rose *goes out.*

Edward : I think I should like a little.

Melanie (*pouring it out*) : Here—— (*She motions him to sit.*) There is a little cake, too, if you would care.

Edward : No, thank you.

Melanie (*eating one*) : They are delicious.

Edward : Very well, I will try one. (*He takes a cake.*)

Melanie : What will we speak of ?

Edward : I don't know.

Melanie (*smiling*) : You are so very sweet.

Edward : I don't think we will speak of that, anyhow.

Melanie : And very, very kind.

Edward : No, really I'm not.

MELANIE : And my very, very good friend.

EDWARD : I hope so. I do hope so.

MELANIE : Would you have another small cake ?

EDWARD : Yes, please.

MELANIE : I will also.

They both have another cake.

MELANIE : In Paris there are very lovely cakes.

EDWARD : There must be.

There is a rat-tat-tat at the front door. They both put their chocolate cups down hurriedly.

MELANIE : Quickly.

EDWARD : I say, my mouth's full.

MELANIE : Never mind—so is mine.

They fly into each other's arms and stand motionless. Presently ROSE *re-enters.*

ROSE : It's only the girl from Mrs. Baxter's, with a bill.

MELANIE : Send her away.

ROSE : I have.

She goes out.

MELANIE (*going to the window*) : I am so very sorry.

EDWARD : He must come soon, mustn't he ?

MELANIE : Yes, he is late now.

EDWARD : I wish that you loved me, really.

MELANIE : So do I. You would be so easy to love.

EDWARD : Are you unhappy ?

MELANIE : Yes.

EDWARD : Because you love him so much ?

MELANIE : Because he does not love me—enough.

EDWARD : Do you think he ever will ?

MELANIE : Yes. I know it.

EDWARD : I shall remember you always—whatever happens to me.

MELANIE : I will remember you too. I will re-member how you put away your own happiness to help me, and even if we see each other again very little, and even when we become very old people, and even when the day comes when I must die, you will be in my heart truly as a kind and dear friend.

" NEVERMORE."   MELANIE.

Verse.

Dear Friend,
If hearts could only be
Content with love and sympathy.
How sweetly we could live,
We both of us have so much love to give.
No matter how our minds conspire,
Imprisoned by our own desire,
We are not free to choose.
What love we gain,
What love we lose,
We cannot choose.

Refrain.

Nevermore. Nevermore,
Can life be quite the same.
The lights and shadows change,
All the old familiar world is strange,
Evermore. Evermore,
Our hearts are in the flame.
Others may regain their freedom,
But for you and me,
Never-nevermore.

EDWARD : Melanie !

294

He takes her in his arms and kisses her. PAUL *enters
quietly and sees them. He looks angry for a moment, and
then assumes a charming smile.*

PAUL : I hope I am not intruding.

MELANIE (*breaking away*) : Paul !

PAUL : I see that you have returned to reason.

MELANIE : Yes, Paul.

PAUL : I am glad.

MELANIE : Yes, Paul.

PAUL : Lord Sheere, I congratulate you.

EDWARD (*stiffly*) : Thank you.

PAUL : It is so pretty to see Youth—in love.

EDWARD : Love is a very strange sensation, Monsieur
le Duc—for Youth, particularly so. When one is young
one feels things so strongly. One feels—foolishly
perhaps—that the very fact of loving is enough—
worth making all sacrifices for. It is sad—almost tragic
—to think that with age so much of the best in life
loses its savour. You have my sympathy, Monsieur
le Duc.

He bows abruptly to both of them and goes out. PAUL
goes to the writing table.

PAUL : You should be very happy with him. He
seems to be quite suitably unbalanced.

MELANIE : Yes, Paul.

PAUL : You are going to marry him ?

MELANIE : Yes, Paul.

PAUL : I am very glad.

MELANIE : Yes, Paul.

PAUL : But I think it is a little vulgar of you to fall
into his arms with such abandon, so soon after the
scene you made last night.

MELANIE : Yes, Paul.

PAUL : The game is over now, so you can speak in French if you like.

MELANIE : Oui, Paul.

PAUL (*irritably*) : Qu'est-ce que vous avez ce matin ?

MELANIE : I think I would prefer to talk in English.

PAUL : Pourquoi ?

MELANIE : Because it feels more happy—to-day.

PAUL : You are in love ?

MELANIE : Yes, Paul.

PAUL : So am I.

MELANIE : Oh ! (*She laughs.*)

PAUL : Why do you laugh ?

MELANIE : I thought you would say that.

PAUL : I am going to marry Lady Julia.

MELANIE (*calmly*) : Yes, Paul.

PAUL : Can you say nothing else but " Yes, Paul " ?

MELANIE : There is nothing else to say.

PAUL : The whole thing has been a mistake—a ridiculous horrible mistake.

MELANIE : Yes, Paul.

PAUL : When are you going to be married ?

MELANIE : Soon—very soon.

PAUL : What about money ?

MELANIE : That will not matter. It never does.

PAUL : I will see that you have everything you want.

MELANIE : That is very kind—of Lady Julia.

PAUL : Why do you stare at me like that ?

MELANIE : I am sorry.

PAUL : Have you anything to reproach me with ?

MELANIE : No.

She shrugs her shoulders and walks away.

PAUL : Melanie—— (*He goes to her.*)

MELANIE : Yes, Paul.

PAUL : I am sorry—very sorry.

MELANIE : No, no, I am good now—you cannot make me cry.

PAUL : I don't want to make you cry. I wish with all my heart for you to be happy.

MELANIE : I will be happy then.

He stirs a cup of chocolate.

PAUL : Will you stay here? The rent is paid for six weeks more.

MELANIE : I do not know.

PAUL : I am going to London.

MELANIE : When?

PAUL : To-morrow.

MELANIE : So soon?

PAUL : But I will come back—in a little while—to make all arrangements for your marriage.

MELANIE : Very well.

PAUL : Does that satisfy you? (*He drops a spoon noisily.*)

MELANIE : Yes, Paul. (*She turns away.*)

PAUL : Please don't look sad.

She walks away.

MELANIE : It is not real sadness.

PAUL : All comedies must come to an end.

MELANIE (*turning again*) : I have one thing to ask— it is very small.

PAUL : What is it?

MELANIE : Come once more to see me before you go.

PAUL : No—no——

MELANIE : Please—it is not much to ask—come this evening to a little supper—I will invite Lady Julia also, and Edward, my fiancé—it will be to celebrate that we are all so happy.

PAUL : C'est un enfantillage.

MELANIE : It will be very gay, and at the same time it will be a little sad—but please, please in memory of our happy days together—please say you will come ?

PAUL : But, Melanie—my dear child——

MELANIE (*very softly*) : Please ?

PAUL : Very well.

MELANIE : Merci, mon cher, cher ami——

> *She goes up to him quite simply and kisses him on the mouth. He instinctively succumbs to her kiss for a moment, and then, breaking away from her abruptly, he goes hurriedly from the room. She is left standing still for a moment, and then, with an expression of triumph on her face, she runs to the window to see him go. She begins to sing gaily and a trifle hysterically, and she is still singing as she runs towards her room as the lights fade.*

ACT III

SCENE III

The following Scene is cued to music.

> *This Scene is the gardens again. It is evening, and although most of the lights are still shining, there are very few people about. Occasionally a couple stroll across and are lost to sight among the shadows. The orchestra plays softly and sentimentally. Presently* PAUL *enters. He stands looking about him for a moment, as though he were lost. Two lovers cross in front of him, so engrossed*

*in each other that they do not even notice him. He walks
slowly down to the bench left. As he is about to sit down
upon it, two more lovers pass. They stop still for a
moment in a close embrace and then go on their way.*
PAUL *sits down disconsolately. Somewhere in the distance* MELANIE'S *voice is heard singing.* PAUL *starts
to his feet sharply, and then sinks back again, realising
that the voice is only in his mind. The little boy who
bowled the hoop in the first scene comes on, but this time
his hoop is looped over his left arm while his right
encircles the waist of a little girl. They giggle happily
across the stage and disappear. The music swells, and
with it,* MELANIE'S *voice grows louder.* PAUL *rises with
his hands to his ears and starts to move away, but wherever
he turns he is met by lovers. The whole scene slides almost
imperceptibly into a form of ballet. Finally with all the
lovers circling round him and tormenting him, he breaks
away and runs off the stage, as the lights fade.*

ACT III

SCENE IV

The Scene is MELANIE'S *room again. The room has been
completely dismantled. There are neither curtains, rugs,
nor furniture left. The floor is covered with straw and
shavings and pieces of rope, all the paraphernalia of
packing. The windows are wide open, and strong moon-
light floods into the room, which, itself, is lit only by
a few meagre candles. The noise of the waves on the*

*shingle can be plainly heard. Arranged round the room
are various boxes and trunks and packing cases. At
one of these* ROSE *is kneeling, with a pile of clothes on
the floor beside her.*
There is a knock on the door.

ROSE (*over her shoulder*): Come in.
      EDWARD *enters. He gives a little start of astonish-
ment.* ROSE *rises to her feet.*
EDWARD: The front door was open, so I came
straight——
ROSE: I left it open on purpose, in case I didn't
hear.
EDWARD: What has happened?
ROSE: There is a note for you.
EDWARD: Where is Mademoiselle?
ROSE: She has gone.
EDWARD: Gone!
ROSE: The note will explain everything. Here it is.
      *She hands him a note, which is lying on one of the
packing cases.*
EDWARD: Thank you. (*He opens it and reads it by
the light of one of the candles.*)
      ROSE *resumes her packing.*
EDWARD: Where has she gone? She doesn't say.
ROSE: France. She left on the evening boat for
Dieppe. You can see its lights out there, the sea is
calm, so it isn't going very fast.
      *He crosses sadly to the opposite window, looks out,
then reverently kisses the note. While he is standing
looking out of the window there are footsteps on the stairs
and* LADY JULIA *sweeps into the room.*
JULIA: Good Heavens!

EDWARD : I fear that Mademoiselle is not entertaining this evening after all.

JULIA : Obviously.

EDWARD : She has gone.

JULIA : Do you know, I almost gathered that.

ROSE : There is a note for you, Madame.

JULIA : How polite. It would have saved me considerable inconvenience if she had sent it to my house.

ROSE (*curtly*) : Here it is, anyhow.

JULIA (*taking it*) : Thank you.

> *She, too, reads by the light of one of the candles. When she has finished it, she laughs.*

JULIA : Extraordinarily well phrased for a gutter-snipe.

EDWARD (*hotly*) : Melanie was not a gutter-snipe.

JULIA : I'm so sorry. I had forgotten your great tenderness for her.

EDWARD : I never shall.

JULIA (*smiling*) : Faithful unto death !

EDWARD : Yes. I am her friend, for always.

JULIA : How touching. All the same I cannot help feeling that it is just as well for you that she has gone away.

EDWARD (*turning away*) : I wouldn't expect you to understand, Madame.

JULIA (*loosening her cloak*) : Well, I suppose we had better wait here and break the news to Paul.

ROSE (*still packing*) : That would be waste of time, Madame.

JULIA : Why, what do you mean ?

ROSE : Monsieur le Dook sailed with Mademoiselle on the evening boat for France.

JULIA (*sharply*) : What !

301

Rose : You can still see the lights from the window. They look ever so pretty reflected in the water.

Julia (*furiously*) : You're lying ! Monsieur le Duc couldn't possibly have sailed.

Rose : That's as may be, but I did happen to see him on to the boat myself. They was very gay—both of them.

Julia (*controlling herself*) : I see. (*Bitterly.*) How very, very amusing.

Rose : A joke's a joke all the world over, I always say.

Julia : Lord Sheere, will you kindly escort me to my house ?

Edward : With pleasure, Lady Julia.

Julia : I fear my cook will be in bed, but I can offer you a little wine.

Edward : Thank you.

Julia : We can drink a toast—to absent friends !

> *Without looking at* Rose, *she walks out of the room.*
> Edward *is about to follow her, then he hesitates and comes back.*

Edward : Good-bye, Rose.

Rose (*jumping to her feet, and curtseying*) : Good-bye, my lord.

Edward (*giving her a little purse of money*) : Will you please keep this in remembrance of me ?

Rose : Oh, yes, my lord—thank you.

> *He goes to the door and turns.*

Edward : If—if you should ever see her again—give her my love.

Rose : Yes, my lord.

> Edward *goes out.*
> Rose *stands looking after him and after a moment*

or two she resumes her packing, humming to herself meanwhile. Presently there are hurried footsteps on the stairs and PAUL bursts into his room. His face is white, and he is trembling.

PAUL : Rose ! What's the matter ? What is happening ?

ROSE (*rising to her feet*) : You've missed them, sir.

PAUL : Missed whom ?

ROSE : Lady Julia and Lord Sheere. They just went out.

PAUL : Where is Mademoiselle ? (*He rushes towards the bedroom door.*) Where is Mademoiselle ?

ROSE : You've missed her too, sir.

PAUL : What do you mean ?

ROSE : She has gone.

PAUL : Gone !—where—where has she gone ?

ROSE : France, sir—she left a note for you—here it is.
She takes a note from the bosom of her dress and gives it to him. He takes it mechanically, with an expression on his face of utter despair. ROSE watches him, she starts to sing quietly. When he has finished reading it, he walks slowly across the stage.

PAUL (*to ROSE—stamping his foot*) : Stop singing ! (*Speaking with great difficulty.*) She doesn't give any address—she doesn't say where I can find her——

He turns slowly round, goes up to the window and looks out at the sea, then, resting his head on his arms he breaks down completely. ROSE looks at him for a moment, and then slams down the lid of the trunk she has been packing and walks into the bedroom, her heels clattering sharply on the bare floor. In a moment or two her footsteps are heard again, but this time it is MELANIE who comes out of the bedroom. She clatters in with the same tread as ROSE. *She is dressed for travelling and carries a paper bag of humbugs in her hand. She looks at* PAUL *in indecision for a second, then she marches across the room and slams down the lid of another trunk. He does not look round. She goes to another box and slams down the lid of that. Still he pays no attention. Finally, when she has slammed all the lids of all the boxes, she goes quietly up to him, and sinks on to the floor behind him. She takes his hand which is hanging down by his side, and very tenderly kisses it. He turns slowly, and she proffers him the paper bag.*

MELANIE : Mon cher amour—would you like a oomboog ?

CURTAIN.

HANDS ACROSS THE SEA

A Light Comedy in One Scene

from

TO-NIGHT AT 8.30

CHARACTERS:
LADY MAUREEN GILPIN (Piggie)
COMMANDER PETER GILPIN, R.N., *her husband*
THE HON. CLARE WEDDERBURN
LIEUT. COMMANDER ALASTAIR CORBETT, R.N.
MAJOR GOSLING (Bogey)
MR. WADHURST
MRS. WADHURST
MR. BURNHAM
WALTERS

The action of the play takes place in the drawing-room of the
GILPINS' *flat in London.*
Time: Present Day.

The Scene is the drawing-room of the GILPINS' *flat in London.*
   The room is nicely furnished and rather untidy. There is a
   portable gramophone on one small table and a tray of cock-
   tail things on another; apart from these, the furnishing
   can be left to the discretion of the producer.
   When the Curtain rises the telephone is ringing.
   WALTERS, *a neat parlourmaid, enters and answers it.*
   The time is about six p.m.

WALTERS (*at telephone*): Hallo—yes—no, her ladyship's not back yet—she said she'd be in at five, so she
ought to be here at any minute now—what name,
please?—Rawlingson—Mr. and Mrs. Rawlingson——
(*She scribbles on the pad.*) Yes—I'll tell her——
   She hangs up the receiver and goes out. There is the
   sound of voices in the hall and LADY MAUREEN GILPIN
   enters, followed at a more leisurely pace by her husband,
   PETER GILPIN. MAUREEN, *nicknamed* PIGGIE *by her*
   intimates, is a smart, attractive woman in the thirties.
   PETER *is tall and sunburned and reeks of the Navy.*
PIGGIE (*as she comes in*): —and you can send the car
back for me at eleven-thirty—it's quite simple, darling,
I wish you wouldn't be so awfully complicated about
everything——
PETER: What happens if my damned dinner goes on
longer than that and I get stuck?
PIGGIE: You just get stuck, darling, and then you get
unstuck and get a taxi——

307

PETER (*grumbling*): I shall be in uniform, clinking with medals——

PIGGIE: If you take my advice you'll faint dead away at eleven o'clock and then you can come home in the car and change and have time for everything——

PETER: I can't faint dead away under the nose of the C.-in-C.

PIGGIE: You can feel a little poorly, can't you—anybody has the right to feel a little poorly—— (*She sees the telephone pad.*) My God!

PETER: What is it?

PIGGIE: The Rawlingsons.

PETER: Who the hell are they?

PIGGIE: I'd forgotten all about them—I must get Maud at once—— (*She sits at the telephone and dials a number.*)

PETER: Who are the Rawlingsons?

PIGGIE: Maud and I stayed with them in Samolo, I told you about it, that time when we had to make a forced landing—they practically saved our lives—— (*At telephone.*) Hullo—Maud—darling, the Rawlingsons are on us—what—the RAWLINGSONS—yes—I asked them to-day and forgot all about it—you must come at once—but, darling, you *must*—Oh, dear—no, no, that was the Frobishers, these are the ones we stayed with—mother and father and daughter—you must remember—pretty girl with bad legs—— No—they didn't have a son—we swore we'd give them a lovely time when they came home on leave—I know they didn't have a son, that was those other people in Penang—— Oh, all right—you'll have to do something about them, though—let me ask them to lunch with you

to-morrow—all right—one-thirty—I'll tell them——
(*She hangs up.*)—she can't come——

PETER: You might have warned me that a lot of
Colonial strangers were coming trumpeting into the
house——

PIGGIE: I tell you I'd forgotten——

PETER: That world trip was a grave mistake——

PIGGIE: Who can I get that's celebrated—to give
them a thrill?

PETER: Why do they have to have a thrill?

PIGGIE: I'll get Clare, anyway—— (*She dials another
number.*)

PETER: She'll frighten them to death.

PIGGIE: Couldn't you change early and come in your
uniform? That would be better than nothing——

PETER: Perhaps they'd like to watch me having my
bath!

PIGGIE (*at telephone*): I want to speak to Mrs.
Wedderburn, please—yes—— (*To* PETER.) I do wish
you'd be a little helpful—— (*At telephone.*) Clare?—
this is Piggie—I want you to come round at once and
help me with the Rawlingsons—no, I know you
haven't, but that doesn't matter—— Mother, father
and daughter—very sweet—they were divine to us in
the East—I'm repaying hospitality—Maud's having
them to lunch to-morrow and Peter's going to take
them round the dockyard——

PETER: I'm not going to do any such thing——

PIGGIE: Shut up, I just thought of that and it's a
very good idea—— (*At telephone.*) All right, darling—
as soon as you can—— (*She hangs up.*)—I must go and
change——

PETER: You know perfectly well I haven't time to

take mothers and fathers and daughters with bad legs round the dockyard——

PIGGIE: It wouldn't take a minute, they took us all over their rubber plantation.

PETER: It probably served you right.

PIGGIE: You're so disobliging, darling, you really should try to conquer it—it's something to do with being English, I think—as a race I'm ashamed of us— no sense of hospitality—the least we can do when people are kind to us in far-off places is to be a little gracious in return.

PETER: They weren't kind to me in far-off places.

PIGGIE: You know there's a certain grudging, sullen streak in your character—I've been very worried about it lately—it's spreading like a forest fire——

PETER: Why don't you have them down for the week-end?

PIGGIE: Don't be so idiotic, how can I possibly? There's no room to start with and even if there were they'd be utterly wretched——

PETER: I don't see why.

PIGGIE: They wouldn't know anybody—they probably wouldn't have the right clothes—they'd keep on huddling about in uneasy little groups——

PETER: The amount of uneasy little groups that three people can huddle about in is negligible.

    ALASTAIR CORBETT *saunters into the room. He is good-looking and also distinctly Naval in tone.*

ALLY: Hallo, chaps.

PIGGIE: Ally, darling—how lovely—we're in trouble—Peter'll tell you all about it——

    The telephone rings and she goes to it. The following conversations occur simultaneously.

ALLY: What trouble?

PETER: More of Piggie's beach friends.

ALLY: Let's have a drink.

PETER: Cocktail?

ALLY: No, a long one, whisky and soda.

PETER (*going to drink table*): All right.

ALLY: What beach friends?

PETER: People Maud and Piggie picked up in the East.

PIGGIE (*at phone*): Hullo!—Yes—Robert, dear—how lovely! (*To others.*) It's Robert.

ALLY: Piggie ought to stay at home more.

PIGGIE (*on phone*): Where are you?

PETER: That's what I say!

PIGGIE (*on phone*): Oh, what a shame!—No—Peter's going to sea on Thursday—I'm going down on Saturday.

ALLY: Rubber, I expect—everybody in the East's rubber.

PIGGIE (*on phone*): No—nobody particular—just Clare and Bogey and I think Pops; but he thinks he's got an ulcer or something and might not be able to come.

PETER: We thought you might be a real friend and take them over the dockyard.

ALLY: What on earth for?

PETER: Give them a thrill.

PIGGIE (*on phone*): All right—I'll expect you—no, I don't think it can be a very big one—he looks as bright as a button.

ALLY: Why don't you take them over the dockyard?

PETER: I shall be at sea, Thursday onwards—exercises!

PIGGIE (*on phone*): No, darling, what is the use of having her—she only depresses you—oh—all right! (*Hangs up.*) Oh, dear——

PETER: It's quite easy for you—you can give them lunch on board.

ALLY: We're in dry dock.

PETER: They won't mind. (*To* PIGGIE.) What is it?

PIGGIE: Robert—plunged in gloom—he's got to do a course at Greenwich—he ran into a tram in Devonport—and he's had a row with Molly—he wants me to have her for the week-end so that they can make it up all over everybody. Have you told Ally about the Rawlingsons?

PETER: Yes, he's taking them over the dockyard, lunching them on board and then he's going to show them a submarine——

PIGGIE: Marvellous! You're an angel, Ally—I must take off these clothes, I'm going mad——

> She goes out of the room at a run.
> There is the sound of the front-door bell.

PETER: Let's go into my room—I can show you the plans——

ALLY: Already? They've been pretty quick with them.

PETER: I made a few alterations—there wasn't enough deck space—she ought to be ready by October, I shall have her sent straight out to Malta——

ALLY: Come on, we shall be caught——

> They go off on the left as WALTERS *ushers in* MR. *and* MRS. WADHURST *on the right.*
> The WADHURSTS *are pleasant, middle-aged people, their manner is a trifle timorous.*

WALTERS: Her ladyship is changing, I'll tell her you are here.

MRS. WADHURST: Thank you.

MR. WADHURST: Thank you very much.

WALTERS goes out.

The WADHURSTS *look round the room.*

MRS. WADHURST: It's a very nice flat.

MR. WADHURST: Yes—yes, it is.

MRS. WADHURST (*scrutinising a photograph*): That must be him.

MR. WADHURST: Who?

MRS. WADHURST: The Commander.

MR. WADHURST: Yes—I expect it is.

MRS. WADHURST: Sailors always have such nice open faces, don't they?

MR. WADHURST: Yes, I suppose so.

MRS. WADHURST: Clean-cut and look you straight in the eye—I like men who look you straight in the eye.

MR. WADHURST: Yes, it's very nice.

MRS. WADHURST (*at another photograph*): This must be her sister—I recognise her from the *Tatler*—look— she was Lady Hurstley, you know, then she was Lady Macfadden and I don't know who she is now.

MR. WADHURST: Neither do I.

MRS. WADHURST: What a dear little boy—such a sturdy little fellow—look at the way he's holding his engine.

MR. WADHURST: Is that his engine?

MRS. WADHURST: He has rather a look of Donald Hotchkiss, don't you think?

MR. WADHURST: Yes, dear.

MRS. WADHURST: I must say they have very nice things—oh, dear, how lovely to be well off—I must write to the Brostows by the next mail and tell them all about it.

MR. WADHURST: Yes, you must.

MRS. WADHURST: Don't you think we'd better sit down?

MR. WADHURST: Why not?

MRS. WADHURST: You sit in that chair and I'll sit on the sofa.

She sits on the sofa. He sits on the chair.

MR. WADHURST: Yes, dear.

MRS. WADHURST: I wish you wouldn't look quite so uncomfortable, Fred, there's nothing to be uncomfortable about.

MR. WADHURST: She does expect us, doesn't she?

MRS. WADHURST: Of course, I talked to her myself on the telephone last Wednesday, she was perfectly charming and said that we were to come without fail and that it would be divine.

MR. WADHURST: I still feel we should have telephoned again just to remind her. People are always awfully busy in London.

MRS. WADHURST: I do hope Lady Dalborough will be here, too—I should like to see her again—she was so nice.

MR. WADHURST: She was the other one, wasn't she?

MRS. WADHURST (*irritably*): What do you mean, the other one?

MR. WADHURST: I mean not this one.

MRS. WADHURST: She's the niece of the Duke of Frensham, her mother was Lady Merrit, she was a great traveller too—I believe she went right across the Sahara dressed as an Arab. In those days that was a very dangerous thing to do.

MR. WADHURST: I shouldn't think it was any too safe now.

WALTERS *enters and ushers in* MR. BURNHAM, *a nondescript young man carrying a longish roll of cardboard.*

WALTERS: I'll tell the Commander you're here.

MR. BURNHAM: Thanks—thanks very much.

WALTERS *goes out.*

MRS. WADHURST (*after a slightly awkward silence*): How do you do?

MR. BURNHAM: How do you do?

MRS. WADHURST (*with poise*): This is my husband.

MR. BURNHAM: How do you do?

MR. WADHURST: How do you do?

They shake hands.

MRS. WADHURST (*vivaciously*): Isn't this a charming room—so—so lived in.

MR. BURNHAM: Yes.

MR. WADHURST: Are you in the Navy, too?

MR. BURNHAM: No.

MRS. WADHURST (*persevering*): It's so nice to be home again—we come from Malaya, you know.

MR. BURNHAM: Oh—Malaya.

MRS. WADHURST: Yes, Lady Maureen and Lady Dalborough visited us there—my husband has a rubber plantation up-country—there's been a terrible slump, of course, but we're trying to keep our heads above water —aren't we, Fred?

MR. WADHURST: Yes, dear, we certainly are.

MRS. WADHURST: Have you ever been to the East?

MR. BURNHAM: No.

MRS. WADHURST: It's very interesting really, although the climate's rather trying until you get used to it, and of course the one thing we do miss is the theatre——

MR. BURNHAM: Yes—of course.

MRS. WADHURST: There's nothing my husband and I enjoy so much as a good play, is there, Fred?

MR. WADHURST: Nothing.

MRS. WADHURST: And all we get is films, and they're generally pretty old by the time they come out to us—— (*She laughs gaily.*)

MR. WADHURST: Do you go to the theatre much?

MR. BURNHAM: No.

There is silence which is broken by the telephone ringing. Everybody jumps.

MRS. WADHURST: Oh, dear—do you think we ought to answer it?

MR. WADHURST: I don't know.

The telephone continues to ring. CLARE WEDDER-BURN *comes in. She is middle-aged, well-dressed and rather gruff. She is followed by* "BOGEY" GOSLING, *a Major in the Marines, a good-looking man in the thirties.*

CLARE: Hallo—where's the old girl?

MRS. WADHURST (*nervously*): I—er, I'm afraid I——

CLARE (*going to the telephone*): Mix a cocktail, Bogey—I'm a stretcher case—— (*At telephone.*) Hallo—no, it's me—Clare—— God knows, dear—shall I tell her to call you back?—all right—no, it was bloody, darling—a gloomy dinner at the Embassy, then the worst play I've ever sat through and then the Café de Paris and that awful man who does things with a duck—I've already seen him six times, darling—oh, you know, he pinches its behind and it quacks 'Land of Hope and Glory'—I don't know whether it hurts it or not—I minded at first but I'm past caring now, after all, it's not like performing dogs, I mind about the performing dogs terribly—all right—good-bye—— (*She hangs up and*

316

turns to MRS. WADHURST.) Ducks are pretty bloody anyway, don't you think?

MRS. WADHURST: I don't know very much about them.

CLARE: The man swears it's genuine talent, but I think it's the little nip that does it.

MRS. WADHURST: It sounds rather cruel.

CLARE: It's a gloomy form of entertainment any-how, particularly as I've always hated 'Land of Hope and Glory'——

BOGEY: Cocktail?

CLARE (*taking off her hat*): Thank God!

> BOGEY *hands round cocktails, the* WADHURSTS *and* MR. BURNHAM *accept them and sip them in silence.*

BOGEY: I suppose Piggie's in the bath.

CLARE: Go and rout her out.

BOGEY: Wait till I've had a drink.

CLARE (*to* MRS. WADHURST): Is Peter home or is he still darting about the Solent?

MRS. WADHURST: I'm afraid I couldn't say—you see——

BOGEY: I saw him last night with Janet——

CLARE: Hasn't she had her baby yet?

BOGEY: She hadn't last night.

CLARE: That damned baby's been hanging over us all for months——

> *The telephone rings—*CLARE *answers it.*

(*At telephone.*) Hallo—yes—hallo, darling—no, it's Clare—yes, he's here—— No, I really couldn't face it—yes, if I were likely to go to India I'd come, but I'm not likely to go to India—— I think Rajahs bumble up a house-party so terribly—yes, I know *he's* different, but the other one's awful—Angela had an agonising time with him—all the dining-room chairs had to be changed because they were leather and his religion prevented him sitting on them—all the dogs had to be kept out of the house because they were unclean, which God knows was true of the Bedlington, but the other ones were clean as whistles—and then to round everything off he took Laura Merstham in his car and made passes at her all the way to Newmarket—all right, darling—here he is—— (*To* BOGEY.) It's Nina, she wants to talk to you——

> *She hands the telephone to* BOGEY, *who reaches for it and lifts the wire so that it just misses* MRS. WAD-HURST'S *hat. It isn't quite long enough so he has to bend down to speak with his face practically touching her.*

BOGEY (*at telephone*): Hallo, Nin—— I can't on Wednesday, I've got a Guest Night—it's a hell of a long way, it'd take hours——

> PIGGIE *comes in with a rush.*

PIGGIE: I am so sorry——

CLARE: Shhh!

BOGEY: Shut up, I can't hear——

PIGGIE (*in a shrill whisper*): Who is it?

CLARE: Nina.

BOGEY (*at telephone*): Well, you can tell George to leave it for me—and I can pick it up.

PIGGIE: How lovely to see you again!

BOGEY (*at telephone*): No, I shan't be leaving till about ten, so if he leaves it by nine-thirty I'll get it all right——

PIGGIE: My husband will be here in a minute—he has to go to sea on Thursday, but he's arranged for you to be taken over the dockyard at Portsmouth——

BOGEY (*at telephone*): Give the old boy a crack on the jaw.

PIGGIE: It's the most thrilling thing in the world. You see how the torpedoes are made—millions of little wheels inside, all clicking away like mad—and they cost thousands of pounds each——

BOGEY (*at telephone*): No, I saw her last night—not yet, but at any moment now—I should think—— All right—— Call me at Chatham—if I can get away I shall have to bring Mickie, too——

PIGGIE: How much do torpedoes cost each, Clare?

CLARE: God knows, darling—something fantastic—ask Bogey— —

PIGGIE: Bogey——

BOGEY: What?

PIGGIE: How much do torpedoes cost each?

BOGEY: What?—(*at telephone*)—wait a minute, Piggie's yelling at me——

PIGGIE: Torpedoes—— (*She makes a descriptive gesture.*)

BOGEY: Oh, thousands and thousands—terribly expensive things—ask Peter—— (*At telephone*)—If I do bring him you'll have to be frightfully nice to him, he's been on the verge of suicide for weeks——

PIGGIE: Don't let her go, I must talk to her——

BOGEY (*at telephone*): Hold on a minute, Piggie wants to talk to you—all right—I'll let you know—here she is——

> PIGGIE *leans over the sofa and takes the telephone from* BOGEY, *who steps over the wire and stumbles over* MRS. WADHURST.

BOGEY: I'm most awfully sorry——

MRS. WADHURST: Not at all——

PIGGIE (*to* MRS. WADHURST): It's so lovely you being in England—— (*At telephone.*) Darling—what was the meaning of that sinister little invitation you sent me?

BOGEY: You know what Mickey is.

PIGGIE (*at telephone*): No, dear, I really can't—I always get so agitated——

CLARE: Why does he go on like that? It's so tiresome.

PIGGIE (*at telephone*): I'll come if Clare will—— (*To* CLARE.) Are you going to Nina's Indian ding-dong?

CLARE: Not without an anæsthetic.

PIGGIE (*at telephone*): She's moaning a bit, but I'll persuade her—what happens after dinner?—the man with the duck from the Café de Paris—— (*To the room in general.*) She's got that sweet duck from the Café de Paris——

CLARE: Give me another cocktail, Bogey, I want to get so drunk that I just can't hear any more——

PIGGIE (*at telephone*): But, darling, do you think it's quite *wise*—I mean Maharajahs are terribly touchy and there's probably something in their religion about ducks being mortal sin or something—you know how difficult they are about cows and pigs—just a minute— (*To the* WADHURSTS.) You can tell us, of course——

MR. WADHURST: I beg your pardon?

PIGGIE: Do Indians mind ducks?

MR. WADHURST: I—I don't think so——

BOGEY: Do you come from India?

MRS. WADHURST: No, Malaya.

PIGGIE: It's the same sort of thing, though, isn't it? —if they don't mind them in Malaya it's unlikely that they'd mind them in India—— (*At telephone.*) It'll probably be all right, but you'd better get Douglas Byng as a standby.

CLARE: There might be something in their religion about Douglas Byng.

PIGGIE: Shh! (*At telephone.*) Everyone's making such a noise! The room's full of the most frightful people. Darling, it definitely *is* Waterloo Station—— No, I'm almost sure he can't—he's going to sea on Thursday—don't be silly, dear, you can't be in the Navy without going to sea *sometimes*——

PETER *enters, followed by* ALLY.

(*At telephone.*) Here he is now, you can ask him yourself—— (*To* PETER.) Peter, it's Nina, she wants to talk to you—— (*To the* WADHURSTS.) This is my husband and Commander Corbett—he's been longing to meet you and thank you for being so sweet to us—I told him all about your heavenly house and the plantation——

MRS. WADHURST (*bridling—to* ALLY): It was most delightful, I assure you, to have Lady Maureen with us——

PIGGIE: Not him, him—that's the wrong one——

MRS. WADHURST: Oh, I'm so sorry——

PETER (*shaking hands with* MRS. WADHURST): It was so kind of you—my wife has talked of nothing else——

PIGGIE (*grabbing him*): Here—Nina's yelling like a banshee——

PETER: Excuse me. (*He takes the telephone.*) Hallo, Nin—what for?—— No, I can't, but Piggie probably can—— (*To* PIGGIE.) Can you go to Nina's party for the Rajahs?

PIGGIE: We've been through all that——

PETER: All right—I didn't know—— (*At*

telephone.) No, I shall be at sea for about three days—it isn't tiresome at all, I like it——

PIGGIE (*to* MRS. WADHURST): How's your daughter?

MRS. WADHURST (*surprised*): She's a little better, thank you.

PIGGIE: Oh, has she been ill? I'm so sorry.

MR. WADHURST (*gently*): She's been ill for five years.

PIGGIE (*puzzled*): How dreadful for you—are you happy with that cocktail, or would you rather have tea?

MRS. WADHURST: This is delicious, thank you.

PETER (*at telephone*): I honestly can't do anything about that, Nina, you might be able to find out from the Admiral—well, if his mother was mad too that is an extenuating circumstance—he'll probably be sent home—— (*To* CLARE.) Did you know that Freda Bathurst had once been in an asylum?

CLARE: No, but it explains a lot.

PIGGIE: Why?

PETER: Her son went mad in Hong Kong.

CLARE: What did he do?

PETER: I don't know, but Nina's in a state about it.

PIGGIE: I don't see what it's got to do with Nina——

PETER: He's a relation of some sort—— (*At telephone*.) What did he do, Nina?—— Oh—— Oh, I see—— Oh—well, he'll certainly be sent home and a good job too, we can't have that sort of thing in the Service—— If I were you I'd keep well out of it—all right—— Good-bye. (*He hangs up.*)

PIGGIE: What was it?

PETER: I couldn't possibly tell you.

PIGGIE: Poor boy, I expect the climate had something to do with it—the climate's awful in Hong Kong —look at poor old Wally Smythe——

ALLY (*to the* WADHURSTS): Did you ever know Wally Smythe?

MRS. WADHURST: No, I'm afraid not.

CLARE: You didn't miss much.

PIGGIE: I adored Wally, he was a darling.

CLARE: He kept on having fights all the time—I do hate people hitting people—— (*To* MRS. WADHURST.) Don't you?

MRS. WADHURST: Yes.

> *There is suddenly complete silence*—PIGGIE *breaks it with an effort.*

PIGGIE (*vivaciously to the* WADHURSTS): Maud was so frightfully sorry that she couldn't come to-day—she's pining to see you again and she asked me to ask you if you'd lunch there to-morrow?

MRS. WADHURST: How very kind of her.

PIGGIE: She's got a divine little house hidden away in a mews, it's frightfully difficult to find—— (*The telephone rings.*) I've got millions of questions I want to ask you, what happened to that darling old native who did a dance with a sword?—— (*At telephone.*) Hallo— (*Continuing to everyone in general.*) It was the most exciting thing I've ever seen, all the villagers sat round in torchlight and they beat—— (*At telephone.*) Hallo— yes, speaking—— (*Continuing*) beat drums and the—— (*At telephone*) hallo—darling, I'd no idea you were back—— (*to everybody*) and the old man tore himself to shreds in the middle, it was marvellous—— (*At telephone.*) I can't believe it, where are you speaking from?—— My dear, you're *not!*—— (*To everybody.*) It's Boodie, she's got back last night and she's staying with Norman——

CLARE: Is Phyllis there?

PIGGIE (*at telephone*): Is Phyllis there?—— She's away?—— (*To* CLARE.) She's away.

PETER (*to* MR. WADHURST): That's the best joke I ever heard.

CLARE: It's made my entire season that's all, it's just made it.

PIGGIE (*at telephone*): You'd better come and dine to-night—I'm on a diet, so there's only spinach, but we can talk—— Yes, she's here—absolutely worn out—we all are—— Oh yes, it was pretty grim, it started all right and everything was going beautifully when Vera arrived, unasked, my dear, and more determined than Hitler—of course there was the most awful scene—Alice flounced upstairs with tears cascading down her face and locked herself in the cook's bedroom—— Clare tried to save the situation by dragging Lady Borrowdale on to the terrace——

CLARE (*sibilantly*): That was *afterwards!*——

PIGGIE (*at telephone*): Anyhow hell broke loose—you can imagine—Janet was there, of course, and we were all worried about her—no, it hasn't arrived yet, but the odds are mounting—— (*To everybody.*) She hasn't had it yet, has she, Peter?

PETER: If she has it was born in the gramophone department at Harrods—I left her there at four-thirty——

PIGGIE (*at telephone*): No, it's still what's known as on the way—I'll expect you about eight-thirty—I've got to do my feet and then I'm going to relax—all right—yes, she's here—— (*To* CLARE.) Here, Clare, she wants to talk to you——

CLARE *in order to reach the telephone comfortably has to kneel on the sofa.*

CLARE: Excuse me.

MRS. WADHURST: I'm so sorry.

CLARE (*at telephone*): Darling—I'm dead with surprise——

PIGGIE (*to* MRS. WADHURST): Now you must tell me some more——

MRS. WADHURST: Well, really, I don't——

CLARE: Shhh!—I can't hear a word—— (*At telephone.*) He what?—when?—— He must be raving——

PIGGIE (*in a harsh whisper*): Have you still got that sweet dog?

MRS. WADHURST (*also whispering*): Yes, we've still got Rudolph.

PIGGIE (*to everybody*): Rudolph's an angel, I can never tell you how divine he was—he used to come in every morning with my breakfast tray and jump on to the bed——

MRS. WADHURST (*horrified*): Oh, you never told me that, how very naughty of him—he's very seldom allowed in the house at all——

PIGGIE (*puzzled*): But—but——

MR. WADHURST: Perhaps you're thinking of some other dog, Lady Maureen—Rudolph is a Great Dane——

PIGGIE (*bewildered*): Oh, yes, of course, how idiotic of me——

CLARE (*at telephone*): —Well, all I can say is she ought to be deported—you can't go about making scenes like that, it's so lacking in everything—all right, darling—call me in the morning—I've got a hairdresser in the afternoon, why don't you make an appointment at the same time?—lovely—— Good-bye. (*She hangs up.*)

PIGGIE: Do sit down, Clare, and stop climbing

about over everybody. (*To* MRS. WADHURST.) You must forgive me—this is a mad-house—it's always like this—I can't think why——

CLARE (*in a whisper to* PETER, *having noticed* MR. BURNHAM): Why's that man got a roll of music, is he going to sing?

PETER (*also in a whisper*): I don't know—he ought by rights to be a lovely girl of sixteen——

MRS. WADHURST: Have you been in London for the whole season?

PIGGIE: Yes, it's been absolutely frightful, but my husband is getting leave soon, so we shall be able to pop off somewhere——

ALLY (*to* MR. WADHURST): I suppose you've never run across a chap in Burma called Beckwith?

MR. WADHURST: No, I've never been to Burma.

ALLY: He's in rubber, too, I believe—or tea—he's very amusing.

MRS. WADHURST (*to* PIGGIE): We did hope you'd come and lunch with us one day—but I expect you're terribly busy——

PIGGIE: My dear, I'd worship it—— (*The telephone rings.*) Oh really, this telephone never stops for one minute—— (*At telephone.*) Hallo—yes, speaking—— Who?—Mrs. Rawlingson—— Oh, yes, yes, yes—— (*She hands the telephone to* MRS. WADHURST.) Here—it's for you——

MRS. WADHURST (*astonished*): For me? How very curious——

PIGGIE: Give me a cocktail, Bogey—I haven't had one at all yet and I'm exhausted——

MRS. WADHURST (*at telephone*): Hallo—what—who? —I'm afraid I don't quite understand——

BOGEY (*giving* PIGGIE *a cocktail*): Here you are—it's a bit weak——

MRS. WADHURST (*still floundering*): —I think there must be some mistake—just a moment—— (*To* PIGGIE.) It's for you, Lady Maureen—a Mrs. Rawlingson——

PIGGIE (*laughing*): Now isn't that the most extraordinary coincidence—— (*She takes the telephone.*)— Hallo—yes—speaking—— (*She listens and her face changes.*)—Oh yes, of course, how stupid of me—— (*She looks hurriedly at the* WADHURSTS, *then at* PETER.) I'm so awfully sorry, I only just came in—— Oh, what a shame—no, no, no, it doesn't matter a bit—— No—indeed you must call me up the first moment he gets over it—— Yes—I expect it was—yes—— Good-bye.

> *She slowly hangs up the receiver, looking at the* WADHURSTS *in complete bewilderment. She makes a sign to* PETER *over* MRS. WADHURST'S *shoulder, but he only shakes his head.*

PIGGIE (*brightly, but with intense meaning*): That was Mrs. Rawlingson.

PETER: Good God!

PIGGIE (*with purpose, sitting next to* MRS. WADHURST): Did you ever meet the Rawlingsons out East?

MRS. WADHURST: No—I don't know them.

PIGGIE: Maud and I stayed with them too, you know.

MRS. WADHURST: Where?

PIGGIE: It was in Malaya somewhere, I think—I do get so muddled.

MRS. WADHURST: I think we should have heard of them if they lived in Malaya.

> PETER *meanwhile has gone to the piano and started to strum idly—he begins to hum lightly at the same time.*

PETER (*humming to a waltz refrain, slightly indistinctly, but clearly enough for* PIGGIE *to hear*): If these are not them who are they? Who are they? Who are they?

PIGGIE *rises and saunters over to the piano.*

PIGGIE: Play the other bit, dear, out of the second act—— (*She hums*)—you know—"I haven't the faintest idea—— Oh no—I haven't the faintest idea".

PETER (*changing tempo*): "Under the light of the moon, dear—you'd better find out pretty soon, dear".

CLARE: What on earth's that out of?

PIGGIE: Don't be *silly*, Clare—all I ask is that you shouldn't be *silly*!

CLARE (*understanding*): Oh yes—I see.

There is silence except for PETER'S *playing—everyone looks covertly at the* WADHURSTS. PIGGIE *goes over to* MR. WADHURST.

PIGGIE (*with determination*): What ship did you come home in?

MR. WADHURST: The *Naldera*.

ALLY: P & O?

MRS. WADHURST: Yes.

PIGGIE: I suppose you got on at Singapore?

MR. WADHURST: No, Penang.

PIGGIE (*the light breaking*): Penang! Of course, Penang.

MRS. WADHURST: Yes, we have some friends there, so we went by train from Singapore and stayed with them for a couple of days before catching the boat.

PIGGIE (*sunk again*): Oh yes—yes, I see.

PETER (*at piano, humming to march time*): "When you hear those drums rat-a-plan—rat-a-plan—find out the name of the place if you can—la la la la la la la la——"

PIGGIE (*persevering*): How far is your house from the

328

sea? Maud and I were arguing about it for hours the other day——

MR. WADHURST: It's right on the sea.

PIGGIE: That's exactly what I said, but you know Maud's so vague—she never remembers a thing——

CLARE: I suppose it's hell hot all the year round where you are?

MRS. WADHURST: Yes, the climate is a little trying, but one gets used to it.

BOGEY: Are you far from Kuala Lumpur.

MRS. WADHURST: Yes, a long way.

BOGEY: Oh, I knew some people in Kuala Lumpur once.

MR. WADHURST: What were their names?

BOGEY: Damn it, I've forgotten—something like Harrison——

PIGGIE (*helpfully*): Morrison?

ALLY: Williamson?

PETER: Lightfoot?

BOGEY: No, it's gone——

PIGGIE (*irritably*): Never mind—it couldn't matter less really, could it?

MRS. WADHURST (*rising*): I'm afraid we must really go now, Lady Maureen——

PIGGIE: Oh no—please——

MRS. WADHURST: We have to dress because we're dining and going to the theatre—that's the one thing we do miss dreadfully in Pendarla—the theatre——

CLARE: We miss it a good deal here, too.

PIGGIE (*remembering everything*): Pendarla—oh dear, what a long way away it seems—dear Mrs. Wadhurst— (*She shoots a triumphant glance at* PETER.)—it's been so lovely having this little peep at you—you and Mr.

Wadhurst must come and dine quietly one night and we'll go to another theatre——

MRS. WADHURST: That would be delightful—Fred——

MR. WADHURST: Good-bye.

PIGGIE: Peter—come and say good-bye to Mr. and Mrs. Wadhurst.

PETER (*coming over and shaking hands*): Good-bye—I can never tell you how grateful I am to you for having been so kind and hospitable to my wife——

MRS. WADHURST: Next time, I hope you'll come and call on us too.

PETER: I should love to.

MRS. WADHURST: Good-bye.

CLARE: Good-bye——

> *Everybody says good-bye and shakes hands,* PETER *opens the door for the* WADHURSTS *and they go out on a wave of popularity. He goes out into the hall with them closing the door after him.* PIGGIE *collapses on to the sofa.*

PIGGIE (*hysterically*): Oh, my God, that was the most awful half an hour I've ever spent——

CLARE: I thought it all went down like a dinner.

PIGGIE: I remember it all now, we stayed one night with them on our way from Siam—a man in Bangkok had wired to them or something——

ALLY: That was a nice bit you did about the old native dancing with a sword——

PIGGIE: Oh dear, they must have thought I was drunk.

> PETER *re-enters.*

PETER: Next time you travel, my darling, I suggest you keep a diary.

PIGGIE: Wasn't it frightful—poor angels—I must ring up Maud—— (*She dials a number.*) I think they had a heavenly time though, don't you—I mean they couldn't have noticed a thing——

PETER: Oh no, the whole affair was managed with the utmost subtlety—I congratulate you——

PIGGIE: Don't be sour—Peter (*At telephone.*) Hallo—Maud?—darling, it's not the Rawlingsons at all, it's the Wadhursts—— (*To everybody.*) Good heavens, I never gave them Maud's address. (*At telephone.*) I forgot to give them your address—how can you be so unkind, Maud, you ought to be ashamed of yourself—they're absolute pets, both of them——

PETER: Come on, Ally, I've got to dress——

ALLY: All right——

CLARE: Shall I see you on Sunday?

ALLY: Yes—I'll be over——

PIGGIE (*at telephone*): —they had a lovely time and everybody was divine to them——

CLARE: Come on, Bogey, we must go, too——

PIGGIE: Wait a minute, don't leave me—I've got to do my feet—— (*At telephone*)—no, I was talking to Clare—— My dear, I know, she rang me up too—she's staying with Norman—Phyllis will be as sour as a quince——

PETER *and* ALLY *go off talking.*

CLARE: Darling, I really *must* go——

PIGGIE (*at telephone*): —all right—I'll try to get hold of them in the morning and put them off—I do think it's horrid of you though, after all, they were frightfully sweet to us—I've done all I can—well, there's no need to get into a rage, I'm the one to get into a rage—yes, you are, I can hear you—your teeth are chattering like dice in a box—— Oh, all right! (*She hangs up.*) Maud's impossible——

CLARE: Listen, Piggie——

PIGGIE: Wait just one minute, I've got to get the things to do my feet——

She rushes out of the room.

CLARE: I really don't see why we should all wait about—— (*She suddenly sees* MR. BURNHAM.) Oh—hallo.

MR. BURNHAM (*nervously*): Hallo.

CLARE: I thought you'd left with your mother and father.

MR. BURNHAM: They weren't my mother and father —I'm from Freeman's. I've brought the designs for the Commander's speed boat—Mr. Driscoll couldn't come——

CLARE: Well, you'd better wait—he'll be back soon——

MR. BURNHAM: I'm afraid I can't wait much longer —I have to get back to the shop——

CLARE: You should have piped up before——

BOGEY: Listen, Clare, we must push off——

CLARE: All right.

MR. BURNHAM *retires again into the shadows as* PIGGIE *returns with several bottles, a towel and a pair of scissors. She sits on the sofa and takes her shoes and stockings off.*

PIGGIE: —The trouble with Maud is, she's too insular——

CLARE: Are you driving down on Saturday?

PIGGIE: Yes—I promised to stop off at Godalming and have a cutlet with Freda on the way—do you want to come?

CLARE: You know perfectly well I hate Freda's guts.

PIGGIE (*beginning on her feet*): All right, darling—I'll expect you in the afternoon——

The telephone rings—PIGGIE *reaches for it with one hand and goes on painting her toe nails with the other—at telephone:*

Hallo—yes. Oh, David, I'm *so* sorry—I completely forgot——

CLARE *and* BOGEY *hiss good-bye at her, she waves to them, and they go out.*

I couldn't help it, I had to be sweet to some people that Maud and I stayed with in Malaya—— Oh! David darling, don't be so soured-up—yes, of course I do, don't be so silly—— No, I'm quite alone doing my feet —well, I can't help that, I happen to *like* them red—well, after all they are my feet, I suppose I can paint them blue if I want to——

MR. BURNHAM *begins to tiptoe out of the room, he leaves his roll of designs on the table.* PIGGIE *catches sight of him just as he is gingerly opening the door.*

(*To* MR. BURNHAM.) Oh, good-bye—it's been absolutely lovely, you're the sweetest family I've ever met in my life——

CURTAIN

333

STILL LIFE

A Play in Five Scenes

from

TO-NIGHT AT 8.30

CHARACTERS:
LAURA JESSON
MYRTLE BAGOT
BERYL WATERS
STANLEY
ALBERT GODBY
ALEC HARVEY
YOUNG MAN
BILL
JOHNNIE
MILDRED
DOLLY MESSITER

The action of the play takes place in the refreshment room of Milford Junction Station.

Time: The Present.

SCENE I

The scene is the refreshment room of Milford Junction Station.
On the left of the stage is a curved counter piled with glass
cases containing sandwiches, rock cakes, etc. There are
rows of tea-cups and glasses symmetrically arranged, an
expression of the fanciful side of MYRTLE'S *imagination.*
Schweppes' bottles of soda and Tonic water have been
placed in circles and squares. Even the rock cakes mount
each other on the glass stands in a disciplined pattern.
There is a metal machine which gushes hot tea, a sort of
cylindrical samovar.

For drinking hours there are the usual appurtenances for
the drawing of draught beer, and the wall behind the
counter, except for a door upstage, is lined with looking-
glass shelves supporting bottles, packets of chocolate,
packets of cigarettes, etc.

There are two windows in the back wall. Their lower
panes are frosted and their upper ones tastefully plastered
with stained glass paper. There is another similar
window on the right-hand wall which is at a slight angle.
In this there is also a door leading on to the platform.
There are three tables against the back wall, a stove in the
corner, and two more tables against the right-hand wall,
then the door and another table set below it. There are
several advertisements and calendars in frames, and
artificial flowers.

MYRTLE BAGOT *herself is a buxom and imposing*
widow. Her hair is piled high, and her expression

337

reasonably jaunty except on those occasions when her strong sense of refinement gets the better of her.

BERYL WATERS, *her assistant, is pretty but dimmed, not only by* MYRTLE'S *personal effulgence, but by her firm authority.*

When the curtain rises it is about 5.25 *p.m. on an evening in April. The evening sunlight streams through the right-hand window illuminating gaily the paraphernalia on the counter.*

A YOUNG MAN *in a mackintosh is finishing his tea at one of the upstage tables and reading an evening paper.*

LAURA JESSON *is sitting at the downstage table having tea. She is an attractive woman in the thirties. Her clothes are not particularly smart but obviously chosen with taste. She looks exactly what she is, a pleasant, ordinary married woman, rather pale, for she is not very strong, and with the definite charm of personality which comes from natural kindliness, humour and reasonable conscience. She is reading a Boot's library book at which she occasionally smiles. On the chair beside her there are several parcels as she has been shopping.*

STANLEY *enters from the platform. He wears a seedy green uniform and carries a tray strapped to his shoulders. He goes to the counter. He addresses* MYRTLE *with becoming respect,* BERYL, *however, he winks at lewdly whenever the opportunity.*

STANLEY: I'm out of "Marie's", Mrs. Bagot, and I could do with some more Nestlé's plain.

MYRTLE (*scrutinising the tray*): Let me see.

STANLEY: An old girl on the 4.10 asked if I'd got an ice-cream wafer. I didn't 'arf laugh.

MYRTLE: I don't see that there was anything to

laugh at—a very natural request on a faine day.

STANLEY: What did she think I was, a 'Stop me and buy one?'

BERYL *sniggers.*

MYRTLE: Be quiet, Beryl—and as for you, Stanley, don't you be saucy—you were saucy when you started to work here, and you've been getting saucier and saucier ever since. Here you are—— (*She gives him some packets of biscuits and Nestlé's chocolate.*) Go on now.

STANLEY (*cheerfully*): Righto.

He winks at BERYL *and goes out.*

MYRTLE: And see here, Beryl Waters, I'll trouble you to remember you're on duty——

BERYL: I didn't do anything.

MYRTLE: Exactly—you just stand there giggling like a fool—did you make out that list?

BERYL: Yes, Mrs. Bagot.

MYRTLE: Where is it?

BERYL: I put it on your desk.

MYRTLE: Where's your cloth?

BERYL: Here, Mrs. Bagot.

MYRTLE: Well, go and clean off Number 3. I can see the crumbs on it from here.

BERYL: It's them rock cakes.

MYRTLE: Never you mind about the rock cakes, just you do as you're told and don't argue.

BERYL *goes over to clean No. 3 table.*

ALBERT GODBY *enters. He is a ticket inspector, somewhere between thirty and forty. His accent is north country.*

ALBERT: Hullo!

MYRTLE: Quite a stranger, aren't you?

ALBERT: I couldn't get in yesterday.

339

MYRTLE (*bridling*): I wondered what had happened to you.

ALBERT: I 'ad a bit of a dust-up.

MYRTLE (*preparing his tea*): What about?

ALBERT: Saw a chap getting out of a first-class compartment, and when he come to give up 'is ticket it was third-class, and I told 'im he'd 'ave to pay excess, and then he turned a bit nasty and I 'ad to send for Mr. Saunders.

MYRTLE: Fat lot of good he'd be.

ALBERT: He ticked him off proper.

MYRTLE: Seeing's believing——

ALBERT: He's not a bad lot, Mr. Saunders, after all you can't expect much spirit from a man who's only got one lung and a wife with diabetes.

MYRTLE: I thought something must be wrong when you didn't come.

ALBERT: I'd have popped in to explain but I had a date and 'ad to run for it the moment I went off.

MYRTLE (*frigidly*): Oh, indeed!

ALBERT: A chap I know's getting married.

MYRTLE: Very interesting, I'm sure.

ALBERT: What's up with you, anyway?

MYRTLE: I'm sure I don't know to what you're referring.

ALBERT: You're a bit unfriendly all of a sudden.

MYRTLE (*ignoring him*): Beryl, hurry up—put some coal in the stove while you're at it.

BERYL: Yes, Mrs. Bagot.

MYRTLE: I'm afraid I really can't stand here wasting my time in idle gossip, Mr. Godby.

ALBERT: Aren't you going to offer me another cup?

MYRTLE: You can 'ave another cup and welcome

when you've finished that one. Beryl'll give it to you—
I've got my accounts to do.

ALBERT: I'd rather you gave it to me.

MYRTLE: Time and Taide wait for no man, Mr.
Godby.

ALBERT: I don't know what you're huffy about, but
whatever it is I'm very sorry.

MYRTLE: You misunderstand me—I'm not——

> ALEC HARVEY *enters. He is about thirty-five. He
> wears a moustache, a mackintosh and a squash hat, and
> he carries a small bag. His manner is decisive and un-
> flurried.*

ALEC: A cup of tea, please.

MYRTLE: Certainly. (*She pours it out in silence.*) Cake
or pastry?

ALEC: No, thank you.

MYRTLE: Threepence.

ALEC (*paying*): Thank you.

> *He takes his cup of tea and goes over to a table. He
> takes off his hat and sits down.* LAURA *glances at the
> clock, collects her parcels in a leisurely manner and goes
> out on to the platform.* BERYL *returns to her place behind
> the counter.*

BERYL: Minnie hasn't touched her milk.

MYRTLE: Did you put it down for her?

BERYL: Yes, but she never came in for it.

MYRTLE: Go out the back and see if she's in the
yard.

ALBERT (*conversationally*): Fond of animals?

MYRTLE: In their place.

ALBERT: My landlady's got a positive mania for
animals—she's got two cats, one Manx and one
ordinary, three rabbits in a hutch in the kitchen, they

belong to her little boy by rights, and one of them foolish-looking dogs with hair over its eyes.

MYRTLE: I don't know to what breed you refer.

ALBERT: I don't think it knows itself——

There is a rumbling noise in the distance, and the sound of a bell.

MYRTLE: There's the boat train.

There is a terrific clatter as the express roars through the station.

ALBERT: What about my other cup? I shall have to be moving—the five-forty-three will be in in a minute.

MYRTLE: Who's on the gate? (*She pours him out another cup.*)

ALBERT: Young William.

MYRTLE: You're neglecting your duty, you know—that's what you're doing.

ALBERT: A bit of relaxation never did anyone any harm——

LAURA enters hurriedly holding a handkerchief to her eye.

LAURA: Please could you give me a glass of water—I've got something in my eye and I want to bathe it.

MYRTLE: Would you like me to have a look?

LAURA: Please don't trouble. I think the water will do it.

MYRTLE (*handing her a glass of water*): Here.

MYRTLE and ALBERT watch her in silence as she bathes her eye.

ALBERT: Bit of coal dust, I expect.

MYRTLE: A man I knew lost the sight of one eye through getting a bit of grit in it.

ALBERT: Painful thing—very painful.

MYRTLE (*as LAURA lifts her head*): Better?

LAURA (*obviously in pain*): I'm afraid not—oh!

 ALEC *rises from his table and comes over.*

ALEC: Can I help you?

LAURA: Oh, no, please—it's only something in my eye.

MYRTLE: Try pulling down your eyelid as far as it'll go.

ALBERT: And then blowing your nose.

ALEC: Please let me look. I happen to be a doctor.

LAURA: It's very kind of you.

ALEC: Turn round to the light, please—now—look up—now look down—I can see it. Keep still—— (*He twists up the corner of his handkerchief and rapidly operates with it.*) There——

LAURA (*blinking*): Oh, dear—what a relief—it was agonising.

ALEC: It looks like a bit of grit.

LAURA: It was when the express went through—thank you very much indeed——

ALEC: Not at all.

 There is the sound of a bell on the platform.

ALBERT (*gulping down his tea*): There we go—I must run.

LAURA: How lucky for me that you happened to be here.

ALEC: Anybody could have done it.

LAURA: Never mind, you did and I'm most grateful. There's my train. Good-bye.

  She puts out her hand and he shakes it politely. She goes out followed at a run by ALBERT GODBY.

  ALEC *looks after her for a moment and then goes back to his table. There is the noise of the train rumbling into the station as the lights fade.*

343

Scene II

The scene is the same and the time is about the same.

> *Nearly three months have passed since the preceding scene, and it is now July.*

> MYRTLE *is resplendent in a light overall.* BERYL'S *appearance is unaltered. The tables are all unoccupied.*

MYRTLE (*slightly relaxed in manner*): It's all very faine, I said, expecting me to do this that and the other, but what do *I* get out of it? You can't expect me to be a cook-housekeeper and char rolled into one during the day, and a loving wife in the evening just because you feel like it. Oh, dear no. There are just as good fish in the sea, I said, as ever came out of it, and I packed my boxes then and there and left him.

BERYL: Didn't you ever go back?

MYRTLE: Never. I went to my sister's place at Folkestone for a bit, and then I went in with a friend of mine and we opened a tea-shop in Hythe.

BERYL: And what happened to him?

MYRTLE: Dead as a door-nail inside three years!

BERYL: Well, I never!

MYRTLE: So you see, every single thing she told me came true—first them clubs coming together, an unexpected journey, then the Queen of diamonds and the ten—that was my friend and the tea-shop business. Then the Ace of spades three times running——

> STANLEY *enters.*

STANLEY: Two rock and an apple.

MYRTLE: What for?

STANLEY: Party on the up platform.

MYRTLE: Why can't they come in here for them?

STANLEY: Ask me another. (*He winks at* BERYL.)

MYRTLE: Got something in your eye?

STANLEY: Nothing beyond a bit of a twinkle every now and again.

BERYL (*giggling*): Oh, you are awful!

MYRTLE: You learn to behave yourself, my lad. Here are your rock cakes. Beryl, stop sniggering and give me an apple off the stand.

> BERYL *complies.*

Not off the front, silly, haven't you got any sense. Here—— (*She takes one from the back of the stand so as to leave the symmetry undisturbed.*)

STANLEY: This one's got a hole in it.

MYRTLE: Tell 'em to come and choose for themselves if they're particular—go on now.

STANLEY: All right—give us a chance.

MYRTLE: What people want to eat on the platform for I really don't know. Tell Mr. Godby not to forget his tea.

STANLEY: Righto!

> *He goes out as* ALEC *and* LAURA *come in.* LAURA *is wearing a summer dress,* ALEC, *a grey flannel suit.*

ALEC: Tea or lemonade?

LAURA: Tea, I think—it's more refreshing, really. (*She sits down at the table by the door.*)

> ALEC *goes to the counter.*

ALEC: Two teas, please.

MYRTLE: Cakes or pastry?

ALEC (*to* LAURA): Cakes or pastry?

LAURA: No, thank you.

ALEC: Are those bath buns fresh?

MYRTLE: Certainly they are—made this morning.

ALEC: Two, please.

MYRTLE *puts two bath buns on a plate, meanwhile* BERYL *has drawn two cups of tea.*

MYRTLE: That'll be eightpence.

ALEC: All right. (*He pays her.*)

MYRTLE: Take the tea to the table, Beryl.

ALEC: I'll carry the buns.

BERYL *brings the tea to the table.* ALEC *follows with the buns.*

ALEC: You must eat one of these—fresh this morning.

LAURA: Very fattening.

ALEC: I don't hold with such foolishness.

BERYL *returns to the counter.*

MYRTLE: I'm going over my accounts. Let me know when Albert comes in.

BERYL: Yes, Mrs. Bagot.

BERYL *settles down behind the counter with* Peg's Paper.

LAURA: They do look good, I must say.

ALEC: One of my earliest passions—I've never outgrown it.

LAURA: Do you like milk in your tea?

ALEC: Yes, don't you?

LAURA: Yes—fortunately.

ALEC: Station refreshments are generally a wee bit arbitrary, you know.

LAURA: I wasn't grumbling.

ALEC (*smiling*): Do you ever grumble—are you ever sullen and cross and bad-tempered?

LAURA: Of course I am—at least not sullen exactly— but I sometimes get into rages.

ALEC: I can't visualise you in a rage.

LAURA: I really don't see why you should,

ALEC: Oh, I don't know—there are signs, you know—one can usually tell——

LAURA: Long upper lips and jaw lines and eyes close together?

ALEC: You haven't any of those things.

LAURA: Do you feel guilty at all? I do.

ALEC (*smiling*): Guilty?

LAURA: You ought to more than me, really—you neglected your work this afternoon.

ALEC: I worked this morning—a little relaxation never did anyone any harm. Why should either of us feel guilty?

LAURA: I don't know—a sort of instinct—as though we were letting something happen that oughtn't to happen.

ALEC: How awfully nice you are!

LAURA: When I was a child in Cornwall—we lived in Cornwall, you know—May, that's my sister, and I used to climb out of our bedroom window on summer nights and go down to the cove and bathe. It was dreadfully cold but we felt very adventurous. I'd never have dared do it by myself, but sharing the danger made it all right —that's how I feel now, really.

ALEC: Have a bun—it's awfully bad for you.

LAURA: You're laughing at me!

ALEC: Yes, a little, but I'm laughing at myself, too.

LAURA: Why?

ALEC: For feeling a small pang when you said about being guilty.

LAURA: There you are, you see!

ALEC: We haven't done anything wrong.

LAURA: Of course we haven't.

ALEC: An   accidental   meeting—then   another

accidental meeting—then a little lunch—then the movies—what could be more ordinary? More natural?

LAURA: We're adults, after all.

ALEC: I never see myself as an adult, do you?

LAURA (*firmly*): Yes, I do. I'm a respectable married woman with a husband and a home and three children.

ALEC: But there must be a part of you, deep down inside, that doesn't feel like that at all—some little spirit that still wants to climb out of the window—that still longs to splash about a bit in the dangerous sea.

LAURA: Perhaps we none of us ever grow up entirely.

ALEC: How awfully nice you are!

LAURA: You said that before.

ALEC: I thought perhaps you hadn't heard.

LAURA: I heard all right.

ALEC (*gently*): I'm respectable too, you know. I have a home and a wife and children and responsibilities—I also have a lot of work to do and a lot of ideals all mixed up with it.

LAURA: What's she like?

ALEC: Madeleine?

LAURA: Yes.

ALEC: Small, dark, rather delicate——

LAURA: How funny! I should have thought she'd be fair.

ALEC: And your husband? What's he like?

LAURA: Medium height, brown hair, kindly, unemotional and not delicate at all.

ALEC: You said that proudly.

LAURA: Did I? (*She looks down.*)

ALEC: What's the matter?

LAURA: The matter? What could be the matter?

ALEC: You suddenly went away.

LAURA (*brightly*): I thought perhaps we were being rather silly.

ALEC: Why?

LAURA: Oh, I don't know—we are such complete strangers, really.

ALEC: It's one thing to close a window, but quite another to slam it down on my fingers.

LAURA: I'm sorry.

ALEC: Please come back again.

LAURA: Is tea bad for one? Worse than coffee, I mean?

ALEC: If this is a professional interview, my fee is a guinea.

LAURA (*laughing*): It's nearly time for your train.

ALEC: I hate to think of it, chugging along, interrupting our tea party.

LAURA: I really am sorry now.

ALEC: What for?

LAURA: For being disagreeable.

ALEC: I don't think you could be disagreeable.

LAURA: You said something just now about your work and ideals being mixed up with it—what ideals?

ALEC: That's a long story.

LAURA: I suppose all doctors ought to have ideals, really—otherwise I should think the work would be unbearable.

ALEC: Surely you're not encouraging me to talk shop?

LAURA: Do you come here every Thursday?

ALEC: Yes. I come in from Churley, and spend a day in the hospital. Stephen Lynn graduated with me— he's the chief physician here. I take over from him once a week, it gives him a chance to go up to London and me a chance to observe and study the hospital patients.

LAURA: Is that a great advantage?

ALEC: Of course. You see I have a special pigeon.

LAURA: What is it?

ALEC: Preventive medicine.

LAURA: Oh, I see.

ALEC (*laughing*): I'm afraid you don't.

LAURA: I was trying to be intelligent.

ALEC: Most good doctors, especially when they're young, have private dreams—that's the best part of them, sometimes though, those get over-professionalised and strangulated and—am I boring you?

LAURA: No—I don't quite understand—but you're not boring me.

ALEC: What I mean is this—all good doctors must be primarily enthusiasts. They must have, like writers and painters, and priests, a sense of vocation—a deep-rooted, unsentimental desire to do good.

LAURA: Yes—I see that.

ALEC: Well, obviously one way of preventing disease is worth fifty ways of curing it—that's where my ideal comes in—preventive medicine isn't anything to do with medicine at all, really—it's concerned with conditions, living conditions and common-sense and hygiene. For instance, my speciality is pneumoconiosis.

LAURA: Oh, dear!

ALEC: Don't be alarmed, it's simpler than it sounds —it's nothing but a slow process of fibrosis of the lung due to the inhalation of particles of dust. In the hospital here there are splendid opportunities for observing cures and making notes, because of the coal mines.

LAURA: You suddenly look much younger.

ALEC (*brought up short*): Do I?

LAURA: Almost like a little boy.

ALEC: What made you say that?

LAURA (*staring at him*): I don't know—yes, I do.

ALEC (*gently*): Tell me.

LAURA (*with panic in her voice*): Oh, no—I couldn't, really. You were saying about the coal mines——

ALEC (*looking into her eyes*): Yes—the inhalation of coal dust—that's one specific form of the diseases—it's called Anthracosis.

LAURA (*hypnotised*): What are the others?

ALEC: Chalicosis—that comes from metal dust—steel works, you know——

LAURA: Yes, of course. Steel works.

ALEC: And Silicosis—stone dust—that's gold mines.

LAURA (*almost in a whisper*): I see.
        There is the sound of a bell.
There's your train.

ALEC (*looking down*): Yes.

LAURA: You mustn't miss it.

ALEC: No.

LAURA (*again the panic in her voice*): What's the matter?

ALEC (*with an effort*): Nothing—nothing at all.

LAURA (*socially*): It's been so very nice—I've enjoyed my afternoon enormously.

ALEC: I'm so glad—so have I. I apologise for boring you with those long medical words——

LAURA: I feel dull and stupid, not to be able to understand more.

ALEC: Shall I see you again?
        There is the sound of a train approaching.

LAURA: It's the other platform, isn't it? You'll have to run. Don't worry about me—mine's due in a few minutes.

ALEC: Shall I see you again?

LAURA: Of course—perhaps you could come over to Ketchworth one Sunday. It's rather far, I know, but we should be delighted to see you.

ALEC (*intensely*): Please—please——

The train is heard drawing to a standstill.

LAURA: What is it?

ALEC: Next Thursday—the same time——

LAURA: No—I can't possibly—I——

ALEC: Please—I ask you most humbly——

LAURA: You'll miss your train!

ALEC: All right. (*He gets up.*)

LAURA: Run——

ALEC (*taking her hand*): Good-bye.

LAURA (*breathlessly*): I'll be there.

ALEC: Thank you, my dear.

He goes out at a run, colliding with ALBERT GODBY, *who is on his way in.*

ALBERT: 'Ere—'ere—take it easy now—take it easy—— (*He goes over to the counter.*)

LAURA *sits quite still staring in front of her as the lights fade.*

SCENE III

It is now October. Three months have passed since the preceding scene.

The refreshment room is empty except for MYRTLE, *who is bending down putting coal into the stove.*

ALBERT GODBY *enters. Upon perceiving her slightly vulnerable position, he slaps her lightly on the behind—she springs to her feet.*

352

MYRTLE: Albert Godby, how dare you!

ALBERT: I couldn't resist it.

MYRTLE: I'll trouble you to keep your hands to yourself.

ALBERT: You're blushing—you look wonderful when you're angry, like an avenging angel.

MYRTLE: I'll give you avenging angel—coming in here taking liberties——

ALBERT: I didn't think after what you said last Monday you'd object to a friendly little slap.

MYRTLE: Never you mind about last Monday—I'm on duty now. A nice thing if Mr. Saunders had happened to be looking through the window.

ALBERT: If Mr. Saunders is in the 'abit of looking through windows, it's time he saw something worth looking at.

MYRTLE: You ought to be ashamed of yourself!

ALBERT: It's just high spirits—don't be mad at me.

MYRTLE (*retiring behind the counter*): High spirits indeed!

ALBERT (*singing*):

"I'm twenty-one to-day—I'm twenty-one to-day,
  I've got the key of the parlour door—
  I've never been twenty-one before——"

MYRTLE (*retiring behind the counter*): Don't make such a noise—they'll hear you on the platform.

ALBERT (*singing*):

"Picture you upon my knee and tea for two and two
      for tea".

MYRTLE: Now look here, Albert Godby, once and for all, will you behave yourself!

ALBERT (*singing*):

"Sometimes I'm 'appy—sometimes I'm blue-oo——"

(*He breaks off.*) This is one of my 'appy moments——

MYRTLE: Here, take your tea and be quiet.

ALBERT: It's all your fault, anyway.

MYRTLE: I don't know to what you're referring, I'm sure.

ALBERT: I was thinking of to-night——

MYRTLE: If you don't learn to behave yourself there won't be a to-night—or any other night, either——

ALBERT (*singing*):

"I'm in love again, and the spring is coming.

  I'm in love again, hear my heart-strings humming——"

MYRTLE: Will you hold your noise?

ALBERT: Give us a kiss.

MYRTLE: I'll do no such thing.

ALBERT: Just a quick one—across the counter. (*He grabs her arm across the counter.*)

MYRTLE: Albert, stop it!

ALBERT: Come on—there's a love.

MYRTLE: Let go of me this minute.

ALBERT: Come on, just one.

> They scuffle for a moment, upsetting a neat pile of cakes on to the floor.

MYRTLE: Now look at me Banburys—all over the floor.

> ALBERT bends down to pick them up. STANLEY enters.

STANLEY: Just in time—or born in the vestry.

MYRTLE: You shut your mouth and help Mr. Godby pick up them cakes.

STANLEY: Anything to oblige. (*He helps* ALBERT.)

> ALEC *and* LAURA *come in.* LAURA *goes to their usual table.* ALEC *goes to the counter.*

ALEC: Good afternoon.

MYRTLE (*grandly*): Good afternoon.

ALEC: Two teas, please.

MYRTLE: Cake or pastry?

ALEC: No, thank you—just the tea.

ALBERT (*conversationally*): Nice weather.

ALEC: Very nice.

ALBERT: Bit of a nip in the air, though.

> MYRTLE, *having given* ALEC *two cups of tea, and taken the money for it, turns to* STANLEY.

MYRTLE: What are you standing there gaping at?

STANLEY: Where's Beryl?

MYRTLE: Never you mind about Beryl, you ought to be on Number 4, and well you know it.

ALBERT (*reflectively*): Love's young dream!

> ALEC, *meanwhile, has carried the two cups of tea over to the table and sat down.*

STANLEY: There's been a run on the Cadbury's nut milk this afternoon; I shall need some more.

MYRTLE (*looking at his tray*): How many have you got left?

STANLEY: Only three.

MYRTLE: Take six more then, and don't forget to mark 'em down.

STANLEY: Righto.

> STANLEY *goes behind the counter and collects six packets of chocolate, then he goes out whistling.*

ALEC: I didn't mean to be unkind.

LAURA: It doesn't matter.

> *A* YOUNG MAN *comes in and goes to the counter.*

YOUNG MAN: Cup of coffee, please, and a beef sandwich.

MYRTLE: We're out of beef—will ham do?

YOUNG MAN: Yes—ham'll do.

> ALBERT *winks at* MYRTLE *over his tea-cup.*
> MYRTLE *draws a cup of coffee for the* YOUNG MAN *and*
> *takes a sandwich out of one of the glass stands.*

ALEC: We can't part like this.

LAURA: I think it would be better if we did.

ALEC: You don't really mean that?

LAURA: I'm trying to mean it—I'm trying with all my strength.

ALEC: Oh, my dearest dear——

LAURA: Don't—please don't——

MYRTLE (*to* YOUNG MAN): Fourpence, please.

YOUNG MAN: Thank you. (*He pays, and carries his coffee and sandwich over to the table near the stove.*)

ALBERT: It is all right about to-night, isn't it?

MYRTLE: I'll think about it.

ALBERT: It's Claudette Colbert, you know.

MYRTLE: Fat chance I shall get of enjoying Claudette Colbert with you hissing in me ear all the time.

ALBERT: I'll be as good as gold.

> BERYL *enters in a coat and hat—she goes behind the*
> *counter.*

ALEC: It's no use running away from the truth, darling—we're lovers, aren't we? If it happens or if it doesn't, we're lovers in our hearts.

LAURA: Can't you see how wrong it is? How dreadfully wrong!

ALEC: I can see what's true—whether it's wrong or right.

BERYL (*taking off her hat and coat*): Mr. Saunders wants you, Mr. Godby.

ALBERT: What for?

BERYL: I don't know.

MYRTLE: You'd better go, Albert, you know what he is.

ALBERT: I know 'e's a bloody fool, if that's what you mean.

MYRTLE: Be quiet, Albert—in front of Beryl.

BERYL: Don't mind me.

MYRTLE: Go on—finish up your tea.

ALBERT: No peace for the wicked——

MYRTLE: Go on——

ALBERT: I'll be back——

MYRTLE: That'll be nice, I'm sure——

> ALBERT *goes.*
>
> MYRTLE *retires to the upper end of the counter.* BERYL *goes off and comes on again laden with various packages of comestibles. She and* MYRTLE *proceed to stack them on the upstage end of the counter.*

ALEC (*urgently*): There's no chance of Stephen getting back until late—nobody need ever know.

LAURA: It's so furtive to love like that—so cheap—much better not to love at all.

ALEC: It's too late not to love at all—be brave—we're both in the same boat—let's be generous to each other.

LAURA: What is there brave in it—sneaking away to someone else's house, loving in secret with the horror of being found out hanging over us all the time. It would be far braver to say good-bye and never see each other again.

ALEC: Could you be as brave as that? I know I couldn't.

LAURA (*breathlessly*): Couldn't you?

ALEC: Listen, my dear. This is something that's never happened to either of us before. We've loved before and been happy before, and miserable and contented and reckless, but this is different—something lovely and strange and desperately difficult. We can't measure it along with the values of our ordinary lives.

LAURA: Why should it be so important—why should we let it be so important?

ALEC: We can't help ourselves.

LAURA: We can—we can if only we're strong enough.

ALEC: Why is it so strong to deny something that's urgent and real—something that all our instincts are straining after—mightn't it be weak and not strong at all to run away from such tremendous longing?

LAURA: Is it so real to you? So tremendous?

ALEC: Can't you see that it is.

LAURA: It's so difficult, so strained. I'm lost.

ALEC: Don't say that, darling.

LAURA: Loving you is hard for me—it makes me a stranger in my own house. Familiar things, ordinary things that I've known for years like the dining-room curtains, and the wooden tub with a silver top that holds biscuits and a water-colour of San Remo that my mother painted, look odd to me, as though they belonged to someone else—when I've just left you, when I go home, I'm more lonely than I've ever been before. I passed the house the other day without noticing and had to turn back, and when I went in it seemed to draw away from me—my whole life seems to be drawing away from me, and—and I don't know what to do.

ALEC: Oh, darling——

LAURA: I love them just the same, Fred I mean and the children, but it's as though it wasn't me at all—as though I were looking on at someone else. Do you know what I mean? Is it the same with you? Or is it easier for men——

ALEC: I don't know.

LAURA: Please, dear, don't look unhappy. I'm not grumbling, really I'm not——

ALEC: I don't suppose being in love has ever been easy for anybody.

LAURA (*reaching for his hand*): We've only got a few more minutes—I didn't mean to be depressing.

ALEC: It isn't any easier for me, darling, honestly it isn't.

LAURA: I know, I know—I only wanted reassuring.

ALEC: I hold you in my arms all the way back in the train—I'm angry with every moment that I'm not alone —to love you uninterrupted—whenever my surgery door opens and a patient comes in, my heart jumps in case it might be you. One of them I'm grateful to—he's got neuritis, and I give him sun-ray treatment—he lies quite quietly baking, and I can be with you in the shadows behind the lamp.

LAURA: How silly we are—how unbearably silly!

ALEC: Friday — Saturday — Sunday — Monday — Tuesday—Wednesday——

LAURA: Thursday——

ALEC: It's all right, isn't it?

LAURA: Oh, yes—of course it is.

ALEC: Don't pass the house again—don't let it snub you. Go boldly in and stare that damned water-colour out of countenance.

LAURA: All right—don't bake your poor neuritis man too long—you might blister him.

The continuation of their scene is drowned by the noisy

entrance of two soldiers, BILL *and* JOHNNIE. *They go to the counter.*

BILL: Afternoon, lady.

MYRTLE (*grandly*): Good afternoon.

BILL: A couple of splashes, please.

MYRTLE: Very sorry, it's out of hours.

JOHNNIE: Come on, lady—you've got a kind face.

MYRTLE: That's neither here nor there.

BILL: Just sneak us a couple under cover of them poor old sandwiches.

MYRTLE: Them sandwiches were fresh this morning, and I shall do no such thing.

BILL: Come on, be a sport.

JOHNNIE: Nobody'd know.

MYRTLE: I'm very sorry, I'm sure, but it's against the rules.

BILL: You could pop it into a couple of tea-cups.

MYRTLE: You're asking me to break the law, young man.

JOHNNIE: I think I've got a cold coming on—we've been mucking about at the Butts all day—you can't afford to let the army catch cold, you know.

MYRTLE: You can have as much as you want after six o'clock.

BILL: An 'eart of stone—that's what you've got, lady—an 'eart of stone.

MYRTLE: Don't you be cheeky.

JOHNNIE: My throat's like a parrot's cage—listen! (*He makes a crackling noise with his throat.*)

MYRTLE: Take some lemonade then—or ginger-beer.

BILL: Couldn't touch it—against doctor's orders— my inside's been most peculiar ever since I 'ad trench feet—you wouldn't give a child carbolic acid, would you? That's what ginger-beer does to me.

MYRTLE: Get on with you!

JOHNNIE: It's true—it's poison to him, makes 'im make the most 'orrible noises—you wouldn't like anything nasty to 'appen in your posh buffay——

MYRTLE: May licence does not permit me to serve alcohol out of hours—that's final!

JOHNNIE: We're soldiers we are—willing to lay down our lives for you—and you grudge us one splash——

MYRTLE: You wouldn't want to get me into trouble, would you?

BILL: Give us a chance, lady, that's all—just give us a chance.

    They both roar with laughter.

MYRTLE: Beryl, ask Mr. Godby to come 'ere for a moment, will you?

BERYL: Yes, Mrs. Bagot.

    She comes out from behind the counter and goes on to the platform.

BILL: Who's 'e when 'e's at home?

MYRTLE: You'll soon see—coming in here cheeking me.

JOHNNIE: Now then, now then, naughty naughty——

MYRTLE: Kaindly be quiet!

BILL: Shut up, Johnnie——

JOHNNIE: What about them drinks, lady?

MYRTLE: I've already told you I can't serve alcoholic refreshment out of hours——

JOHNNIE: Come off it, mother, be a pal!

MYRTLE (*losing her temper*): I'll give you mother, you saucy upstart——

BILL: Who are you calling an upstart!

MYRTLE: You—and I'll trouble you to get out of here double quick—disturbing the customers and making a nuisance of yourselves.

JOHNNIE: 'Ere, where's the fire—where's the fire!

ALBERT GODBY *enters, followed by* BERYL.

ALBERT: What's going on in 'ere!

MYRTLE (*with dignity*): Mr. Godby, these gentlemen are annoying me.

BILL: We 'aven't done anything.

JOHNNIE: All we did was ask for a couple of drinks——

MYRTLE: They insulted me, Mr. Godby.

JOHNNIE: We never did nothing of the sort—just 'aving a little joke, that's all.

ALBERT *laconically*): 'Op it—both of you.

BILL: We've got a right to stay 'ere as long as we like.

ALBERT: You 'eard what I said—'Op it!

JOHNNIE: What is this, a free country or a bloody Sunday school?

ALBERT (*firmly*): I checked your passes at the gate—your train's due in a minute—Number 2 platform——'Op it.

JOHNNIE: Look 'ere now——

BILL: Come on, Johnnie—don't argue with the poor little basket.

ALBERT (*dangerously*): 'Op it!

BILL *and* JOHNNIE *go to the door*. JOHNNIE *turns*.

JOHNNIE: Toodle-oo, mother, and if them sandwiches were made this morning, you're Shirley Temple——

They go out.

MYRTLE: Thank you, Albert.

BERYL: What a nerve talking to you like that!

MYRTLE: Be quiet, Beryl—pour me out a nip of Three Star—I'm feeling quite upset.

ALBERT: I've got to get back to the gate.

MYRTLE (*graciously*): I'll be seeing you later, Albert.

ALBERT (*with a wink*): Okay!

> *He goes out.*
>
> *A train bell rings.* BERYL *brings* MYRTLE *a glass of brandy.*

MYRTLE (*sipping it*): I'll say one thing for Albert Godby—he may be on the small side, but 'e's a gentleman.

> *She and* BERYL *retire once more to the upper end of the counter and continue their arrangement of bottles, biscuits, etc. There is the sound of a train drawing into the station.*

LAURA: There's your train.

ALEC: I'm going to miss it.

LAURA: Please go.

ALEC: No.

LAURA (*clasping and unclasping her hands*): I wish I could think clearly. I wish I could know—really know what to do.

ALEC: Do you trust me?

LAURA: Yes—I trust you.

ALEC: I don't mean conventionally—I mean really.

LAURA: Yes.

ALEC: Everything's against us—all the circumstances of our lives—those have got to go on unaltered. We're nice people, you and I, and we've got to go on being nice. Let's enclose this love of ours with real strength, and let that strength be that no one is hurt by it except ourselves.

LAURA: Must we be hurt by it?

ALEC: Yes—when the time comes.

LAURA: Very well.

ALEC: All the furtiveness and the secrecy and the hole-in-corner cheapness can be justified if only we're strong enough—strong enough to keep it to ourselves, clean and untouched by anybody else's knowledge or even suspicious—something of our own for ever—to be remembered——

LAURA: Very well.

ALEC: We won't speak of it any more—I'm going now—back to Stephen's flat. I'll wait for you—if you don't come I shall know only that you weren't quite ready—that you needed a little longer to find your own dear heart. This is the address.

> *He scribbles on a bit of paper as the express thunders through the station. He gets up and goes swiftly without looking at her again. She sits staring at the paper, then she fumbles in her bag and finds a cigarette. She lights it— the platform bell goes.*

MYRTLE: There's the 5.43.

BERYL: We ought to have another Huntley and Palmer's to put in the middle, really.

MYRTLE: There are some more on the shelf.

> *BERYL fetches another packet of biscuits and takes it to MYRTLE. There is the noise of the 5.43—LAURA'S train—steaming into the station. LAURA sits puffing her cigarette. Suddenly she gets up—gathers up her bag quickly, and moves towards the door. She pauses and comes back to the table as the whistle blows. The train starts, she puts the paper in her bag and goes quietly out as the lights fade.*

SCENE IV

The time is about 9.45 on an evening in December.

> *There are only two lights on in the refreshment room as it is nearly closing time.*
>
> *When the scene starts the stage is empty. There is the noise of a fast train rattling through the station.*
>
> BERYL *comes in from the upstage door behind the counter armed with several muslin cloths which she proceeds to drape over the things on the counter. She hums breathily to herself as she does so.* STANLEY *enters, he has discarded his uniform and is wearing his ordinary clothes.*

STANLEY: Hallo!

BERYL: You made me jump.

STANLEY: Are you walking home?

BERYL: Maybe.

STANLEY: Do you want me to wait?

BERYL: I've got to go straight back.

STANLEY: Why?

BERYL: Mother 'll be waiting up.

STANLEY: Can't you say you've been kept late?

BERYL: I said that last time.

STANLEY: Say it again—say there's been a rush on.

BERYL: Don't be so silly—Mother's not that much of a fool.

STANLEY: Be a sport, Beryl—shut down five minutes early and say you was kept ten minutes late—that gives us a quarter of an hour.

BERYL: What happens if Mrs. Bagot comes back?

STANLEY: She won't—she's out having a bit of a slap and tickle with our Albert.

BERYL: Stan, you are awful!

STANLEY: I'll wait for you in the yard.

BERYL: Oh, all right.

STANLEY goes out.

BERYL resumes her song and the draping of the cake stands. LAURA enters—she looks pale and unhappy.

LAURA: I'd like a glass of brandy, please.

BERYL: We're just closing.

LAURA: I see you are, but you're not quite closed yet, are you?

BERYL (*sullenly*): Three Star?

LAURA: Yes, that'll do.

BERYL (*getting it*): Tenpence, please.

LAURA (*taking money from her bag*): Here—and—have you a piece of paper and an envelope?

BERYL: I'm afraid you'll have to get that at the bookstall.

LAURA: The bookstall's shut—please—it's very important—I should be so much obliged——

BERYL: Oh, all right—wait a minute.

She goes off.

LAURA sips the brandy at the counter, she is obviously trying to control her nerves. BERYL returns with some notepaper and an envelope.

LAURA: Thank you so much.

BERYL: We close in a few minutes, you know.

LAURA: Yes, I know.

She takes the notepaper and her brandy over to the table by the door and sits down. She stares at the paper for a moment, takes another sip of brandy and then begins to write. BERYL looks at her with exasperation and goes off through the upstage door. LAURA falters in her writing, then breaks down and buries her face in her hands. ALEC *comes in—he looks hopelessly round for a moment, and then sees her.*

ALEC: Thank God oh, darling!

LAURA: Please go away—please don't say anything.

ALEC: I can't let you go like this.

LAURA: You must. It'll be better—really it will.

ALEC (*sitting down beside her*): You're being dreadfully cruel.

LAURA: I feel so utterly degraded.

ALEC: It was just a beastly accident that he came back early—he doesn't know who you are—he never even saw you.

LAURA: I listened to your voices in the sitting-room —I crept out and down the stairs—feeling like a prostitute.

ALEC: Don't, dearest—don't talk like that, please——

LAURA (*bitterly*): I suppose he laughed, didn't he— after he got over being annoyed? I suppose you spoke of me together as men of the world.

ALEC: We didn't speak of you—we spoke of a nameless creature who had no reality at all.

LAURA (*wildly*): Why didn't you tell him the truth? Why didn't you say who I was and that we were lovers —shameful secret lovers—using his flat like a bad house because we had nowhere else to go, and were afraid of being found out! Why didn't you tell him we were cheap and low and without courage—why didn't you——

ALEC: Stop it, Laura—pull yourself together!

LAURA: It's true—don't you see, it's true!

ALEC: It's nothing of the sort. I know you feel horrible, and I'm deeply, desperately sorry. I feel horrible, too, but it doesn't matter really—this—this unfortunate, damnable incident—it was just bad luck. It couldn't affect us really, you and me—we know the truth—we know we really love each other—that's all that matters.

LAURA: It isn't all that matters—other things matter, too, self-respect matters, and decency—I can't go on any longer.

ALEC: Could you really—say good-bye—not see me any more?

LAURA: Yes—if you'd help me.

> *There is silence for a moment.* ALEC *gets up and walks about—he stops and stands staring at a coloured calendar on the wall.*

ALEC (*quietly, with his back to her*): I love you, Laura— I shall love you always until the end of my life—all the shame that the world might force on us couldn't touch the real truth of it. I can't look at you now because I know something—I know that this is the beginning of the end—not the end of my loving you—but the end of our being together. But not quite yet, darling—please not quite yet.

LAURA: Very well—not quite yet.

ALEC: I know what you feel—about this evening, I mean—about the beastliness of it. I know about the strain of our different lives, our lives apart from each other. The feeling of guilt—of doing wrong is a little too strong, isn't it? Too persistent—perhaps too great a price to pay for the few hours of happiness we get out of it. I know all this because it's the same for me, too.

LAURA: You can look at me now—I'm all right.

ALEC (*turning*): Let's be careful—let's prepare ourselves—a sudden break now, however brave and admirable, would be too cruel—we can't do such violence to our hearts and minds.

LAURA: Very well.

ALEC: I'm going away.

LAURA: I see.

ALEC: But not quite yet.

LAURA: Please not quite yet.

BERYL *enters in hat and coat.*

BERYL: I'm afraid it's closing time.

ALEC: Oh, is it?

BERYL: I shall have to lock up.

ALEC: This lady is catching the 10.10—she's not feeling very well, and it's very cold on the platform.

BERYL: The waiting-room's open.

ALEC (*going to counter*): Look here—I'd be very much obliged if you'd let us stay here for another few minutes.

BERYL: I'm sorry—it's against the rules.

ALEC (*giving her a ten-shilling note*): Please—come back to lock up when the train comes in.

BERYL: I'll have to switch off the lights—someone might see 'em on and think we were open.

ALEC: Just for a few minutes—please!

BERYL: You won't touch anything, will you?

ALEC: Not a thing.

BERYL: Oh, all right.

She switches off the lights. The lamp from the platform shines in through the window so it isn't quite dark.

ALEC: Thank you very much.

BERYL *goes out by the platform door, closing it behind her.*

LAURA: Just a few minutes.

ALEC: Let's have a cigarette, shall we?

LAURA: I have some. (*She takes her bag up from the table.*)

ALEC (*producing his case*): No, here. (*He lights their cigarettes carefully.*) Now then—I want you to promise me something.

LAURA: What is it?

ALEC: Promise me that however unhappy you are, and however much you think things over that you'll meet me next Thursday as usual.

LAURA: Not at the flat.

ALEC: No—be at the Picture House café at the same time. I'll hire a car—we'll drive out into the country.

LAURA: All right—I promise.

ALEC: We've got to talk—I've got to explain.

LAURA: About going away?

ALEC: Yes.

LAURA: Where are you going? Where can you go? You can't give up your practice!

ALEC: I've had a job offered me—I wasn't going to tell you—I wasn't going to take it—but I must—I know now, it's the only way out.

LAURA: Where?

ALEC: A long way away—Johannesburg.

LAURA (*hopelessly*): Oh God!

ALEC (*hurriedly*): My brother's out there—they're opening a new hospital—they want me in it. It's a fine opportunity, really. I'll take Madeleine and the boys, it's been torturing me for three weeks, the necessity of making a decision one way or the other—I haven't told anybody, not even Madeleine. I couldn't bear the idea of leaving you, but now I see—it's got to happen soon, anyway—it's almost happening already.

LAURA (*tonelessly*): When will you go?

ALEC: In about two months' time.

LAURA: It's quite near, isn't it?

ALEC: Do you want me to stay? Do you want me to turn down the offer?

LAURA: Don't be foolish, Alec.

ALEC: I'll do whatever you say.

LAURA: That's unkind of you, my darling. (*She suddenly buries her head in her arms and bursts into tears.*)

ALEC (*putting his arms round her*): Oh, Laura, don't, please don't!

LAURA: I'll be all right—leave me alone a minute.

ALEC: I love you—I love you.

LAURA: I know.

ALEC: We knew we'd get hurt.

LAURA (*sitting up*): I'm being very stupid.

ALEC (*giving her his handkerchief*): Here.

LAURA (*blowing her nose*): Thank you.

> *The platform bells goes.*

There's my train.

ALEC: You're not angry with me, are you?

LAURA: No, I'm not angry—I don't think I'm anything, really—I feel just tired.

ALEC: Forgive me.

LAURA: Forgive you for what?

ALEC: For everything—for having met you in the first place—for taking the piece of grit out of your eye—for loving you—for bringing you so much misery.

LAURA (*trying to smile*): I'll forgive you—if you'll forgive me——

> *There is the noise of a train pulling into the station.*
> BERYL *enters.* LAURA *and* ALEC *get up.*

ALEC: I'll see you into the train.

LAURA: No—please stay here.

ALEC: All right.

LAURA (*softly*): Good-night, darling.

ALEC: Good-night, darling.

> *She goes hurriedly out on to the platform without looking back.*

ALEC: The last train for Churley hasn't gone yet, has it?

BERYL: I couldn't say, I'm sure.

ALEC: I'll wait in the waiting-room—thank you very much.

BERYL: I must lock up now.

ALEC: All right. Good-night.

BERYL: Good-night.

> *The train starts as he goes out on to the platform. BERYL locks the door carefully after him, and then goes off upstage as the lights fade.*

SCENE V

The time is between 5 and 5.30 on an afternoon in March. MYRTLE is behind the counter. BERYL is crouching over the stove putting coals in it. ALBERT enters.

ALBERT (*gaily*): One tea, please—two lumps of sugar, and a bath bun, and make it snappy.

MYRTLE: What's the matter with you?

ALBERT: Beryl, 'op it.

MYRTLE: Don't you go ordering Beryl about—you haven't any right to.

ALBERT: You heard me, Beryl—'Op it.

BERYL (*giggling*): Well, I never!

MYRTLE: Go into the back room a minute, Beryl.

BERYL: Yes, Mrs. Bagot.

　　She goes.

MYRTLE: Now then, Albert—you behave—we don't want the whole station laughing at us.

ALBERT: What is there to laugh at?

MYRTLE: Here's your tea.

ALBERT: How d'you feel?

MYRTLE: Don't talk so soft—how should I feel?

ALBERT: I only wondered—— (*He leans towards her.*)

MYRTLE: Look out—somebody's coming in.

ALBERT: It's only Romeo and Juliet.

　　LAURA *and* ALEC *come in.* LAURA *goes to the table,* ALEC *to the counter.*

ALEC: Good afternoon.

MYRTLE: Good afternoon—same as usual?

ALEC: Yes, please.

MYRTLE (*drawing tea*): Quite Springy out, isn' it?

ALEC: Yes—quite.

　　He pays her, collects the tea and carries it over to the table—something in his manner causes ALBERT *to make a grimace over his tea-cup at* MYRTLE. ALEC *sits down at the table, and he and* LAURA *sip their tea in silence.*

ALBERT: I spoke to Mr. Saunders.

MYRTLE: What did he say?

ALBERT: 'E was very decent as a matter-of-fact—said it'd be all right——

　　MILDRED *comes in hurriedly. She is a fair girl wearing a station overall.*

MILDRED: Is Beryl here?

MYRTLE: Why, Mildred, whatever's the matter?

373

MILDRED: It's her mother—she's bad again—they telephoned through to the Booking Office.

MYRTLE: She's inside—you'd better go in. Don't go yelling in at her now—tell her gently.

MILDRED: They said she'd better come at once.

MYRTLE: I thought this was going to happen—stay here, Mildred. I'll tell her. Wait a minute, Albert.

MYRTLE *vanishes into the inside room.*

ALBERT: Better get back to the bookstall, hadn't you?

MILDRED: Do you think she's going to die?

ALBERT: How do I know?

MILDRED: Mr. Saunders thinks she is—judging by what the doctor said on the telephone.

ALBERT: 'Ow do you know it was the doctor?

MILDRED: Mr. Saunders said it was.

ALBERT: She's always being took bad, that old woman.

MILDRED: Do you think Beryl would like me to go along with her?

ALBERT: You can't, and leave nobody on the papers.

MILDRED: Mr. Saunders said I might if it was necessary.

ALBERT: Well, go and get your 'at then, and don't make such a fuss.

MYRTLE *comes back.*

MYRTLE: She's going at once, poor little thing!

ALBERT: Mildred's going with her.

MYRTLE: All right, Mildred—go on.

MILDRED (*half-way to the door*): What about me 'at?

MYRTLE: Never mind about your 'at—go this way.

MILDRED *rushes off upstage*.

MYRTLE: Poor child—this has been hanging over her for weeks. (*She puts her head round the door*.) Mildred, tell Beryl she needn't come back to-night, I'll stay on.

ALBERT: 'Ere, you can't do that, we was going to the Broadway Melody of 1936.

MYRTLE: For shame, Albert—thinking of the Broadway Melody of 1936 in a moment of life and death!

ALBERT: But look 'ere, Myrtle——

MYRTLE: I dreamt of a hearse last night, and whenever I dream of a hearse something happens—you mark my words——

ALBERT: I've got reserved tickets——

MYRTLE: Send Stanley to change them on his way home. Come in 'ere when you go off and I'll make you a little supper inside.

ALBERT (*grumbily*): Everybody getting into a state and fussing about——

MYRTLE: You shock me, Albert, you do really—go on, finish up your tea and get back to the gate. (*She turns and goes to the upper end of the counter*.)

ALBERT *gulps his tea*.

ALBERT (*slamming the cup down on the counter*): Women!
He *stamps out on to the platform*.

ALEC: Are you all right, darling?

LAURA: Yes, I'm all right.

ALEC: I wish I could think of something to say.

LAURA: It doesn't matter—not saying anything, I mean.

ALEC: I'll miss my train and wait to see you into yours.

LAURA: No—no—please don't. I'll come over to your platform with you—I'd rather.

375

ALEC: Very well.

LAURA: Do you think we shall ever see each other again?

ALEC: I don't know. (*His voice breaks.*) Not for years, anyway.

LAURA: The children will all be grown up—I wonder if they'll ever meet and know each other.

ALEC: Couldn't I write to you—just once in a while?

LAURA: No—please not—we promised we wouldn't.

ALEC: Please know this—please know that you'll be with me for ages and ages yet—far away into the future. Time will wear down the agony of not seeing you, bit by bit the pain will go—but the loving you and the memory of you won't ever go—please know that.

LAURA: I know it.

ALEC: It's easier for me than for you. I do realise that, really I do. I at least will have different shapes to look at, and new work to do—you have to go on among familiar things—my heart aches for you so.

LAURA: I'll be all right.

ALEC: I love you with all my heart and soul.

LAURA (*quietly*): I want to die—if only I could die.

ALEC: If you died you'd forget me—I want to be remembered.

LAURA: Yes, I know—I do, too.

ALEC: Good-bye, my dearest love.

LAURA: Good-bye, my dearest love.

ALEC: We've still got a few minutes.

LAURA: Thank God——!

> DOLLY MESSITER *bustles into the refreshment room. She is a nicely dressed woman, with rather a fussy manner. She is laden with parcels. She sees* LAURA.

DOLLY: Laura! What a lovely surprise!

LAURA (*dazed*): Oh, Dolly!

DOLLY: My dear, I've been shopping till I'm dropping—that sounds like a song, doesn't it? My feet are nearly falling off, and my throat's parched. I thought of having tea in Spindle's, but I was terrified of losing the train. I'm always missing trains, and being late for meals, and Bob gets disagreeable for days at a time. Oh, dear—— (*She flops down at their table.*)

LAURA: This is Doctor Harvey.

ALEC (*rising*): How do you do!

DOLLY (*shaking hands*): How do you do! Would you be a perfect dear and get me a cup of tea! I don't think I could drag my poor old bones as far as the counter. I must get some chocolates for Tony, too, but I can do that afterwards—here's sixpence——

ALEC (*waving it away*): No, please——

> He goes drearily over to the counter, gets another cup of tea from MYRTLE, pays for it and comes back to the table, meanwhile DOLLY continues to talk.

DOLLY: My dear—what a nice-looking man. Who on earth is he? Really, you're quite a dark horse. I shall telephone Fred in the morning and make mischief—that is a bit of luck. I haven't seen you for ages, and I've been meaning to pop in, but Tony's had measles, you know, and I had all that awful fuss about Phyllis—but of course you don't know—she left me! Suddenly upped and went, my dear, without even an hour's warning, let alone a month's notice.

LAURA (*with an effort*): Oh, how dreadful!

DOLLY: Mind you, I never cared for her much, but still Tony did. Tony adored her, and—but, never mind, I'll tell you all about that in the train.

377

ALEC arrives back at the table with her tea—he sits down again.

Thank you so very much. They've certainly put enough milk in it—but still it's wet and that's all one can really ask for in a refreshment room—— (*She sips it.*) Oh, dear—no sugar.

ALEC: It's in the spoon.

DOLLY: Oh, of course—what a fool I am—Laura, you look frightfully well. I do wish I'd known you were coming in to-day, we could have come together and lunched and had a good gossip. I loathe shopping by myself, anyway.

There is the sound of a bell on the platform.

LAURA: There's your train.

ALEC: Yes, I know.

DOLLY: Aren't you coming with us?

ALEC: No, I go in the opposite direction. My practice is in Churley.

DOLLY: How interesting! What sort of a doctor are you? I mean, are you a specialist at anything or just a sort of general family doctor?

ALEC: I'm a general practitioner at the moment.

LAURA (*dully*): Dr. Harvey is going out to Africa next week.

DOLLY: But, my dear, how thrilling! Are you going to operate on the Zulus or something? I always associate Africa with Zulus, but I may be quite wrong.

There is the sound of ALEC's train approaching.

ALEC: I must go.

LAURA: Yes, you must.

ALEC: Good-bye.

DOLLY: Good-bye.

He shakes hands with DOLLY, looks at LAURA

*swiftly once, then presses her hand under cover of the table
and leaves hurriedly as the train is heard rumbling into the
station.* LAURA *sits quite still.*

DOLLY: He'll have to run—he's got to get right over
to the other platform. How did you meet him?

LAURA: I got something in my eye one day, and he
took it out.

DOLLY: My dear—how very romantic! I'm always
getting things in my eye and nobody the least bit
attractive has ever paid the faintest attention—which
reminds me—you know about Harry and Lucy Jenner,
don't you?

LAURA (*listening for the train to start*): No—what about
them?

DOLLY: My dear—they're going to get a divorce—
at least I believe they're getting a conjugal separation,
or whatever it is to begin with, and the divorce later
on.

 *The train starts, and the sound of it dies gradually
 away in the distance.*

It seems that there's an awful Mrs. Something or other
in London that he's been carrying on with for ages—
you know how he was always having to go up on
business. Well, apparently Lucy's sister saw them,
Harry and this woman, in the Tate Gallery of all places,
and she wrote to Lucy, and then gradually the whole
thing came out.

 There is the sound of a bell on the platform.

Is that our train? (*She addresses* MYRTLE.) Can you tell
me, is that the Ketchworth train?

MYRTLE: No, that's the express.

LAURA: The boat train.

DOLLY: Oh, yes—that doesn't stop, does it? Express

trains are Tony's passion in life—he knows them all by name—where they start from and where they go to, and how long they take to get there. Oh, dear, I mustn't forget his chocolate. (*She jumps up and goes to the counter.*)

      LAURA *remains quite still.*

(*At counter.*) I want some chocolate, please.

MYRTLE: Milk or plain?

DOLLY: Plain, I think—or no, perhaps milk would be nicer. Have you any with nuts in it?

      The express is heard in the distance.

MYRTLE: Nestlé's nut milk—shilling or sixpence?

DOLLY: Give me one plain and one nut milk.

      *The noise of the express sounds louder—*LAURA *suddenly gets up and goes swiftly out on to the platform. The express roars through the station as* DOLLY *finishes buying and paying for her chocolate. She turns.*

DOLLY: Oh! where is she?

MYRTLE (*looking over the counter*): I never noticed her go.

      DOLLY *comes over to the table,* LAURA *comes in again, looking very white and shaky.*

DOLLY: My dear, I couldn't think where you'd disappeared to.

LAURA: I just wanted to see the express go through.

DOLLY: What on earth's the matter—do you feel ill?

LAURA: I feel a little sick.

DOLLY: Have you any brandy?

MYRTLE: I'm afraid it's out of hours.

DOLLY: Surely—if someone's feeling ill——

LAURA: I'm all right, really.

      The platform bell goes.

That's our train.

DOLLY: Just a sip of brandy will buck you up. (*To* MYRTLE.) Please——

MYRTLE: Very well. (*She pours out some brandy.*)

DOLLY: How much?

MYRTLE: Tenpence, please.

DOLLY (*paying her*): There!

> *She takes the brandy over to* LAURA, *who has sat down again at the table.*

Here you are, dear.

LAURA (*taking it*): Thank you.

> *As she sips it the train is heard coming into the station.* DOLLY *proceeds to gather up her parcels as the Curtain falls.*

FUMED OAK

A Comedy in Two Scenes

from

TO-NIGHT AT 8.30

CHARACTERS:

HENRY GOW

DORIS, *his wife*

ELSIE, *his daughter*

MRS. ROCKETT, *his mother-in-law*

Scene I.   Morning.

Scene II.   Evening.

The *action of the play passes in the sitting-room of the* GOWS' *house in South London.*

The *time is the present day.*

The GOWS' *sitting-room is indistinguishable from several thousand other suburban sitting-rooms. The dominant note is refinement. There are french windows at the back opening on to a narrow lane of garden. These are veiled discreetly by lace curtains set off by a pelmet and side pieces of rather faded blue casement cloth. There is a tiled fireplace on the right; an upright piano between it and the window; a fumed oak sideboard on the left and, below it, a door leading to the hall, the stairs and the front door. There is a fumed oak dining-room suite consisting of a table, and six chairs; a sofa; an arm-chair in front of the fire; a radio, and a plentiful sprinkling over the entire room of ornaments and framed photographs.*

When the curtain rises it is about eight-thirty on a spring morning. Rain is trickling down the windows and breakfast is laid on the table.

MRS. ROCKETT *is seated in the arm-chair by the fire; on a small table next to her is a cup of tea, and a work-basket. She is a fattish, grey-looking woman dressed in a blouse and skirt and a pepper and salt jumper of artificial silk. Her pince-nez snap in and out of a little clip on her bosom and her feet are bad which necessitates the wearing of large quilted slippers in the house.*

DORIS, *aged about thirty-five, is seated at the table reading a newspaper propped up against the cruet. She is thin and anæmic and whatever traces of past prettiness she might have had are obscured by the pursed-up, rather sour gentility of her expression. She wears a nondescript coat-frock, a slave bangle and a necklace of amber glass beads. ELSIE, her daughter aged about fourteen, is sitting opposite to her, cutting her toast into strips in order to dip them into her boiled egg. She is a straight-haired ordinary-looking girl dressed in a navy blue school dress with a glacé red leather waist belt.*

There is a complete silence broken only by the occasional rattle of a spoon in a cup or a sniffle from ELSIE who has a slight head cold.

HENRY GOW comes into the room. He is tall and spare, neatly dressed in a blue serge suit. He wears rimless glasses and his hair is going grey at the sides and thin on the top. He sits down at the table without a word. DORIS automatically rises and goes out, returning in a moment with a plate of haddock which she places in front of him and resumes her place. HENRY pours himself out some tea. DORIS, without looking at him, being re-immersed in the paper, passes him the milk and sugar. The silence continues until ELSIE breaks it.

ELSIE: Mum?

DORIS: What?

ELSIE: When can I put my hair up?

DORIS (*snappily*): When you're old enough.

ELSIE: Gladys Pierce is the same age as me and she's got hers up.

DORIS: Never you mind about Gladys Pierce, get on with your breakfast.

ELSIE: I don't see why I can't have it cut. That would be better than nothing.

 This remark is ignored.

Maisie Blake had hers cut last week and it looks lovely.

DORIS: Never you mind about Maisie Blake neither. She's common.

ELSIE: Miss Pritchard doesn't think so. Miss Pritchard likes Maisie Blake a lot, she said it looked ever so nice.

DORIS (*irritably*): What?

ELSIE: Her hair.

DORIS: Get on with your breakfast. You'll be late.

ELSIE (*petulantly*): Oh, Mum——

DORIS: And stop sniffling. Sniffle sniffle sniffle! Haven't you got a handkerchief?

ELSIE: Yes, but it's a clean one.

DORIS: Never mind, use it.

MRS. ROCKETT: The child can't help having a cold.

DORIS: She can blow her nose, can't she, even if she has got a cold?

ELSIE (*conversationally*): Dodie Watson's got a terrible cold, she's had it for weeks. It went to her chest and then it went back to her head again.

MRS. ROCKETT: That's the worst of schools, you're always catching something.

ELSIE: Miss Pritchard's awful mean to Dodie Watson, she said she'd had enough of it.

DORIS: Enough of what?

ELSIE: Her cold.

There is silence again which is presently shattered by the wailing of a baby in the house next door.

MRS. ROCKETT: There's that child again. It kept me awake all night.

DORIS: I'm very sorry, I'm sure.

MRS. ROCKETT (*fiddling in her work-basket*): I wasn't blaming you.

DORIS: The night before last it was the hot-water pipes.

MRS. ROCKETT: You ought to have them seen to.

DORIS: You know as well as I do you can't stop them making that noise every now and then.

MRS. ROCKETT (*threading a needle*): I'm sure I don't know why you don't get a plumber in.

DORIS (*grandly*): Because I do not consider it necessary.

MRS. ROCKETT: You would if you slept in my room —gurgle gurgle gurgle all night long—it's all very fine for you, you're at the end of the passage.

DORIS (*with meaning*): You don't have to sleep there.

MRS. ROCKETT: What do you mean by that?

DORIS: You know perfectly well what I mean.

MRS. ROCKETT (*with spirit*): Listen to me, Doris Gow. I've got a perfect right to complain if I want to and well you know it. It isn't as if I was staying here for nothing.

DORIS: I really don't know what's the matter with you lately, Mother, you do nothing but grumble.

MRS. ROCKETT: Me, grumble! I like that, I'm sure. That's rich, that is.

DORIS: Well, you do. It gives me a headache.

MRS. ROCKETT: You ought to do something about those headaches of yours. They seem to pop on and off at the least thing.

DORIS: And I wish you wouldn't keep passing remarks about not staying here for nothing.

MRS. ROCKETT: Well, it's true, I don't.

DORIS: Anyone would think we was taking advantage of you.

MRS. ROCKETT: Well, they wouldn't be far wrong.

DORIS: Mother, how can you! You're not paying a penny more than you can afford.

MRS. ROCKETT: I never said I was. It isn't the money, it's the lack of consideration.

DORIS: Pity you don't go and live with Nora for a change.

MRS. ROCKETT: Nora hasn't got a spare room.

DORIS: Phyllis has, a lovely one, looking out over the railway. I'm sure her hot-water pipes wouldn't annoy you, there isn't hot water in them.

MRS. ROCKETT: Of course, if I'm not wanted here, I can always go to a boarding-house or a private hotel.

DORIS: Catch you!

MRS. ROCKETT: I'm not the sort to outstay my welcome anywhere——

DORIS: Oh, for heaven's sake don't start that again——

MRS. ROCKETT (*addressing the air*): It seems as though some of us had got out of bed the wrong side this morning.

ELSIE: Mum, can I have some more toast?

DORIS: No.

ELSIE: I could make it myself over the kitchen fire.

DORIS: No, I tell you. Can't you understand plain English? You've had quite enough and you'll be late for school.

MRS. ROCKETT: Never mind, Elsie, here's twopence, you can buy yourself a sponge-cake at Barret's.

ELSIE (*taking the twopence*): Thanks, Grandma.

DORIS: You'll do no such thing, Elsie. I'm not going to have a child of mine stuffing herself with cake in the middle of the High Street.

MRS. ROCKETT (*sweetly*): Eat it in the shop, dear.

DORIS: Go on, you'll be late.

ELSIE: Oh, Mum, it's only ten to.

DORIS: Do as I tell you.

ELSIE: Oh, all right.

> *She goes sullenly out of the room and can be heard scampering noisily up the stairs.*

MRS. ROCKETT (*irritatingly*): Poor little soul.

DORIS: I'll trouble you not to spoil Elsie, Mother.

MRS. ROCKETT: Spoil her! I like that. Better than half starving her.

DORIS (*hotly*): Are you insinuating——

MRS. ROCKETT: I'm not insinuating anything. Elsie's getting a big girl, she only had one bit of toast for her breakfast and she used that for her egg, I saw her.

DORIS: It's none of your business and in future I'd be much obliged if you'd keep your twopences to yourself.

MRS. ROCKETT (*hurt*): Very well, of course if I'm to be abused every time I try to bring a little happiness into the child's life——

DORIS: Anyone would think I ill-treated her the way you talk.

MRS. ROCKETT: You certainly nag her enough.

DORIS: I don't do any such thing and I wish you'd be quiet.

> *She flounces up from the table and goes over to the window, where she stands drumming her fingers on the pane.* HENRY *quietly appropriates the newspaper she has flung down.*

MRS. ROCKETT (*unctuously*): There's no need to lose your temper.

DORIS: I am not losing my temper.

MRS. ROCKETT: If I'd known when you were Elsie's age what you were going to turn out like I'd have given you what for, I can tell you.

DORIS: Pity you didn't, I'm sure.

MRS. ROCKETT: One thing, I never stinted any of my children.

DORIS: I wish you'd leave me to bring up my own child in my own way.

MRS. ROCKETT: That cold's been hanging over her for weeks and a fat lot you care——

DORIS: I've dosed her for it, haven't I? The whole house stinks of Vapex. What more can I do?

MRS. ROCKETT: She ought to have had Doctor Bristow last Saturday when it was so bad. He'd have cleared it up in no time.

DORIS: You and your Doctor Bristow.

MRS. ROCKETT: Nice thing if it turned to bronchitis. Mrs. Henderson's Muriel got bronchitis, all through neglecting a cold; the poor child couldn't breathe, they had to have two kettles going night and day——

DORIS: I suppose your precious Doctor Bristow told you that.

MRS. ROCKETT: Yes, he did, and what's more he saved the girl's life, you ask Mrs. Henderson.

DORIS: Catch me ask Mrs. Henderson anything, not likely, stuck up thing——

MRS. ROCKETT: Mrs. Henderson's a very nice lady-like woman, just because she's quiet and a bit reserved you say she's stuck up——

DORIS: Who does she think she is anyway, Lady Mountbatten?

MRS. ROCKETT: Really, Doris, you make me tired sometimes, you do really.

DORIS: If you're so fond of Mrs. Henderson it's a pity you don't see more of her. I notice you don't go there often.

MRS. ROCKETT (*with dignity*): I go when I am invited.

DORIS (*triumphantly*): Exactly.

MRS. ROCKETT: She's not the kind of woman that likes people dropping in and out all the time. We can't all be Amy Fawcetts.

DORIS: What's the matter with Amy Fawcett?

> ELSIE *comes into the room wearing a mackintosh and a tam-o'-shanter. She stamps over to the piano and begins to search untidily through the pile of music on it.*

MRS. ROCKETT: Well, she's common for one thing, she dyes her hair for another, and she's a bit too free and easy all round for my taste.

DORIS: She doesn't put on airs, anyway.

MRS. ROCKETT: I should think not, after the sort of life she's led.

DORIS: How do you know what sort of a life she's led?

MRS. ROCKETT: Everybody knows, you only have to look at her; I'm a woman of the world, I am, you can't pull the wool over my eyes——

DORIS: Don't untidy everything like that, what are you looking for?

ELSIE: *The Pixie's Parade*, I had it last night.

DORIS: If it's the one with the blue cover it's at the bottom.

ELSIE: It isn't—oh dear, Miss Pritchard will be mad at me if I can't find it.

MRS. ROCKETT: Perhaps you put it in your satchel, dear, here, let me look—— (*She opens* ELSIE's *satchel,*

which is hanging over the back of a chair and fumbles in it.)
Is this it?

ELSIE: Oh yes, thanks, Grandma.

DORIS: Go along now, for heaven's sake, you'll be
late.

ELSIE: Oh, all right, Mum.   Good-bye, Mum,
good-bye, Grandma, good-bye, Dad.

HENRY: Good-bye.

MRS. ROCKETT: Good-bye, dear, give Grandma a
kiss.

> ELSIE *does so.*

DORIS: Don't dawdle on the way home.

ELSIE: Oh, all right, Mum.

> *She goes out. The slam of the front door shakes the
> house.*

DORIS (*irritably*): There now.

MRS. ROCKETT (*with studied politeness*): If you are
going down to the shops this morning, would it be
troubling you too much to get me a reel of white
cotton?

DORIS: I thought you were coming with me.

MRS. ROCKETT: I really don't feel up to it.

DORIS: I'll put it on my list.

> *She takes a piece of paper out of the sideboard drawer
> and scribbles on it.*

MRS. ROCKETT: If it's out of your way, please don't
trouble, it'll do another time.

DORIS: Henry, it's past nine.

HENRY (*without looking up*): I know.

DORIS: You'll be late.

HENRY: Never mind.

DORIS: That's a nice way to talk, I must say.

MRS. ROCKETT: I'm sure if my Robert had ever

lazed about like that in the mornings, I'd have thought the world had come to an end.

DORIS: Henry'll do it once too often, mark my words.

MRS. ROCKETT (*biting off her thread*): Well, that corner's finished.

DORIS (*to* HENRY): You'll have to move now, I've got to clear.

HENRY (*rising—absently*): All right.

MRS. ROCKETT: Where's Ethel?

DORIS: Doing the bedroom.

> *She takes a tray which is leaning against the wall by the sideboard and proceeds to stack the breakfast things on to it.*
>
> HENRY *quietly goes out of the room.*

DORIS: Look at that wicked waste. (*Throws more scraps in fire.*)

MRS. ROCKETT: What's the matter with him?

DORIS: Don't ask me, I'm sure I couldn't tell you.

MRS. ROCKETT: He came in very late last night, I heard him go into the bathroom. (*There is a pause.*) That cistern makes a terrible noise.

DORIS: Does it indeed!

MRS. ROCKETT: Yes, it does.

DORIS (*slamming the teapot on to the tray*): Very sorry, I'm sure.

MRS. ROCKETT: Where'd he been?

DORIS: How do I know?

MRS. ROCKETT: Didn't you ask him?

DORIS: I wouldn't demean myself.

MRS. ROCKETT: Been drinking?

DORIS: No.

Mrs. Rockett: Sounded very like it to me, all that banging about.

Doris: You know Henry never touches a drop.

Mrs. Rockett: I know he says he doesn't.

Doris: Oh, do shut up, Mother, we're not all like father.

Mrs. Rockett: You watch your tongue, Doris Gow, don't let me hear you saying anything against the memory of your poor father.

Doris: I wasn't.

Mrs. Rockett (*belligerently*): Oh yes, you were, you were insinuating again.

Doris (*hoisting up the tray*): Father drank and you know it—everybody knew it.

Mrs. Rockett: You're a wicked woman.

Doris: It's true.

Mrs. Rockett: Your father was a gentleman, which is more than your husband will ever be, with all his night-classes and his book reading—night-classes indeed!

Doris: Who's insinuating now?

Mrs. Rockett (*angrily*): I am, and I'm not afraid to say so.

Doris: What of it?

Mrs. Rockett (*with heavy sarcasm*): I suppose he was at a night-class last night?

Doris (*loudly*): Mind your own business.

Henry *comes in wearing his mackintosh and a bowler hat.*

Henry: What's up?

Doris: Where were you last night?

Henry: Why?

Doris: Mother wants to know and so do I.

HENRY: I was kept late at the shop and I had a bit of dinner in town.

DORIS: Who with?

HENRY: Charlie Henderson.

He picks up the paper off the table and goes out. After a moment the front door slams.

The baby next door bursts into fresh wails.

MRS. ROCKETT: There goes that child again. It's my belief it's hungry.

DORIS: Wonder you don't go and give it twopence to buy sponge-cake.

She pulls the door open with her foot and goes out with the tray as the lights fade on the scene.

SCENE II

It is about seven-thirty in the evening. ELSIE *is sitting at the piano practising with the loud pedal firmly down all the time.*

MRS. ROCKETT *is sitting in her chair by the fire, but she is dressed in her street things and wearing a black hat with a veil.*

DORIS, *also in street clothes, is clearing some paper patterns and pieces of material from the table.*

There is a cloth across the end of the table on which is set a loaf, a plate of cold ham, a saucer with two tomatoes in it, a bottle of A.1 sauce and a teapot, teacup, sugar basin and milk jug.

HENRY *comes in, taking off his mackintosh. He gives one look round the room and goes out into the hall again to hang up his things.* ELSIE *stops playing and comes over to* DORIS.

ELSIE: Can we go now?

DORIS: In a minute.

ELSIE: We'll miss the Mickey.

DORIS: Put on your hat and don't worry.

ELSIE (*grabbing her hat from the sideboard*): Oh, all right.
      HENRY *re-enters.*

DORIS: Your supper's all ready, the kettle's on the gas stove when you want it. We've had ours.

HENRY: Oh!

DORIS: And you needn't look injured either.

HENRY: Very well.

DORIS: If you managed to get home a bit earlier it'd save a lot of trouble all round.

HENRY (*amiably*): Sorry, dear.

DORIS: It's all very fine to be sorry, you've been getting later and later these last few weeks, they can't keep you overtime every night.

HENRY: All right, dear, I'll tell them.

DORIS: Here, Elsie, put these away in the cupboard.
      She hands her a pile of material and pieces of paper.
      ELSIE *obediently takes them and puts them in the left-hand cupboard of the sideboard.*

HENRY (*sitting at the table*): Cold ham, what a surprise!

DORIS (*looking at him sharply*): What's the matter with it?

HENRY: I don't know, yet.

DORIS: It's perfectly fresh, if that's what you mean?

HENRY: Why are you all so dressed up?

ELSIE: We're going to the pictures.

HENRY: Oh, I see.

DORIS: You can put everything on the tray when you've finished and leave it in the kitchen for Ethel.

HENRY: Good old Ethel.

397

Doris (*surprised*): What?

Henry: I said good old Ethel.

Doris: Well, it sounded very silly, I'm sure.

Mrs. Rockett (*scrutinising him*): What's the matter with you?

Henry: Nothing, why?

Mrs. Rockett: You look funny.

Henry: I feel funny.

Mrs. Rockett: Have you been drinking?

Henry: Yes.

Doris: Henry!

Mrs. Rockett: I knew it.

Henry: I had a whisky and soda in town and another one at the Plough.

Doris (*astounded*): What for?

Henry: Because I felt like it.

Doris: You ought to be ashamed of yourself.

Henry: I'm going to have another one too, a bit later on.

Doris: You'll do no such thing.

Henry: That hat looks awful.

Doris (*furiously*): Don't you speak to me like that.

Henry: Why not?

Doris (*slightly nonplussed*): Because I won't have it, so there.

Henry: It's a common little hat and it looks awful.

Doris (*with an admirable effort at control*): Now listen to me, Henry Gow, the next time I catch you drinking and coming home here and insulting me, I'll——

Henry (*interrupting her gently*): What will you do, Dorrie?

Doris (*hotly*): I'll give you a piece of my mind, that's what I'll do.

HENRY: It'll have to be a very little piece, Dorrie, you can't afford much! (*He laughs delighted at his own joke.*)

DORIS: I'd be very much obliged if you'd kindly tell me what this means?

HENRY: I'm celebrating.

DORIS: What do you mean, celebrating? What are you talking about?

HENRY: To-night's our anniversary.

DORIS: Don't talk so soft, our anniversary's not until November.

HENRY: I don't mean that one. To-night's the anniversary of the first time I had an affair with you and you got in the family way.

DORIS (*shrieking*): Henry!

HENRY (*delighted with his carefully calculated effect*): Hurray!

DORIS (*beside herself*): How dare you say such a dreadful thing, in front of the child, too.

HENRY (*in romantic tones*): Three years and a bit after that wonderful night our child was born! (*Lapsing into his normal voice.*) Considering all the time you took forming yourself, Elsie, I'm surprised you're not a nicer little girl than you are.

DORIS: Go upstairs, Elsie.

HENRY: Stay here, Elsie.

DORIS: Do as I tell you.

ELSIE: But, Mum——

DORIS: Mother, take her for God's sake! There's going to be a row.

HENRY (*firmly*): Leave her alone and sit down.

     MRS. ROCKETT *hesitates.*

Sit down, I tell you.

MRS. ROCKETT (*subsiding into a chair*): Well, I never, I——

HENRY (*happily*): See? It works like a charm.

DORIS: A fine exhibition you're making of yourself, I must say.

HENRY: Not bad, is it? As a matter of fact I'm rather pleased with it myself.

DORIS: Go to bed!

HENRY: Stop ordering me about. What right have you got to nag at me and boss me? No right at all. I'm the one that pays the rent and works for you and keeps you. What do you give me in return, I'd like to know! Nothing! I sit through breakfast while you and mother wrangle. You're too busy being snappy and bad-tempered even to say good morning. I come home tired after working all day and ten to one there isn't even a hot dinner for me; here, see this ham? This is what I think of it! (*He throws it at her feet.*) And the tomatoes and the A.1 bloody sauce! (*He throws them too.*)

DORIS (*screaming*): Henry! All over the carpet.

HENRY (*throwing the butter-dish face downwards on the floor*): And that's what I think of the carpet, now then!

DORIS: That I should live to see this! That I should live to see the man I married make such a beast of himself!

HENRY: Stop working yourself up into a state, you'll need all your control when you've heard what I'm going to say to you.

DORIS: Look here——

HENRY: Sit down. We'll all sit down, I'm afraid you'll have to miss the pictures for once.

DORIS: Elsie, you come with me.

MRS. ROCKETT: Yes, go on, Ducks.

She makes a movement towards the door, but HENRY *is too quick for her. He locks the door and slips the key into his pocket.*

HENRY: I've been dreaming of this moment for many years, and believe me it's not going to be spoilt for me by you running away.

DORIS (*on the verge of tears*): Let me out of this room.

HENRY: You'll stay where you are until I've had my say.

DORIS (*bursting into tears and sinking down at the table*): Oh! Oh! Oh!——

ELSIE (*starting to cry too*): Mum—oh, Mum——

HENRY: Here you, shut up, go and get the port out of the sideboard and give some to your mother—go on, do as I tell you.

ELSIE, *terrified and hypnotised into submission, goes to the sideboard cupboard and brings out a bottle of invalid port and some glasses, snivelling as she does so.*

DORIS *continues to sob.*

That's right.

MRS. ROCKETT (*quietly*): You drunken brute, you!

HENRY (*cheerfully*): Worse than that, Mother, far worse. Just you wait and see.

MRS. ROCKETT (*ignoring him*): Take some port, Dorrie, it'll do you good.

DORIS: I don't want any—it'd choke me——

HENRY (*pouring some out*): Come on—here——

DORIS: Keep away from me.

HENRY: Drink it and stop snivelling.

DORIS: I'll never forgive you for this, never, never, never as long as I live! (*She gulps down some port.*)

HENRY (*noting her gesture*): That's better.

MRS. ROCKETT: Pay no attention, Dorrie, he's drunk.

HENRY: I'm not drunk. I've only had two whiskies and sodas, just to give me enough guts to take the first plunge. You'd never believe how scared I was, thinking it over in cold blood. I'm not scared any more though, it's much easier than I thought it was going to be. My only regret is that I didn't come to the boil a long time ago, and tell you to your face, Dorrie, what I think of you, what I've been thinking of you for years, and this horrid little kid, and that old bitch of a mother of yours.

MRS. ROCKETT (*shrilly*): Henry Gow!

HENRY: You heard me, old bitch was what I said, and old bitch was what I meant.

MRS. ROCKETT: Let me out of this room, I'm not going to stay here and be insulted—I'm not——

HENRY: You're going to stay here just as long as I want you to.

MRS. ROCKETT: Oh, am I? We'll see about that——

> *With astonishing quickness she darts over to the window and manages to drag one open.* HENRY *grabs her by the arm.*

HENRY: No, you don't.

MRS. ROCKETT: Let go of me.

DORIS: Oh, Mother, don't let the neighbours know all your business.

HENRY: Not on your life!

MRS. ROCKETT (*suddenly screaming powerfully*): Help! Help! Police! Help! Mrs. Harrison—help!——

> HENRY *drags her away from the window, turns her round and gives her a light slap on the face, she staggers against the piano, meanwhile he shuts the window again, locks it and pockets the key.*

DORIS (*looking at him in horror*): Oh, God! Oh, my God!

ELSIE (*bursting into tears again*): Oh, Mum, Mum, he hit Grandma! Oh, Mum——

> *She runs to* DORIS *who puts her arm round her protectively.*

MRS. ROCKETT (*gasping*): Oh—my heart! I think I'm going to faint—oh—my heart——

HENRY: Don't worry, I'll bring you round if you faint——

MRS. ROCKETT: Oh—oh—oh, dear——

> MRS. ROCKETT *slides on to the floor, perceptibly breaking her fall by clinging on to the piano stool.*
>
> DORIS *jumps up from the table.*

DORIS: Mother!

HENRY: Stay where you are.

> HENRY *goes to the sideboard and pours out a glass of water.* DORIS, *disobeying him, runs over to her mother.* ELSIE *wails.*

HENRY: Stand out of the way, Doris, we don't all want to get wet.

> *He approaches with the glass of water.* MRS. ROCKETT *sits up weakly.*

MRS. ROCKETT (*in a far-away voice*): Where am I?

HENRY: Number Seventeen Cranworth Road, Clapham.

MRS. ROCKETT: Oh—oh, dear!

HENRY: Look here, Mother, I don't want there to be any misunderstanding about this. I liked slapping you just now, see? It was lovely, and if you don't behave yourself and keep quiet I shall slap you again. Go and sit in your chair and remember if you feel faint the water's all ready for you.

> *He helps her up and escorts her to her chair by the fire. She collapes into it and looks at him balefully.*

Now then. Sit down, Dorrie, you look silly standing
about.

DORIS (*with a great effort at control*): Henry——

HENRY (*slowly, but very firmly*): Sit down! And keep
Elsie quiet or I'll fetch her one, too.

DORIS (*with dignity*): Come here, Elsie. Shut up, will
you!

> *She sits at the table, with* ELSIE.

HENRY: That's right.

> *He walks round the room slowly and in silence, looking
> at them with an expression of the greatest satisfaction on
> his face. Finally he goes over to the fireplace;* MRS.
> ROCKETT *jumps slightly as he approaches her, but he
> smiles at her reassuringly and lights a cigarette. Mean-
> while* DORIS, *recovering from her fear, is beginning to
> simmer with rage, she remains still, however, watching.*

Now then. I'm going to start, quite quietly, explaining
a few things to you.

DORIS: Enjoying yourself, aren't you?

HENRY: You've said it.

DORIS (*gaining courage*): You'll grin on the other side
of your face before I've done with you.

HENRY (*politely*): Very likely, Dorrie, very likely
indeed!

DORIS: And don't you Dorrie me, either! Coming
home here drunk, hitting poor mother and frightening
Elsie out of her wits.

HENRY: Maybe it'll do her good, do 'em both good, a
little excitement in the home. God knows, it's dull
enough as a rule.

DORIS (*with biting sarcasm*): Very clever, oh, very
clever, I'm sure.

HENRY: Fifteen, no sixteen years ago to-night,

Dorrie, you and me had a little rough and tumble in your Aunt Daisy's house in Stansfield Road, do you remember?

DORIS: Henry——

HENRY (*ignoring her*): We had the house to ourselves, it being a Sunday, your Aunt had popped over to the Golden Calf with Mr. Simmonds, the lodger, which, as the writers say, was her wont——

MRS. ROCKETT: This is disgusting, I won't listen to another word.

HENRY (*rounding on her*): You will! Shut up!

DORIS: Pay no attention, Mother, he's gone mad.

HENRY: Let me see now, where was I? Oh yes, Stansfield Road. You'd been after me for a long while, Dorrie, I didn't know it then, but I realised it soon after. You had to have a husband, what with Nora married and Phyllis engaged, both of them younger than you, you had to have a husband, and quick, so you fixed on me. You were pretty enough and I fell for it hook, line and sinker; then, a couple of months later you'd told me you'd clicked, you cried a hell of a lot, I remember, said the disgrace would kill your mother if she ever found out. I didn't know then that it'd take a sight more than that to kill that leathery old mare——

MRS. ROCKETT (*bursting into tears*): I won't stand it, I wont! I won't!

HENRY (*rising above her sobs*): I expect you were in on the whole business, in a refined way of course, you knew what was going on all right, you knew that Dorrie was no more in the family way than I was, but we got married; you both saw to that, and I chucked up all the plans I had for getting on, perhaps being a steward in a ship and seeing a bit of the world. Oh yes, all that had to go and we settled down in rooms and I went into Ferguson's Hosiery.

DORIS: I've given you the best years of my life and don't you forget it.

HENRY: You've never given me the best of anything, not even yourself. You didn't even have Elsie willingly.

DORIS (*wildly*): It's not true—stop up your ears, Elsie, don't listen to him, he's wicked—he's wicked——

HENRY (*grimly*): It's true all right, and you know it as well as I do.

DORIS (*shrilly*): It was only right that you married me. It was only fair! You took advantage of me, didn't you? You took away my innocence. It was only right that you paid for it.

HENRY: Come off it, Dorrie, don't talk so silly. I was the innocent one, not you. I found out you'd cheated me a long, long time ago, and when I found out, realised it for certain, I started cheating you. Prepare yourself, Dorrie, my girl, you're going to be really upset this time. I've been saving! Every week for over ten years I've been earning a little bit more than you thought I was. I've managed, by hook and by crook, to put by five hundred and seventy-two pounds—d'you hear me? —five hundred and seventy-two pounds!

MRS. ROCKETT (*jumping to her feet*): Henry! You never have—it's not true——

DORIS (*also jumping up*): You couldn't have—you'd have given it away—I should have found out——

HENRY: I thought that'd rouse you, but don't get excited, don't get worked up. I haven't got it on me, it's in the bank. And it's not for you, it's for me—all but fifty pounds of it, that much is for you, just fifty pounds, the last you'll ever get from me——

DORIS: Henry! You couldn't be so cruel! You couldn't be so mean!

HENRY: I've done what I think's fair and what I think's fair is damn sight more than you deserve. I've transferred the freehold of this house into your name, so you'll always have a roof over your head—you can take in lodgers at a pinch, though God help the poor bastards if you do!

DORIS: Five hundred and seventy-two pounds! You've got all that and you're going to leave me to starve!

HENRY: Cut out the drama, Dorrie, and have a look at your mother's savings bank book—I bet you'll find she's got enough to keep you in comfort till the day you die. She soaked her old man plenty, I'm sure—before he took to soaking himself!

MRS. ROCKETT: It's a lie!

HENRY: Now listen to me, Mother Machree—you've 'ad one sock in the jaw this evening and you're not just asking for another, you're sitting up and begging for it.

MRS. ROCKETT: I'll have you up for assault. I'll have the police on you, my fine fellow!

HENRY: They'll have to be pretty nippy—my boat sails first thing in the morning.

DORIS (*horrified*): Boat!

HENRY: I'm going away. I've got my ticket here in my pocket, and my passport. My passport photo's a fair scream, I wish I could show it to you, but I don't want you to see the nice new name I've got.

DORIS: You can't do it, I can have you stopped by law. It's desertion.

HENRY: That's right, Dorrie, you've said it. Desertion's just exactly what it is.

DORIS (*breathlessly*): Where are you going, you've got to tell me. Where are you going?

HENRY: Wouldn't you like to know? Maybe Africa, maybe China, maybe Australia. There are lots of places in the world you know nothing about, Dorrie. You've often laughed at me for reading books, but I've found out a hell of a lot from books. There are islands in the South Seas for instance with cocoa palms and turtles and sunshine all the year round—you can live there for practically nothing, then there's Australia or New Zealand, with a little bit of capital I might start in a small way sheep-farming. Think of it; miles and miles of open country stretching as far as the eye can see— good food and fresh air—that might be very nice, that might suit me beautifully. Then there's South America. There are coffee plantations, there, and sugar plantations, and banana plantations. If I go to South America I'll send you a whole crate. 'Ave a banana, Dorrie! 'Ave a banana!

DORIS: Henry, listen to me, you can't do this dreadful thing, you can't! If you don't love me any more, think of Elsie.

HENRY (*still in his dream*): Then there's the sea, not the sea we know at Worthing with the tide going in and out regular and the band playing on the pier. The real sea's what I mean. The sea that Joseph Conrad wrote about, and Rudyard Kipling and lots of other people, too, a sea with whacking great waves and water spouts and typhoons and flying-fish and phosphorus making the foam look as if it was lit up. Those people knew a thing or two I can tell you. They knew what life could be like if you give it a chance. They knew there was a bit more to it than refinement and fumed oak and lace curtains and getting old and miserable with nothing to show for it. I'm a middle-aged man, but my health's not too bad taken all round. There's still time for me to see a little bit of real life before I conk out. I'm still fit enough to do a job of work—real work, mind you—not bowing and scraping and wearing meself out showing fussy old cows the way to the lace and the china ware and the bargain basement.

DORIS (*hysterically*): God will punish you, you just see if He doesn't, you just see——

HENRY: God's been punishing me for fifteen years, it's high time He laid off me now. He's been punishing me good and proper for being damn fool enough to let you get your claws into me in the first place——

DORIS (*changing tactics*): Henry, have pity, please don't be so cruel, please—please——

HENRY: And don't start weeping and wailing either, that won't cut any ice with me, I know what you're like, I know you through and through. You're frightened now, scared out of your wits, but give you half a chance and you'd be worse than ever you were. You're a bad lot, Dorrie, not what the world would call a bad lot, but what I call a bad lot. Mean and cold and respectable. Good-bye, Dorrie——

DORIS (*flinging her arms round him and bursting into tears*): Listen to me, Henry, you've got to listen—you must. You can't leave us to starve, you can't throw us on to the streets—if I've been a bad wife to you, I'm sorry—I'll try to be better, really I will, I swear to God I will—— You can't do this, if you won't forgive me, think of Elsie, think of poor little Elsie——

HENRY: Poor little Elsie, my eye! I think Elsie's awful. I always have ever since she was little. She's never done anything but whine and snivel and try to get something for nothing——

ELSIE (*wailing*): Oh, Mum, did you hear what he said? Oh, Dad, oh dear——

MRS. ROCKETT (*comforting her*): There, there, dear, don't listen to him——

HENRY: Elsie can go to work in a year or so, in the meantime, Dorrie, you can go to work yourself, you're quite a young woman still and strong as an ox.— Here's your fifty pounds——

> *He takes an envelope out of his pocket and throws it on to the table. Then he goes towards the door.* DORIS *rushes after him and hangs on to his arm.*

DORIS: Henry, Henry, you shan't go, you shan't——

HENRY (*struggling with her*): Leave hold of me.

DORIS: Mother, Mother—help—help me, don't let him go——

> HENRY *frees himself from her and, taking her by the shoulders, forces her back into a chair, then he unlocks the door and opens it.*

HENRY: I'm taking my last look at you, Dorrie. I shall never see you again as long as I live——

DORIS: Mother! Oh God!—oh, my God!——

> *She buries her head in her arms and starts to sob loudly.* ELSIE *runs and joins her, yelling.* MRS. ROCKETT *sits transfixed staring at him murderously.*

HENRY (*quietly*): Three generations. Grandmother, Mother and Kid. Made of the same bones and sinews and muscles and glands, millions of you, millions just like you. You're past it now, Mother, you're past the thick of the fray, you're nothing but a music-hall joke, a mother-in-law with a bit of money put by. Dorrie, the next few years will show whether you've got guts or not. Maybe what I'm doing to you will save your immortal soul in the long run, that'd be a bit of all right, wouldn't it? I doubt it, though, your immortal soul's too measly. You're a natural bully and a cheat, and I'm sick of the sight of you; I should also like to take this opportunity of saying that I hate that bloody awful slave bangle and I always have. As for you, Elsie, you've got a chance, it's a slim one, I grant you, but still it's a chance. If you learn to work and be independent and, when the time comes, give what you have to give freely and without demanding life-long payment for it, there's just a bit of hope that you'll turn into a decent human being. At all events, if you'll take one parting piece of advice from your cruel, ungrateful father, you'll spend the first money you ever earn on having your adenoids out. Good-bye, one and all. Nice to have known you!

The wails of DORIS *and* ELSIE *rise in volume as he goes jauntily out, slamming the door behind him.*

CURTAIN

411